FROM AMERICA TO AFRICA
VOICES OF FILIPINO WOMEN OVERSEAS

Edited by
LORNA KALAW-TIROL

Published by
FAI RESOURCE MANAGEMENT INC.

This book is dedicated to
all Filipino women everywhere in the world
who are making a difference.

Published by FAI RESOURCE MANAGEMENT INC.
Unit 607 Cityland 10 Tower I, Ayala Avenue, Makati City, Philippines

Cover design by Joanna Ruiz
Cover painting, "Just Go," by Lina Llaguno Ciani
Design and layout of inside pages by JB de la Peña

ISBN 971-92195-0-5

Printed in the Philippines by RAINTREE TRADING & PUBLISHING

CONTENTS

THIS BOOK is like a river, with many tributaries, rivulets, springs, sources, and undercurrents. One very strong undercurrent present in the book is what we in the National Commission on the Role of Filipino Women (where I was chairperson during the term of President Fidel Ramos, 1992 to 1998) and in women's organizations have called "the feminization of migration."

The diaspora of Filipino workers to lands that offered them better work and income opportunities started during the dictatorship of Ferdinand Marcos, when his power was at its zenith and the country lay prostrate at his feet. Even with the restoration of democracy by President Corazon Aquino in 1986, the slow recovery of what used to be the most robust economy this side of Asia after World War II could not stem the human flow to other lands.

This time, however, migration took on a woman's face. The percentage of women workers inched slowly to become the majority, and today it is hovering in the sixties. This book can hardly do justice to these women, who suffer hardships and heartaches while working and living so far away from their loved ones. Their courage, resiliency, and almost superhuman work are simply beyond words.

The other major tributary of this book is a previously published book which one may call a "prequel," or the first of a series, *Coming to Terms: Essays on Midlife by 15 Women*. I was one of those asked by Lorna Kalaw-Tirol, its editor, to contribute an essay. I did so reluctantly, anxious about baring my soul in the mid-century of my life. But the writing of my essay proved to be surprisingly delightful therapy. I felt a great sense of liberation and wonderment and an appreciation of what I had become and continue to be in the process of becoming.

When Josie Opeña Disterhoft, my sister Loida's college classmate in Manila in the Sixties and a resident of Chicago for almost two decades now, read *Coming to Terms*, she suggested a similar book of essays, this time by Filipino women living and working overseas. I embraced the idea wholeheartedly. Among other reasons, I wanted to pass on the grati-fying experience I had in writing my essay to all the women whose stories needed to be told and shared. Lorna was just as enthusiastic about being the book's editor and co-publisher.

From the very start, we agreed that the essays should reflect the wonderful diversity of Filipino women who have found homes everywhere in the world. Thus, we began the search for women living and/or work-ing in continents other than Asia and North America, and the nostalgia-driven effort to trace the tracks of long-lost friends who had left the moth-erland to follow their own individual guiding stars.

To get a good cross-section of professions, jobs, backgrounds, and lifestyles, we tapped the Commission on Filipinos Overseas, which proved to be an excellent source with its bi-annual Presidential Awards for Out-standing Overseas Filipinos.

The new technology of the Internet and e-mail was another rivulet we could not have done without. For instant communication, it has no equal. As a "detective" looking for clues as to people's whereabouts, it was fun. As the bearer of the *obras maestras* of our writers, it was faith-ful. And as the technology improved by leaps and bounds from month to month, it even carried the writers' digitized photographs for our artist Lynett Villariba's sketches.

Finally, this book would have remained a dried and parched spring were it not for my sister Loida and her husband, Reginald Lewis, who passed away almost seven years ago to this day. In both their lives, but especially Reggie's, they did not allow limitation of any kind, including the color of their skin, to keep them from fulfilling their dreams in lands other than their own. Reggie built his business empire in Europe, and after his death Loida continued his legacy. My sister has asked me to help her in this "grand adventure" and along the way allowed me the time and provided me the wherewithal to publish this book. To Reggie and Loida, therefore, my until-today-unspoken gratitude.

IMELDA M. NICOLAS
Publisher

New York City
January 2, 2000

IN THE BEGINNING came a suggestion.

Less than a year later, we have this book.

We could not have gotten from simple suggestion to actual publication without the support of a number of people. We thank them for their contributions to this project:

the 19 writers, for their full and enthusiastic commitment;

Lina Llaguno Ciani, for the evocative painting on the cover;

Mila Nacionales, for her quiet competence and endless patience;

Joanna Ruiz, for her creativity with the cover design;

Lynett Villariba, for her unique pen-and-ink pointillist portraits;

JB de la Peña, for his striking layout;

Jo-Ed K.Tirol, for his assistance as proofreader and gofer; and

Sylvana Diaz of Galleria Duemila in Manila, for lending us a slide of the cover painting.

L.K.T.

Sharifa Zeannat Ali-Salih

Tausug Nurse in the Holy City

THE KINGDOM of Saudi Arabia has been my home for the past 21 years. During that period, I have seen the facets of life experienced by my fellow Filipinos, our *kababayans*. I have seen their great enthusiasm when they go home once a year; going home erases their torments and dilemmas. But I have also seen how others have had to endure harsh working conditions for two years or more, before they could be eligible for that much needed vacation.

We can't help but count every minute of the remaining days of our vacation. I myself wish I could hold on to time, so that there wouldn't be an end to happiness. And yet, whether we like it or not, the final day comes. I hate the atmosphere at the airport when it is time to say goodbye. The lingering sadness of the overseas workers and their families — the hugs, kisses, and tears — is tormenting. Lucky are those who have enough to bring home because not everyone is blessed with a high salary. Some labor for a pittance, pressured by the debts they left behind, particularly the enormous placement fees imposed by some recruitment agencies in Manila. I once asked our female cleaners in the hospital, when they came to me with their problems, how they allowed themselves to be fooled by such agencies. The exchange rate was only 26 pesos to the dollar then and their employer had not paid them for eight months. Praise be to Allah, the *bayanihan* spirit is alive and well even abroad — the Filipino nurses rallied around the cleaners.

The Filipinos in Holy Makkah, formerly Mecca (population: one million), have a good foundation of unity and brotherhood. More often than not, we share each other's happiness and sorrows. Muslims believe that any service rendered in the Holy City is rewarded a thousand times over. We do have some Christian sisters and brothers assigned to Hera General Hospital, a new hospital a short distance away from Makkah. We are part of the set-up of this hospital. I can assure you that there is no demarcation line between us, for the thought of being "away from home" has consolidated our values, allowing us to transcend religious and ethnic barriers.

I BELONGED to the first batch of professional nurses who arrived in the Kingdom in October 1978. Three of us nurses and one male medical technologist were assigned to King Abdul Aziz Hospital, the first hospital established in the Holy City after the unification of the two states — the former Kingdom of Hijas whose capital is Makkah, and the Sultanate of Nejh whose capital is Riyadh — in 1925 by King Abdul Aziz bin Abdurahman Al Saud. The name Saudi Arabia was adopted in September 1932.

The health service in Holy Makkah is the oldest in the Kingdom. It is also the busiest, considering the annual hajj. With millions of pilgrims from all over the world coming to this Holy Place, the health ministry and other services of the government have a tough responsibility. The Kingdom offers free medical services to citizens and visitors, and there are seven general and specialist hospitals and 34 primary health care centers in Makkah, not to mention private hospitals and clinics. Seven more government hospitals are located just a few kilometers away from the Holy City proper and 80 primary health care centers are opened during the hajj season to serve the health needs of the pilgrims. In addition, rolling clinics are deployed, together with air and land ambulances.

When we first arrived, we were kept waiting for eight hours and offered neither food nor room. The nursing service was run by Egyptian nurses who spoke no English. Finally, at 10 p.m. a warm-hearted Pakistani nurse who couldn't bear to see us in the corridor with our suitcases invited us into her room. She spoke English. Thank Allah, was all we could murmur. She had been there for 10 years, she said, and she was the head nurse of the emergency ward. Her name was Fakharunisah and she became our guardian angel and my best friend. Now she is my secretary in the directorate health office.

With no orientation at all, we were assigned to the ward to handle patients. No standard operational procedure (SOP) nor policy was explained to us. The system in the ward was purely functional and Arabic.

Because of the language barrier, we Filipinos were left to do the leg work and give the medications. A week later, I was given the toughest responsibility of my life — to set up the first intensive care unit (ICU) in Makkah. With the help of a Filipino medical technologist named Teoderico Ballaho, I managed to operate the bedside monitors, including the central system and the ventilators which had been untouched for years. Praise be to Allah, the operating manuals were still intact.

In all my eight years in the nurses' home, our flat became the nerve center and receiving station for practically all newcomers. I saw to it that no one after us would have to go through the difficulties we had. It took us a month to find out where to buy our food supplies such as white rice, fish, and vegetables. The taste of Arabic food was completely new to us. The rapport I established with the other Filipinos made me a mother figure to them. In time I would become known to the Arabs as the mother of the Filipino workers. I became "Mommy" even to our Arab counterparts. Even the Moro National Liberation Front chairman, Prof. Nur Misuari, couldn't help breaking protocol by addressing me that way.

It is difficult for women to work in the Kingdom because we face many restrictions, especially since this is a holy place. Outdoor recreations such as games or sports are not available to us. All I hear are don'ts — Don't do this, don't do that — never do's. We are allowed to go out only once a week for three hours — to do our marketing and to pray in the great Mosque of Haram. Even then, there is little time left for shopping because the prescribed time covers the two prayers, *Maghrib* (the sunset prayer) and *Isha* (the evening prayer), and no stores are open during prayer time.

The wearing of the *abaya* and the veil to cover ourselves is a must; in fact, it was stressed during the briefings at the Philippine Overseas Employment Administration the day before we left Manila. We may not wear makeup to work, so grooming is out of the question. Association with the opposite sex is not allowed. This was an outrage, especially to people of Western orientation. Praise be to Allah, we were born Muslims, and so we understand. I didn't realize the importance of all these restrictions until one day, while waiting in the emergency room for transport to get me home, an Arab bystander grabbed me and kissed me. It was a terrible humiliation for me as I had barely started my first year. The man was jailed for three years, but I eventually agreed to his release out of consideration for his family.

4

Language and other cultural differences presented problems to us in our work as health providers, but we found ways to recognize Arabic symbols and do the health charts in Arabic too. A number of non-Arab nurses quickly developed a good command of the Arabic language because they saw the effect of the language barrier on the provision of total quality care. Eventually, however, charting in English was accepted in the ICU.

The inadequacies I saw in nursing were shattering. We had to raise the nursing standards in the ICU. Standard operational procedures were eventually enforced. We were very lucky to have a sensible chief, Dr. Hassan Zaid from Alexandria, Egypt, who had great faith in Filipino nurses. It was during his term that we started the first educational program in the ICU.

To a certain extent, the multinational set-up generated constructive competition among the workers. The Filipinos' professionalism and positive attitudes enhanced rapport and were widely recognized. I'm proud to say that the performance of our nursing staff in the entire Kingdom impressed the authorities and increased the demand for Filipino personnel.

ONE OF THE RISKS pilgrims face during the hot season is heatstroke. The most vulnerable are the pilgrims from the cold countries. Being unaccustomed to heat is a predisposing factor; other factors are obesity, old age, overfatigue, lack of sleep, lack of exercise, dehydration, and infection and other diseases. Heatstroke is a very complex clinical condition in which an elevated body temperature causes tissue damage. It is characterized by hot, dry and flushed skin, disturbance of consciousness, and a rectal temperature of 40 degrees Centigrade and above. If prompt and effective treatment is not given to the patient, he has as much as an 80 percent chance of dying.

I was appointed nursing supervisor of the heatstroke working forces along with three others who included my sister, Sharifa Soraya. The letter order containing our appointments came from the Directorate General Office of the Western Region in Jeddah. We were made to join the official delegation and to follow the itinerary of the hajj (from Makkah to Arafat, Muzdalifa, Mina, and back to Makkah).

The last ritual of the hajj is the throwing of pebbles in Mina (on the 10th, 11th, and 12th of the month of Dul Hijah), symbolic of Abraham's strong rejection of the temptations of the three devils (thus, he threw stones at them) in the sacrifice in which he offered his son to God. We consider those three days as the peak times for heatstroke cases. At one time the temperature in Makkah had reached 50 degrees Centigrade. By 10 in the morning, we could hear the penetrating sound of the ambulance sirens. Heatstroke cases started to arrive one after the other until they filled the casualty room, and still they kept coming. We were left alone to attend to the patients, most of whom were unconscious, and we must have done our job so well that even the Filipino cleaners and porters whom we had trained earlier greatly impressed our doctors during the emergency. Dr Adnan Jamjoom, the regional director of health affairs for the Western Region, would say repeatedly afterward, "That was extremely laudable." He joked, "That was the first time I saw stretchers running like jet planes."

The prescribed working time during the hajj is 12 hours, but due to the urgency of the situation we were forced to work eight hours more. Some of our Arab counterparts were so exhausted they would sneak out one by one, leaving the Heatstroke Treatment Center in Mina General Hospital to the Filipinos. At two in the morning, we were still attending to pilgrims coming from Egypt, Turkey, and Indonesia. Some patients who could not be accommodated in the treatment centers had to be content with simple fanning. Our Filipino staff had to climb the body-cooling machine in order to position unconscious patients who were obese.

Amidst all the work, we had to crack jokes to keep ourselves alive; one of us imagined himself to be in a slaughterhouse, drawing amused laughter from us. At that very moment, the minister of health and his party came in. The minister was surprised to see the same faces he had seen that morning and marveled that we still had the grace to laugh. It was a hilarious scene — our tiny nurses on top of the Makkah body-cooling machines positioning huge patients — and one that won the admiration of the officials. Two days later, just before the health minister left for Riyadh, he posed for pictures with each of the heatstroke staff. Two weeks later, we received by official pouch our pictures with a personal dedication for each one of us from the minister. That gracious gesture from a respected person was the first and last of its kind, because taking photographs is not allowed in the Kingdom. That remarkable gentleman is now the Saudi ambassador to the United Kingdom, His Excellency Dr. Gazi Al Gosaiby, who is also noted for his poetry.

I considered our years with heatstroke cases as golden years, the best of our prime time in nursing. It led me to conduct studies on a

6

patho-physiology program entitled "Heatstroke from the Nurse's Point of View." The title itself, which I used in my presentation, earned me a standing ovation during the MOH Hajj Workshop in Jeddah on March 18, 1982. The workshop was attended by 12 well-known medical scientists from the United States, Canada, Germany, Switzerland, and the UK. I wasn't even supposed to be a speaker, but after the afternoon session on the first day, Dr. Mustafa Khogali of Sudan, who is an institution in the treatment of heatstroke as well as a political figure, approached me and said, "Sister Sharifa, can we ask you to speak on the nursing side of heatstroke tomorrow?" I was speechless. Then he explained that the distinguished speakers were asking about the nurses' viewpoint. All I could answer was, "I just can't say no to you, Sir." I paused, then added, "I'll try my best anyway, but please don't expect too much from me, okay?"

At that moment I wasn't aware of the enormous commitment I got myself into, until I realized that I had to prepare myself. That night I had to skip the banquet in honor of our visiting speakers. The following day, my companions and I were a little tense and nervous. I could only smile at Dr. Khogali when I saw him trapped in conversation with our health officials. Suddenly, it was time for the first session. I was the third speaker for that day. All I wanted was to give the best of myself for I felt my being a Filipino deeply.

Do you know that except in 1986, 1990, 1994, and 1996, when there were one or two adults, there have been no recorded cases of heatstroke among the Filipino pilgrims? Generally, there are more older people who come for the hajj, some of them even wishing to die in the holy land. What helps Filipino pilgrims is that they never fail to bring with them umbrellas, native fans, and medicines. That's how health-conscious Filipinos are.

But during the hajj in the summer of 1990 our former ambassador to the Kingdom, lawyer Abraham Rasul, almost lost his life. Praise be to Allah, he was given immediate intervention right in the Philippine tent. He was not supposed to go to Makkah that day because the heat was intense. I tried to convince his wife, former senator Santanina Rasul, to persuade him to stay in Jeddah. I was concerned about his hypertension and diabetes. It was my lucky year as I was excused from my office so that I could make my own hajj. The two Rasul sons were also around: Jun, a doctor in sports medicine who had come all the way from New York, and Yusuf, a member of the embassy staff. We all proceeded to

Arafat Valley (on the 8th of the month of Dul Hijah) without the ambassador. The temperature was 50 degrees Centigrade. Early morning the following day, we were all surprised when the ambassador arrived with two companions. After greeting us, he left immediately to meet all the Filipino pilgrims. I tried to catch Mrs. Rasul's eye, if only to warn her to get ready. I also tried to ignore my strong intuition, and hoped things would go well. I started to feel restless toward noon, then at one in the afternoon the ambassador came, accompanied by two members of the Philippine delegation. I knew something was wrong. The ambassador looked pale and exhausted. All of a sudden he approached his wife and said, "Nen, I don't feel good." Then he collapsed.

The tent was thrown into a commotion, except for Mrs. Rasul who maintained her composure all throughout the ordeal. I told everyone to relax and calm down and give us space for ventilation. We managed to give the ambassador immediate emergency management. It was frightening, but I had to be strong and confident. Indeed, I could only turn to the Great Almighty Allah at that moment. I could also feel the love and care of everyone around. Some made excellent fanners, as fanning was our only recourse in that situation. I used cold modulated water to cool the ambassador. At that point, the only thing that mattered to me was to bring back his level of consciousness, for at least I could be certain of a healthy response. Praise be to Allah, after 15 minutes he regained consciousness. We rushed him to Makkah immediately.

ALL THESE YEARS, I have stressed to my nurses the importance of giving psychological support to both the patient and his or her family. This is an aspect of health care often neglected by most health providers. It is not difficult to understand the basic anxieties of the acutely traumatized person — his fear of death, mutilation, and loss. All these can surely lead to loss of control, whether emotional, physical, or intellectual. How well we can alleviate their anxieties and increase their confidence speaks of our values and essence as nurses.

In 1984 the first English program was carried out by the new director of health affairs in Makkah, Dr. Mohammad Amin Mojaddadi. A Western-oriented Saudi, he gave us full and equal recognition with our Arab counterparts. The breakthrough was a great source of relief to the Filipino personnel. Under the new hospital director, another Western-trained Saudi doctor named Dr. Mohammad Ahmed Jamal, the medical department was placed under the full management of the Filipino staff who met his challenge by becoming a model section. From head nurse, I was promoted not long after to nurse supervisor. I found myself taking the lead role in setting up new hospitals (Zaher Maternity Center, Rusaifa Maternity Center, Hera General Hospital, all in Makkah, the Heatstroke Treatment Center in Madina, and finally, the Al Sulaimana Surgical Hospital in Riyadh). My team stayed in Riyadh for almost two months. In just one month the Al Sulaimana Surgical Hospital was all set for inauguration. But we felt restless for Makkah, which we considered home. Days passed, and still there was no word about our departure. Until one day the director general of the Central Region came and, after the usual Islamic greetings, said "Alas! you're all leaving tomorrow, Sharifa. Do you know that your regional office in Jeddah is willing to give me 10 nurses in place of you?" It was all I wanted to hear. I heaved a sigh of relief and wept tears of joy.

Three months after the Riyadh venture, our team was booked again to go to Jeddah, this time to tackle the problem of the nursing service in Al Shaty Hospital. To my surprise, the problem was just one of understaffing. This time, 30 nurses from the three other hospitals in Makkah were added to our group. The nursing director was a British national who later resigned. There were other Filipino permanent staff in the hospital. The place was relaxing and professional; better yet, it was near the sea.

To us who came from a "less permissive" area, Jeddah offered a great change and relief. It is one of the most beautiful and safest cities in the world, a preferred destination for foreigners. We stayed in Jeddah for more than three months, and have accomplishments and happy memories of the period to cherish. I shall always look back to it as a time that gave me a good foundation and inspiration. It was also a time when I became instrumental in promoting the standards of our nursing profession. I shall always remember the challenges we faced strongly and, of course, the good times, the parties we enjoyed and acquaintances we made, which all added color to our new horizon. Jeddah remains in the hearts of overseas Filipino workers. I always tell friends that they would be lucky to be assigned there.

THE OUTBREAK of the Gulf War in 1990 shook the entire world. Among the expatriates, there were mixed emotions. Some wanted to go home immediately; others could not, and felt helpless. Some remained true to the call of duty and responsibility. Though Makkah was outside the war zone, we prayed hard for the safety of those in the affected areas, including my brother.

One significant thing about the Gulf War that I can never forget was the strong faith in Allah of the people here. They remained calm and confident, and helped ease our ordeal. The nationwide emergency drills and warnings on chemical warfare, however, gave us an occasional scare. One day my husband arrived from Riyadh and gave me a gas mask; he insisted that I wear it while in the car. I imagined myself looking awkward in that mask as I traveled to Makkah (around 120 kilometers from Jeddah). I imagined, too, what a funny sight I would be to the other commuters and the policemen at the checkpoints. It was only when he started to laugh that I realized my husband was only kidding. I wonder now how true it was that the cattle in three of the Kingdom's leading dairy farms were provided with especially designed gas masks.

To some Filipinos in the eastern and central regions, the encounters between the Iraqis' Scud missiles and the Americans' Patriots were spectacular events. As chairperson of the medical committee (contingency program) of the Philippine Mission in Jeddah, I was in Riyadh at that time. Once, when I heard a Scud coming, I rushed out of the embassy premises to have a good view of it. Some people took pictures; others clapped their hands excitedly. There were those who stayed on rooftops just to wait for the encounter while having their usual barbecue session. They seemed not to realize the great danger to which they were exposing themselves. Did you know that one of the Scuds landed just 150 meters away from the Philippine Embassy building? Another landed a short distance from the Philippine ambassador's residence. For lack of space I cannot go into greater detail here about the other events. All I know is that if the war had gone full scale, not even the contingency plan of the Philippine government could have saved the approximately 750,000 overseas Filipino workers (OFWs) in the Kingdom at that time.

WE IN MAKKAH certainly had our share of ups and downs, adventures, and escapades in the Eighties. Most of them are gone now, after having served for more than a decade. One thing is sure — they just couldn't bear the thought of being away from home longer. For one thing, the loss of an immediate family member while one is away is heartbreaking and traumatic. Very few can go home to pay their final respects to the dead, because plane fares are so expensive. The more practical prefer to send money home instead.

We ourselves went through bad times when we lost four of our dearest friends and colleagues. They are all buried in Makkah. Joy died in a car accident on the day of the Edil Fitri, the feast day after the month of Ramadan. My brother-in-law, Nixon Uy, succumbed to myocardial infarction (MI) at the age of 35. The third was Judith Matingka, a doctor's wife, who died of cancer. Two years ago, we lost Grace Joe, also to MI. Two other Filipino nurses in Makkah died in a fire that struck the private hospital where they worked. The body of Zenaida Adiyad was recovered, but a baby who was found at the same time miraculously survived the fire. The other victim, Saadeya Dima, was asphyxiated. In the case of cancer-stricken OFWs, some chose to go home when their cancer reached the terminal stage.

To every OFW, being away from home is unsettling, devastating, and agonizing. We all have our insecurities and suffer when we are deprived of love and attention. It is primarily the family that suffers the consequences, the children especially. Lucky are those whose marriages are not affected by the so-called "price of money." The presence of parents is necessary and important to the growth and development of children. A working parent who goes home once a year tends to shower his or her children with material gifts, if only to compensate for the long absence. Parents fail to see that this kind of love is wrong. Children may grow up spoiled and demanding; some are even drawn to drugs. When the spouse back home gets involved with another man or woman, one result could be delinquent children. Sad to say, absence from home has upset, if not destroyed, the families of about 75 percent of OFWs.

Even those who are lucky to have their families with them must bear the burden of high tuition imposed by the Philippine International Schools in Jeddah, Riyadh, and Al Khobar. This seems contradictory to the purpose for establishing these schools. What does this make of the constitutional right of every Filipino citizen to free public education?

In 1988 I was on a flight bound for Manila with a close friend who had finished her contract. I was going home for my annual vacation. To my surprise, my friend opened up to me about her problem with her son. He was only six years old when she first left for Saudi Arabia, and every time she went home for a vacation, it was agony to go back to her job in

Saudi. But now that she was going home for good, he didn't want her to. She said she was afraid, and she asked me what I thought. It was difficult for me to answer. I was caught in a situation where I believed I shouldn't encroach on someone else's personal life, that whatever I said should warm rather than hurt the heart. All I could say was that her son must be all grown up now.

Life indeed is full of trials. I have had my own predicaments. Behind all my achievements are frustrations. Yet, whenever something overwhelms me, my first natural response is acceptance. I believe that life has to go on and that we should always make the best of what remains. Perhaps it is for this reason that I've turned to the nursing profession. My strong inclination to music (I belong to a family of musically minded people) has often eased my homesickness and sorrow. I love to play the piano and the guitar, and I love to sing. I compose songs for friends and loved ones and I like to sing our *kundiman* love songs. I love to cook as well, especially *pinakbet* and *sinigang*. I also do oil paintings. For my first painting I did multicolored sails at sea with Jolo's famous Mount Tumantangis in the background. My second work, "Nursing in Islam," shows the heroism of the first Muslim nurses during the battles of Islam.

WHEN WORKING in a country like Saudi Arabia, one often has to forego educational and professional advancement, for educational opportunities are available only to citizens of the Kingdom. This is a big sacrifice for those who aspire to earn master's and doctoral degrees. Even study grants are not available to us foreign workers even if we're willing to go on leave without pay.

So far I have been able to conduct three research studies — on a patho-physiology program in nursing, on general management for quality assurance, and on the history and development of nursing in Holy Makkah. I always thank the Great Almighty Allah for the guidance and blessings he gives me every day.

When my father, Said Mohammad Ali, was still alive, he often wished that I would serve abroad, particularly in Makkah. At his deathbed in May 1976, he insisted that I go to the Kingdom. Finally, in 1978, Filipino medical personnel were recruited for Saudi Arabia for the first time. That was when I realized that my father's dream was written in my destiny. How I wish he were still alive so that I could tell him how much I love him. He was a simple man, but he ingrained in us the values of honesty and decency.

I was born in Turtle Island (Taganak), Sulu, on November 26, 1948, the third of 11 children and the eldest of the girls. We were blessed with adorable parents. Our father became the first mayor of the seven Turtle islands (formerly under Malaysia) which were turned over to the Philippine government during the presidency of Elpidio Quirino. Father realized the importance of a good education for us and so he gave up his political career and returned to Jolo. A member of the royal adviser to the Sultanate of Sulu, he established a good reputation. His philanthropic spirit influenced us a great deal.

My high school days in Notre Dame were a glorious time in Jolo. I can still recall how I hurdled the hard times, such as when I saw Mother Enriqueta, the mother superior, with her sharp eyes. I couldn't seem to get away from her. I didn't realize that she loved me until graduation night, when she hugged and kissed me. Her tears and her sad face are all I remember of this person who played such an important part in my life. Mothers Norberta and Imelda and Miss Paulate were heartwarming to talk to. My classmates and friends were nice too. I miss them all.

Now everything is gone, and not even the peace settlement and development programs of our government can bring back the glory of my beloved hometown. Our people have suffered the consequences of war. Twice we have been victimized by fire. We lost our first house to a fire in 1960, and our second during the war in 1974. The loss of many lives, including that of my maternal grandfather, Serapion Uztani Puquiz, was very traumatic for us.

MY ULTIMATE DREAM is to see Jolo regain its former glory. How, and when? Only time will tell. The search for peace and tranquility is what forced me to be away from home. This is what has driven some of our peace-loving citizens to search for new horizons.

Where are the users? Where are the manipulators? The advocates of what they claim to be *jihad* (religious wars)? Are they away from home?

I promised myself that I wouldn't end this essay without mentioning my sentiments about the so called "social force" in our country. I have borne this within me from the time I first learned right from wrong. How many times and in how many different ways shall we endure the loss and the grief brought on by our Muslim identity?

Will it be a barrier forever? When will the media stop identifying us in terms of that barrier? When will the time for rectification come? Aren't we Muslims Filipinos too?

I belong to the Tausug tribe which regards men as superior to women. Our heritage has a great deal to do with the conservative manners of our women. Yet I believe that in this age of enlightenment no intelligent Filipino woman will allow herself to stagnate or become a liability to her community. Whether we can stand up to the stresses and strains of life I cannot say, but we have lasted far longer than I expected.

Holy Makkah was a breakthrough in my life because I was given the task of handling one of the most important services in the Ministry of Health. In fact, when health officials invited me to become the chief of the newly created Regional Nursing Committee, it took me several days to decide to accept the offer. There were many considerations to think about, chiefly my being a foreigner and a woman in a society where men are thought to be superior to women and in an office with a purely male staff. There were also the high expectations of everyone, as I was endorsed by all the hospital directors. All these were more than enough reason for me to say no. But my ultimate vision — of uplifting the standards of the nursing profession in this region — convinced me to face the new challenge. I also wanted to protect the interests of the other nurses and to be their voice in time of need. I knew that the coming days, months, and years would call for sacrifices, and would be challenging because I would be starting from zero.

It has been a decade since. Praise be to Allah, I'm still here. The recognition, awards, and honors I have achieved are my only proof of my commitment and the fulfillment of our goals (not mine alone), in the service of humanity. Let it be remembered that once there were overseas Filipino workers who served in the Kingdom to the best of their abilities, despite the dire consequences of being away from home. Let there be "peace and prosperity" in our country, for only then will our people stop leaving home in search of a living.

Tita Angangco

From Lit to IT:
An Immigrant
Experience

THERE ARE TWO things I wished for my children. The first was that at an early age they would know what kind of work they wanted to do. Barring that, my second wish was that they would love whatever it was they ended up doing.

My education was rich in books, cultural events, and social expectations. I had a sense of the many different social and professional stereotypes I could be: married — single; housewife — worker; lawyer — doctor. But there was something missing. All the talk and the expectations were about the external rewards of being: being wealthy, being respected, being revered, being powerful. There was hardly any talk of the internal rewards of simply doing, of the pleasure of working on something for the sheer enjoyment of working on it.

My first intimation of this pleasure was when I fell in love with fiction. I read relentlessly and with passion. In the beginning I read to get to the end of a story. But no sooner had one story ended than I was on to the next one. I read story after story, writer after writer, always in anticipation of the next plot line, the next arresting insight. There were many rewards to reading — learning new things, sharing found knowledge with friends and strangers, feeling accomplished and in touch. But for me the purest of these rewards lay in the simple act of reading — that moment of absorption, the flight from one's self, the pleasure of being somewhere other than within one's own skin.

I was not blessed with knowing what I wanted to be, let alone do. Growing up middle class and female in Manila in the Sixties was confusing. It was like being between too many things. Between being allowed to be smart but not smart enough to know more than the men. Between being progressive enough to want a career but not progressive enough to be ambitious. Between being able to know in your heart what you wanted without the courage to ask for it. It was a time poised between two worlds – my parents' world and my world – and I walked the tightrope between the comfort of theirs and the uncertainty of mine.

My parents wanted me to be a doctor like them. I couldn't relate to being a doctor. I couldn't relate to being anything, really, because I didn't know what that meant. I was looking for something other than inert images of being — being a doctor, a lawyer, an academic. So I started a long and tortuous journey in search of (more often in flight from) what I wanted to be.

LITERATURE WAS my first love. So after college I taught English in high school for a very brief while, then went on to do graduate work in comparative literature. I spent a year reading literature. It was probably one of the best years of my life. I could do what I liked doing best — reading — and I could do it with impunity. But no one would pay me just to read, and I didn't fancy doing the other stuff that went with it, like teaching, writing, research. When the department offered me a scholarship, I panicked. The thought of sitting in one of those tiny, musty carrels in the English department for the rest of my life, single and loveless, jettisoned me out of my English Lit dream world into something more practical — psychology.

I soon found out that reading psychology was not easy. It took me three days to get past Hebb's article on the reticular formation of the brain. The phrasing was awkward, the language turgid. I was also not used to reading nonfiction. I needed to keep a D.H. Lawrence novel by me at all times to break the monotony. I probably read more Lawrence than psychology that first semester. But for once in my life I stuck to the course. It took me 10 years to complete my postgraduate degree. When I finished, I had gone to four universities and shifted my major five times, but I had done all that within the same field of study.

During those 10 years, I settled on a pattern of working some years and studying other years. I worked in an insurance company, a primary school for boys, and a research agency, and ran the research department for the Population Commission. I began to develop a sense of what I could be. I liked the idea of becoming a development worker, someone who moved from one Third World country to the next doing good things. The travel was appealing. Equally appealing were the people who worked in development. They were quirky, different, sometimes very smart, never boring. But it was still not clear to me what I would do as a development worker, other than hang around interesting development people pushing the latest trend in development programs at some tired bureaucrats in some poor and desperate Third World country.

I was then in my twenties, clever and fashionably independent. But I lived under the weight of so many people's expectations. Romantic and undisciplined, I had no idea how to go about being what people expected me to be, let alone what I expected myself to be. I didn't know how to be there because I didn't know how to get there. Nothing in my indolent upbringing had prepared me for the getting there. So I muddled through for 10 years trying to figure it out, and along the way I started to learn a few things. I learned how to apply myself, and as I applied myself, I learned to apply myself even more. This was to prove an invaluable skill. I learned how to learn and develop an interest in mastering difficult things which were alien to me, like statistics and methodology. Finally, I learned about the craft of work, about setting one's own standards and working to them, independently of what others might want or expect.

I finally completed my master's at Harvard in 1978, specializing in evaluation research methodologies. Unable to settle on content, I decided to specialize in methods. This left me room to be both a specialist and a generalist. I was still hedging my bets. On hindsight, however, it turned out to be a very good hedge.

I left the Philippines for the US for the second time in 1975. In my gut I knew, from leaving and returning the first time, that if I ever left the Philippines again, I would most likely never go back. But I needed to leave for many reasons, heart-wise and other-wise. And there was the hope that my would-be development career might take me back home again. At that time I didn't realize what not going back home again really meant. I knew it meant not working in the Philippines. I hadn't thought through what it meant beyond that — that it meant working elsewhere, that elsewhere was a distant place where I knew no one and no one knew me.

MY FIRST JOB abroad was in the summer of 1978. I worked for a consulting firm in Boston writing the evaluation research component for proposals responding to federal government contract requests. In four months I worked on more than 30 proposals. I achieved an average output of five to seven pages a day, exclusive of research. I was so terrified of

18

failing I worked like I had never worked before in my life. I overperformed. At the end of the proposal writing season, I was considered one of the most productive proposal writers in the company. I was also exhausted. I knew then what it meant to work elsewhere. Connectionless, you had only yourself and your skills, and they would be tested again and again and again.

In January 1979, my husband Tim and I left Boston for Toronto, where he joined the faculty of business at York University. Tim's mission was to modernize York's MIS (management information systems, code name for computing) curriculum. In turn, York offered us and my children, who were still in the Philippines, safe passage to Canada without the trials and abuses of immigration. It was to be an interim move. Tim and I both wanted to work in development. I wanted it perhaps more than Tim did, but he had worked internationally for 10 years and was known in the development community and was in demand. He was going to be the passport to my new career. We planned to stay two years in Canada, just enough time to settle the family.

Needing an interim job, I settled on two options: market research in the private sector or program research in the public sector. I opted for the public sector since it was more in line with my development career aspirations. I landed my first job in Canada as a research analyst with the provincial Ministry of Corrections. I didn't know it then, but Corrections offered perhaps the best research opportunities in the Ontario provincial government at that time. Outside of Corrections, the research pickings would be slim. This was Canada in the Eighties, after all, not America in the heyday of the Seventies when social programming was a serious government concern and knowing what worked and didn't work was still considered an empirical issue.

The moment of truth for us came when we got a call from Boston. Tim was offered a two-year assignment in Egypt to head up an oral rehydration (code name: diarrhea killer) program. I was to play the lead evaluation role. It was to be my first and only offer in the area I had trained for. The subject of going to Egypt came up at dinner that evening. Tears flowed. The children were distraught. They had been uprooted from the Philippines and were not about to be uprooted again. We did not insist. Tim made comforting noises about other future opportunities. But in my heart I knew that interim had shifted to permanent. I would have to make the most of Canada and the Ontario provincial government.

By that time, I had moved from Corrections to Housing. I was to stay in Housing for the next 14 years. Because I had never worked continuously and in any one place for more than two years, those 14 years would become my boot camp years. I started out in Housing as a research officer, an empty title. Housing was not a place where the empirical counted for more than the paper on which a report was written. However, I was determined to do research and so did whatever I could dream up in the way of surveys and data analysis projects. I hustled a computer terminal from the information technology (IT) department and when the micro-computers came, I was one of the first in the ministry to get a personal computer on her desk.

My computing skills were hard won. I was one of 10 guinea pigs in a seminar research course at Harvard where the use of a new statistical software called SAS was piloted. (SAS is now one of the best known and most profitable analytical and decision support products on the market.) Since none of the instructors knew the product, all we had to go by was one slim flawed draft of a manual. I spent that semester in the computer room. I was there when it opened and I was there when it closed. I remember that experience as one where my ability to master an alien skill was honed to its finest.

I had managed to get support for a sizeable research project on utility consumption costs in public housing projects. I worked independently, had access to resources, and was enjoying myself. Looking back, I would say my first initial work years were halcyon years. I worked in a relatively obscure space, was fairly competent, occupied the bottom of the pecking hierarchy, and posed no threat to anyone. This, however, was about to change.

IT WAS AROUND 1986 when I was approached by Murray Wilson, the executive director of the division I worked for. He had heard about these new microcomputers and, being a progressive man, wanted to trial run a number of them in his regional offices. The IT department had turned down his request for support — it had no plans of deploying microcomputers widely across the ministry, their position being that the micro was a passing fad. But not wanting to completely alienate Murray, who was a powerful man, IT suggested that perhaps the Asian research analyst who seemed to know her way around these devices and worked in his division would not mind supporting his micros.

Murray (bless his heart) bought the first six micros in the operations division. I installed and supported them in each of the six regional offices across the province. I still had my research job; the micros were kind of my side business. In less than a year, the original six micros grew to about 40. In two years, the 57 housing authorities across the province, all reporting to the same Murray Wilson, bought the new computers; my micro farm grew to more than 100. By the third year, I was responsible for more than 500 micro computers and a staff of some 30 computer professionals. All this was accomplished through one man's vision and resolve and a very firm handshake. I would never meet anyone like Murray Wilson again in my career in the Ontario public service.

My users, who were field personnel, did not see me as an IT professional. They believed I was one of them, having come out of a non-IT background. They gave me tremendous support and in turn I worked to serve their interests. As I did more and more for my field clients, my empire grew and my relationship with the corporate IT department began to deteriorate. I was about to get my first serious lesson in organizational realities.

Organizations are static microcultures. They don't like change. They don't like new ways of doing things. And they don't like upstarts. The microcomputer was an upstart technology. It behaved differently from traditional mainframe forms. It threatened established patterns of ownership and power. It marked the beginning of a fundamental sea change in the contract between the technology providers and the people who used the technology. Today, many of us take our computing independence for granted, but only 15 years ago the computer department controlled everything — purchase, access, and knowledge.

It was not by design that I found myself in the midst of this sea change. It was not entirely by accident, either. Having gone through so many changes in my life, both personal and professional, I happen to like change. I embraced this job with all the energy and enthusiasm I could muster. I recruited the youngest, smartest people I could find and together we built a new and very different IT organization, a service organization. My methods and success were celebrated by my division. But I paid a price. I was not recognized nor compensated appropriately for the work I did. This was the trade-off with corporate IT.

I wonder now whether I would have had to pay the same price had I not been foreign. I'm not talking about discrimination. I'm talking about stereotypes and expectations. I believe I deeply disappointed some people. I wasn't the Asian they had come to know and love. I smoked, drank, sometimes swore, and challenged the status quo.

During this period of my career, I held two jobs — my renegade computer job and a program job. My program job was my safety net. It was mainstream and respectable. I ran the corporate planning section for the division I worked for. This section led the divisional planning function and did projects related to new program directions and requests for program funding. I learned a lot in this job: about the role housing plays in the social economy; about social safety nets and what we can reasonably achieve with blunt government instruments; about political expediency and fragile bureaucracies.

I came upon my next job under serendipitous circumstances. The housing program branch needed revitalizing, having lost most of its key people. I was offered the job of manager, nonprofit programs, but I turned it down. Later, I was given two choices: report to corporate IT or take the manager job. It was a gentle form of blackmail and one for which I will be forever grateful. I took the manager job and gave up my upstart computing career.

I spent the next five years designing a new nonprofit program for Ontario, 20,000 units of new social housing valued at roughly two billion dollars. The old program had come under considerable public scrutiny for its "irresponsible expenditure of public funds and loose administration" (their words, not mine). Even as we labored under a socialist government, the political winds were changing. We were entering a different, dramatically more conservative, and meaner era.

My mandate was to design a program which could survive the scrutiny of Cabinet, the provincial auditor, the media, and anyone else who may have thought that yet another nonprofit program in Ontario was reckless and wasteful. To this end I brought to program design the "stuff" I had learned from my computer days: stuff like structured analysis, process decomposition, flowcharting. It was an exciting experiment in cross-disciplinary methods, and it worked. When the Conservatives finally took over, the rigor built into the program's design allowed them to dismantle what was left of the program. Ironically, the strategy we devised to keep the program going provided the mechanism which allowed it to be stopped.

SHORTLY BEFORE the new government took over, I left Housing for a computer job in Management Board Secretariat (MBS), the central agency of the provincial government. MBS had been looking for quite a while for a director to manage computer services for the secretariat. It needed someone who understood IT management and how to position IT for cost-effective client service delivery. What I had done five years ago in Housing had become mainstream. I was hired.

My colleagues in Housing were appalled. In Housing I was in operations and part of "the line," the people who actually made things happen. The line has and will always have a healthy and well-deserved contempt for anything "corporate," i.e., staff. I was not just joining the corporate part of Housing; I was joining the mother of all corporates — the central agency, the group that manufactured all the rules for all the other people to follow.

I fled Housing for all kinds of reasons, the most significant of which was the sense of an impending ideological shift in government policy and directions. Housing had become my social justice work, the reason I worked for government. I was now part of a large stakeholder community of housing advocates who saw housing as one of the primary building blocks toward the creation of a healthy social economy in Ontario. However, the political winds were about to shift such that it was going to become impossible to continue to do this work within government.

I was also about to shift, from missionary to someone who simply worked for a living. For the past 10 years in Housing, I had worked on average 55- to 60-hour weeks. I had spent most of my forties trying to understand this thing called work, developing the skills needed to survive it, and not achieving any balance between work, status, mission, and personal life. I had come full circle back to the questions about being and doing that had plagued me earlier on in my career.

I now understood the "doing" side. I understood what I could do and what I enjoyed doing. The "being" part of it continued to perplex and elude me. I had worked for more than 10 years in Housing, had done two full-time jobs for the better part of that time, had managed some of the largest and most complex policy and implementation projects in that Ministry, but my status had advanced only to the position of manager. I had not managed my career. And for someone like me, a visible minority and a woman, managing one's career is profoundly important. The challenge for me was to understand and accept the personal responsibility and implications of not having done that.

There was another part to the "being" side, the part of what I stood for, the reason I worked for government. That, too, needed reformulation. When I first joined government, I didn't appreciate the extent of its pluralism nor the elasticity with which it shapes and reshapes its responses in line with the political texture of the day. Working in government can thus never be truly satisfying, and I found aspects of the work deeply frustrating. I needed to find a different way of fulfilling that part of me. I also needed to learn to accept government for the flawed and often helpless institution it can be.

The MBS job was perfect. It did two things for me. One, it offered me a promotion. Two, it gave me a way of separating the work from the mission. The job had no pretensions to saving the world. It was just a job.

But I needed to continue to do some of the work I had done in Housing. I had done some community work in the mid-Eighties when I helped organize the building of two social housing projects for the Filipino community. As my role in housing became more central, however, I had to leave my community work behind for conflict of interest reasons. Leaving Housing meant I could resume my housing community work. So I joined the board of an organization called Homes First which houses the homeless and the hard to house. Over the next five years, Homes First would provide me the opportunity to make my social contribution.

Today, I am a full-fledged IT professional. I define myself in terms of the industry I work in — the computer industry. Being part of government is secondary and happenstance. I have laboriously learned a big lesson that wasn't apparent to the *activista* flower-child: there are more ways of changing the world than through work, nine to five. I stumbled across, or maybe was subconsciously attracted to, an industry that doesn't much care about anything except the application of technology to solving problems of efficiency and productivity. It doesn't care, for example, whether its minions are black, brown, or beige. On the Internet, famously, no one knows (or cares) if you're a dog, or even a small, retiring Filipino woman. And so it is in my job.

Here, then, is my wisdom on the subject of the immigrant experience. I have seen that the migrant is uniquely disadvantaged, by reason of cultural dislocation, rootlessness, discrimination, and starting over, late. I have also seen that aspirations don't travel well. What you might have wished to achieve in your homeland may be impossible, or irrelevant, in your adopted country. You have to recast your dreams, and recast the means you adopt to achieve them.

But the immigrant in North America is also blessed in more than an obvious material sense. She is free of significant societal expectations. In the great anonymous cities, where every third person is an immigrant, she is free to craft a life (or not), free to leave a husband (or not), free to raise a family (or not), free to make a contribution (or not), free to dream again.

Dr. Nini Bautista de Garcia

A Nuclear Scientist I Never Meant to Be

IT IS A MONDAY morning, and I am sitting, peacefully content, in my little garden in one of the private enclaves of expatriates living in Vienna, a mixed community of mostly United Nations staff, with a sprinkling of Austrian professionals and businessmen. My neighbor writes a column in the *Bezirks Journal* (each of the 23 districts in Vienna has its own newspaper, mostly ads). Too bad my incessant duty travels for the UN and my unflagging interest in and involvement with the Philippine community in Vienna keep me from going that extra mile to participate more in the district affairs, except for Sunday Mass in the local parish. I walk to the church in fair or foul weather with my cleaning lady, a part-time domestic helper, friend, and occasional confidante.

Ahh, this is the life... Am I ever so lucky, and don't I know it! How many writers, frustrated or otherwise, would give an arm and a leg to be able to find the time and the wherewithal to sit in their garden on a workday, and luxuriate after a leisurely breakfast of American waffles and English tea with milk, and to indulge, indulge?

Yes, one must be extremely lucky to be able to do this, and one need not assuage any pangs of guilt by rationalizing and defensively saying, "Why, I deserve it...after all, I have been working hard all my life."

And now, nearing retirement from the International Atomic Energy Agency (IAEA) after 14 years of service, haven't I earned enough Brownie points by finishing a Philippine centennial project, a coffee- table book in full color, the first ever about the Filipino migrant community in Austria or elsewhere? How we sweated blood and tears for this book, which almost never was! It showcases the proud history and fascinating multicultural heritage of the Filipino people so that Austro-Filipino children too often saddled with identity crisis, incredulous Austrian or foreign spouses, and nonchalant Filipinos themselves can become a little prouder of being Filipinos.

As a tribute to the first Filipino migrants in Austria some 25 years ago, no less than the Austrian Chancellor said during the state visit of President Fidel Ramos that he knew, from personal experience, that healing was much faster with the loving care of Filipino nurses. A survey made by the University of Vienna also pointed out that the Filipinos are a more accepted group in Austria compared to the other cultural minorities there like the Turks, the Poles, the Peruvians, and the Chinese.

The singing of the birds in the neighbor's garden on such a lovely summer day, so rare in Wien, inspires, but I do not need much inspiration or further encouragement to write my story. I am driven instead by a need to tell those who will come after me, not about the successes I have had and how I achieved them, but more about how to cope and how to accomplish what one wants while being one's own person. Anything else would have been a cop-out, a waste of life even, for the nebulous and dubious rewards of a seemingly successful life of career, home and family, friends, loyal or otherwise, peer acceptance, and all such other indicators of "Hey, I'm okay... you're okay," or "Hey, I've got it made, and I am better than you are..."

It is not even a case of "What does it profit a man if he gains the whole world..." Modesty aside, I might even have had it all: envious friends jabbing left-handed compliments; career, home and family, friends; a modicum of creature comforts, travel, awards, community involvement. But I have also had my share of frenzy, of hectic workaholism, co-dependence, frustrations, disappointments, intrigues, almost legal battles, broken relationships, cheating boyfriends, envious friends, and ruthless backbiting — the whole gamut of human existence. In fact, that's the whole caboodle that's called life. And one learns and tries to remember the lessons well, and one forgives again and yet again, and tries to forget. One is wounded and embittered, and then is healed. One stumbles again and again, limps and finally gets back on one's feet. And oh yes, mistakes, I've made a lot, some too painful to remember, maybe for a later retelling or, like Scarlett O'Hara, "tomorrow"....

My involvement with the Filipinos in Austria started with a bang. I do not even quite recall how I got sucked into the community. There was the big earthquake of 1986 in the Philippines and like all true patriots, the Filipinos in Vienna rallied to the survivors' call for help. I organized a fund-raising evening with dinner and dancing, in addition to a cultural show, at the Palais Ferstel in Imperial Vienna's first district. The hefty proceeds from the evening were gratefully acknowledged by the coordinators of the relief efforts through the Department of Foreign Affairs. I had been in Vienna barely a year, having joined the International Atomic Energy Agency (IAEA) on April Fools' Day, 1985, a Sunday. It was rather cold in Vienna and my coat was still packed. Mercifully, I was staying with the Palabricas, my former colleagues at the Philippine Atomic Energy Commission (PAEC). Offie and I were together in Spain at the Junta de Energia Nuclear (Nuclear Energy Board). At one time there were hundreds of *becarios,* or fellows, at the Instituto de Studios Nucleares, a magnet for the bright and willing to go into the then glamorous field of atomic energy. The socialist government later diminished the role and the anti-nukes saw to it that the many brilliant careers were crushed and dismissed, and replaced by socialist nonscientists. One cannot argue with the powers that be, but that's another story.

SINCE I WAS no beauty queen, I perhaps unconsciously chose the other path of, ahem, brains (or would you call it chutzpah?), to make my mark in this world. I did not make a conscious effort to excel, but try I did. I was lucky that there were always lots of things to read as Dad had tons of books. He was always reading when he was not working in his laboratory after a full day in his dental clinic, or if he was not attending meetings of the Masonic Lodge, Eastern Star, Rotary, etc. Between them, Dad and Mom must have founded, or helped found, most of the charitable and civic organizations in Cavite — Rotary Club, Inner Wheel Club, Order of the Eastern Star, Order of the Rainbow for Girls, Woman's Club, Young Men's Christian Association, among others. I devoured whatever I could lay my hands on and at age five discovered the great American magazines and got lost in their bright, unachievable world.

But I digress. Let's look at the story of one who did not want a career in nuclear science.

Early on, a mentor, Professor Rosel, a pioneer soil scientist, told me that when you apply for a job make sure you are not only qualified but overqualified. For my first job I was surely more than qualified. It was the lowest rank of the government service with the dubious title of technical and editorial aide in an office publication called Irrigation News. I made it to the cover of the magazine, which reached all the farmers and administrators of irrigation projects under the Department of Public Works and Highways. I wrote a series of articles on the proposed salinity study of the Pampanga and Bulacan rivers which was later expanded into a research study funded by the National Science Development Board jointly with the Bureau of Soils where I did the chemical analysis. It was a sort of one-woman enterprise. I was project proponent, project leader, chief scientist, chief researcher, and I did even the menial jobs of field work. I did get help from my thesis students who did part of the lab work in exchange for tutorial and thesis advice. I would put in long hours at the old Bureau of Soils in Ermita, and had to stay in town to be able to go on early sampling trips to the Pampanga and Bulacan rivers which were plagued by salt intrusion. From this study I devised a quick method by which to warn farmers against pumping saline waters into their dry fields.

Even then I was the only woman in that world of field men but there was respect, probably because I was a no-nonsense girl who did not want to play — the field men were notorious womanizers, with a girl in every town where there were irrigation projects, plus entertainment from the country stops along the highways. It was grueling work doing kilometers of sampling, but "analysis is only as good as the sample," as any analyst knows. I had to do it myself. What if the field men were too lazy to drive out to the length and breadth of the area under study and just took samples wherever it was convenient? But we had fun talking to the farmers, interviewing them, solving their problems, and we were treated so well, a tribute to the Filipino sense of *utang na loob*. At that time, there was still a healthy respect for government "experts."

Supervisory positions in government required some units of administrative expertise or management. True to my mentor's maxim, I not only took the required units but earned a master's degree in business administration from the Ateneo. We were the last class to graduate from Ateneo Padre Faura before it succumbed to the economic theory of land use and gave way to a shopping center just like nearby Assumption Convent. My group of senior executives and professionals was as congenial as they were topnotch. Again I was the only woman in a class of men older than I who were top guns in their offices. The

MBA again served me in more ways than one. On the strength of this degree I moonlighted at a multinational PVC manufacturing company in Makati under a rather tough control freak.

It was a rare privilege to join the atomic energy world in the Philippines during its early years. The PAEC was founded in 1959 by then colonel Florencio A. Medina, former chief of the Research and Development Center of the Armed Forces of the Philippines, a chemist from UP, a man with vision, and a mover who turned that vision into reality. Together with Deputy Commissioner Pedro Afable, a civil engineer from the DPWH, he gathered all the brains from UP and formed the nucleus of PAEC.

One joined PAEC in those days to see the world. Every scientist candidate already had a proposed career path in the overall scheme of the country's nuclear energy program. Only the brightest were chosen since they had to qualify and be ready, able and willing to go abroad — to the centers of excellence, training grounds in the then emerging field of peaceful uses of atomic energy, and the multidisciplinary applications of nuclear science and technology. When I was interviewed by all these "pioneers," their standards were as exacting as those they had set for themselves. They would make comments such as "intelligent, but not brilliant," maybe tongue-in-cheek at times, that would faze even intrepid summas or magnas.

The Sixties were a glorious, exhilarating time to be at PAEC. It was one big family then, encouraged by the paterfamilias General Medina, who had 13 children of his own but treated the staff, scientists and driver like family and equally. His maxim, "Learning never ends," was the battlecry of PAEC then. Everybody but everybody was being trained for his or her own special and unique expertise. That was a lesson I learned well. My family and friends complained that I was always studying, accumulating a string of titles along the way and training certificates in atomic energy from various centers of excellence — B.S. in chemical engineering, M.S. in chemistry (I was working for an M.S. in nuclear engineering at the UP when I was sent abroad for my Ph.D. in nuclear chemistry), not to mention my MBA from Ateneo.

I was also collecting civil service eligibilities as a hobby, having taken and passed government exams for information writers, information editors, supervisors, cultural attachés, chemical engineers, chemists. I stopped taking government exams only when I went abroad for graduate studies. The eligibilities served me in good stead. Since I was in the government service and did not know any of the influential (appointing) powers that be, my qualifications got me appointed to positions which were much contested. Still, it was a hard and tough climb up the government service ladder. I would have quit PAEC early in the game because of the harassment of an envious person who was determined to stop my promotion. But a mentor and other women colleagues encouraged me to stay on and fight for what was mine. The pattern would be the same wherever I worked. Somehow it would not be an envious or a competitive male colleague (though one encountered one or two along the way) who would block one's progress, but rather a "sister."

I met the challenge of atomic energy head on. In the early days, recruitment at PAEC was made on the basis of one's dura mater as reflected in one's college performance. Being from UP helped, but having an advanced degree from abroad was even better. Much to the envy of the other scientific establishments, PAEC had the creme de la creme of the scientific community. For a while, PAEC was a training ground for local as well as foreign fellows in atomic energy. Dr. Rene Navarro, who had a Ph. D. in nuclear physics from Berkeley, initiated the IPA (India-Philippines-Agency) project, the very first project to demonstrate the successful pooling together of resources available in the region for the synergistic use of the member states. It was later developed by the world organization in atomic energy, the IAEA, into the RCA (Regional Cooperative Agreement in Asia). This model project addressed the technical assistance needs of the region so well that it was replicated in Latin America and Africa. The Philippines provided the research reactor and the venue, the new atomic research center in Quezon City, plus the expertise. India provided the neutron spectrometer and the services of some experts, while the IAEA provided the travel funds and stipends for the training fellows from all over the region. Young scientists from Korea, Indonesia, Thailand and Malaysia trained in neutron scattering research with the best experts and equipment at minimum cost.

I WAS IN Buenos Aires with the Comision Nacional de Energia Atomic at the Centro de Investigacion in Ezeiza, some 40 kilometers away, when I was offered a job at the IAEA, the highest international body dealing with the peaceful uses of the atom. I had earlier applied for the higher post of P-5, chief of chemistry, and thus was in no hurry to take up the offer. But the Philippine ambassador to Austria prevailed upon me to accept the job. He convinced me that it would be better to get a foot in the door, as it were. No country or person had a lien on any position, I was told, and member states took turns filling the vacancies. Obviously, the big donor countries were exempted from such a rule, and director level posts were "reserved" for the bigwigs who rotated the posts among themselves. If strictly based on contribution, the quota for the Philippines would always be oversubscribed since we pay a small amount and a number of highly qualified Filipinos were already in the more accessible general services or G-posts.

As a nuclear safeguards inspector, one has to be physically fit, and I mean truly physically fit: one must be able to carry heavy equipment, plus kilos of documents and papers and supplies while balancing a laptop computer and a suitcase, and be able to run with all these in tow. This means an obstacle course of hundreds of equally harassed Japanese commuters to catch a train as one has only five minutes to maneuver from one track to another, at the same time being alert at all times that one is taking the right train. Mercifully enough, with the help of the special God that protects safeguard inspectors, I rarely missed a train despite all the hazards. Yes, one has to be in tiptop form to be able to walk kilometers inside a nuclear power plant, up and down catwalks, lugging the inevitable equipment and documentation, while dressed in some sort of stifling hot space suit complete with headgear and protective shoes, and sometimes having to breathe through an individually fitted gas mask in areas which hold the possibility of gaseous radioactive contamination.

Though a chemical engineer, I have never had to work on a graveyard shift in plants (but I have had more than one experiment running overnight in the lab which had to be nursed along and recorded periodically, with only a radio announcer on an all-night stand program keeping me company). I was introduced to the wonders of the night shift at the Tokai Mura Plutonium Reprocessing Plant, which uses a continuous process with three shifts of personnel and inspectors. After the initial orientation period of inspection missions and such had given way to regular routine, I caught myself wondering, "What was I doing driving in the wee hours of the morning, from the processing plant on an isolated road back to town to our hotel, or vice versa... going to work at midnight to take the night shift." But everyone assured me it was safe, and thank heavens it was, despite the

32

Yakuza-run bars and Korean mafia pachinko parlors (that stupid game, the plague of all Japanese cities and towns where not a few addicts have committed suicide after heavy losses, or turned to crime to support the vice).

But while in Japan, I did have an experience that almost turned into an international incident. It started innocently enough. I had just come out of the radioactive areas of the plant on a night shift, and was working on reports in our inspectors' office and reviewing some surveillance tapes, when a "new" man came in and chatted me up. He did not introduce himself, and I thought that was odd, since nobody was allowed inside the plant without the proper security clearance. I thought he was one of the plant supervisors. My Japanese counterpart did not know him either, but he did not alert security because he thought the guy was a new management man. Japanese bosses being notorious workaholics, he could have been working overtime.

This guy insisted on talking with me. Out of politeness and thinking that he wanted to practice his English real bad, I talked to him while trying to do my work. When my shift was over, he said he wanted to take me home, but I declined since I was driving myself and did not need any escort. When he insisted, I tried to delay my departure and pretended I had to go back into the radioactive area. I did, and then asked my Japanese counterpart to tell me if the coast was clear. Quickly, I ran to the IAEA car in the deserted parking lot and got in, locked the doors and sped away. Unfortunately, I had to stop by the gate to turn in my plant ID and, lo and behold, the man was there by the guardhouse waiting for me and insisting again on taking me home. I jumped back into the car, and with fearfully pounding heart raced through the dark and lonely road back to the hotel, all the time looking in the rearview mirror to check whether he was following me.

That night, I was so disturbed I couldn't sleep. I had debated with myself whether to report the incident or not, since it might cause some trouble. In the end I decided to report it, in case it should happen again, since I had a lot of graveyard shifts on my schedule. I told my supervisor, the liberated one, and she raised hell and protested to the Japanese management. Later I found out that a full-blown investigation was conducted.

A time-motion study was made of the mystery man, with every move of his retraced, and it turned out to be exactly as I had reported it. The plant's Japanese head of management came to see me and apologized profusely for the incident. A top official from Tokyo, one of the managing directors of the mother company, invited me to dinner by way of an apology, and when he came to Vienna for a meeting again asked me over for dinner and gifted me with a rare Japanese print by a famous artist. It seems that the mystery man was a former auditor or administrator of the plant who was promoted to a post in the Tokyo main office. He had come to Katsuta for the funeral of a relative and decided to visit the plant. Since he was a former boss, he was allowed in at night, in violation of security regulations. What's more, one friendly drink led to another. After the incident, he was demoted for serious misconduct.

I do not know how many other heads rolled as a result of that incident which constituted a breach in security and caused the Japanese management to lose face. I told the vice president that it was a rather harsh punishment, but he said it was an administrative matter and I was not to concern myself with it. I felt so sorry for the guy and regretted having reported him. (Later on I found out that my Japanese counterpart did actually report him, since if I had done so and he had not said anything, things would have been worse.) But was it a case of sexual harassment, or plain bad luck? Maybe the man only wanted to practice his English or to be friendly?

Back at headquarters in Vienna, I did not want to report the incident anymore at the debriefing meeting, as I was the embarrassed party. I did tell the person who had jurisdiction over the Tokyo office, but he thought I was shying away from the night shift. Shades of jingoism, subtle but surely there. I calmly told him that I did not want any privileges. I was going to work just like the male inspectors did and be scheduled for whatever was called for. There is now a rule limiting the number of successive night shifts on our schedules and allowing us a rest day. After all, even female inspectors are not robots and should not try to outdo their male counterparts in testing how much the human body can take before it self-destructs.

A NEW INSPECTOR gets all the wretched assignments, traveling back and forth on a "See (but not see) Japan" schedule to faraway nuclear power plants, most of them in isolated places along the coast. One requirement for nuclear power plant sites is that they should be near a body of water (a sea or lake) for the tons of coolant water needed to cool down the heat generated by the fissioning process in the core fuels, while extracting the hot steam power to run the steam turbines to generate the electric power. Here's a simple household analogy: when you boil water in a whistling teakettle, you use conventional fuel (gas) or a source of heat (electric stove) to heat up the water; when you heat it up further, steam is produced, and it goes through the small hole in the lid and makes the whistling sound.

In a nuclear power plant the heat source or fuel is nuclear fuel — fissionable material like enriched uranium which in a controlled fission reaction releases a tremendous amount of energy as heat. In an uncontrolled fission reaction it can cause a meltdown in the core of the reactor, or in movie parlance, the "China syndrome," referring to the exaggeration and improbability that it would bore a hole straight down to China. Remember, the core of the earth in itself is molten magma which comes out in geological fissures or "boils" called volcanos.

We new inspectors were warned during the Introductory Course on Agency Safeguards (ICAS) that we were working nuclear safeguard inspectors on an inspection mission, not tourists on a holiday. How true that was! Just to get from one plant to another, we had to take the Shinkansen or bullet train which stretches along the spine of Japan from north to south, then transfer to the regular train to get to the nearest city/town, and then to the slower local trains which stop at every small district. A bus ride got us to our hotel, then a taxi took us through winding mountain roads to the inspection site. We had to wake up bright and early for the commute, to arrive at our destinations on time.

The Japanese are quite punctual, but they have the advantage of living in the vicinity of the power plant. Usually the personnel live like bachelors during the week since their families have to live in towns where the children's schools are located. Upon our arrival at the plant site, after much bowing and the formal exchange of business cards, the entrance meeting is opened while the ubiquitous "office lady" serves the ubiquitous "green tea." Though everybody swears that green tea is good for your health, believe you me, one has to acquire a taste for it. Which I did after many, many attempts, so as not to offend my hosts. After a while, I even got to like the green tea cakes and green tea ice cream served in hotels. Talk about adaptation.

After the formal meeting and discussion of the inspection objectives and schedule, we had to prepare the equipment, materials, and documentation to take inside the radiation areas, then go for a whole body count to check for contamination and to get a background count so that we wouldn't claim later that we got contaminated in the plant, causing the Japanese to lose face, which to them is a grievous sin. We then proceeded to the change rooms to be fitted from head to toe with special protective gear, complete with a washable fabric hat which made us look either like cooks or bellboys.

It is a good thing most Japanese facilities have separate change rooms for men and women since they now have female engineers and technical staff. This is not, however, the case in China, a nuclear weapons state, which only recently has acceded to voluntary safeguards inspections of a limited number of facilities. I was the first woman inspector to go to China to see the Qinshan Nuclear Power Plant, which is some kilometers away from Shanghai and requires half a day's travel through the wide plains of the province, the only "sightseeing" possible. Luckily for me, some women from the state energy board in Peking were assigned to accompany me. The facilities at the plant left much to be desired, being meant only for male personnel since there are no female employees. As we came out of the change room, I noticed a huge crowd outside, some of them grumbling, others curious. Most of them were almost belligerent. Only much later did I learn that they had to vacate the entire change room facilities, including the showers (personnel were required to strip and shower down any possible contamination before leaving the premises), to allow us women to shower and change in peace. Naturally the staff had to patiently wait till we had finished, before they themselves could shower and change and finally go home after a long working day. They must have been pretty hungry, too, for their evening meal! It was a rare instance when being female had its privileges.

When inspectors go deeper into a plant, into the more radioactive areas, we have to don yet another layer of a protective monkey suit, usually color-coded to indicate the radioactive contaminant in the area (for example, purple strips on the shoulders to indicate a plutonium area) and so facilitate decontamination and in-house laundering. Over our shoes, we have to wear special overshoes which we exchange for other heavy wear shoes in specific areas. With all that protective gear alone, we waddle not because of weightlessness, like astronauts in space, but because we are weighted down by all that, plus the equipment we need to conduct the inspection. I would strongly recommend that the ICAS include as an important portion, "weightlifting" to build up flabby muscles and "marathon racing" to gain stamina with which to withstand the physical rigors of inspection.

The member states have the right to complain about inspectors' performance or behavior, and therefore inspectors can be assigned elsewhere without any explanation. This was the case with one inspector who was notorious for always being late for inspections (he loved to "party" at night) and sometimes for not showing up at all, which for lesser mortals could have been a cause for dismissal.

What goes on inside the plant is a closely guarded secret, for security reasons, and all reports and documentation emanating from inspection activities are labeled SAFEGUARDS CONFIDENTIAL! In taking care of our reports and paraphernalia at all times, we are like James Bond guarding secret microfilms and the like. Luckily for the new generation of inspectors, computers and high-tech data processing and transmission now allow safeguard materials to be sent electronically by code, so they have less material to handle and guard at all costs.

THROUGHOUT my peripatetic life, the regular crisscrossing of time zones has been both bane and boon as it has enabled me to keep in constant touch with my family and gaggle of relatives and friends in three continents. Strong family ties and the constancy of some friendships, male or otherwise, have often guided me like a beacon of light through murky waters of self-doubt and the hopeless dilemmas in my checkered career. This beacon has worked like an automatic "reality check" in my world, where duty travels sometimes involve some earthshaking or history-changing event.

I was in Pakistan when the Chernobyl nuclear power plant accident was "discovered" by monitors in nearby countries with not a peep from the Russians. That nuclear event changed the system of instant notification to the IAEA and beefed up the worldwide monitoring of nuclear incidents, resulting in an action team for mutual assistance on 24-hour alert. Aware of the dangers of the Chernobyl meltdown, I was glad that at least most of my family were well outside the fallout zone. There was a lot of flak worldwide in the aftermath, and for good reason. Even in faraway Philippines, a row evolved between the importers of baby's milk and the nuclear regulatory body over the acceptable levels of radionuclides in the milk. It was very reassuring to me that my colleagues at the Philippine Nuclear Research Institute stood fast in implementing the strictest limits and disapproved many a shipment that analyzed more than the dose limits.

When the Berlin Wall came down for the eventual reunification of the two Germanys, I was with a new batch of inspector-trainees for an inspection exercise in East Berlin. I joined the hundreds of East Berliners crossing the famous Checkpoint Charlie to the west, each eager to see the "other" side that had been forbidden for so long and to collect the "welcome money" of 20 Deutsch marks per person (enterprising families pooled their bonuses and lugged back western-made TV sets on baby buggies, wheelbarrows, or what have you while loud brass bands oompah-pahed and hot coffee flowed freely). Even ancient *omas* and *opas* (grandfathers and grandmothers) squeaked their wheelchairs through the stream of joyful humanity celebrating freedom. We were with the camera crews of the international press that were billeted in our state-run hotel. I can still feel the tremendous excitement of keeping vigil at Brandenburg Gate, the timeless symbol of divided Berlin and now of reunited Germany. It felt powerful just to be there and reverberate with the jubilation of the Germans. After the reunification, nuclear inspections of facilities in the East led to the closing down of some which did not quite meet the safety standards of the west.

In more recent history, Saddam Hussein's standoff with the US was based primarily on the horrifying discovery of clandestine nuclear facilities and covert activities in Iraq. The Iraqis were that close to producing the bomb. Inspections of weapons of mass destruction also brought to light some sleight of hand: underground secret facilities with hospitals or orphanages above ground as cover, never mind the loss of human lives, that of the sitting targets. Lessons learned from the Iraqi experience led to the strengthening of the whole safeguard system and the unanimous approval of inspections of even undeclared nuclear material.

Colleagues describe Iraqi inspections as a hardship assignment, and work there, as in a hostile environment, almost like in a battle zone. The IAEA inspectors were treated a little better than were the inspectors for weapons of mass destruction. We were looking for nuclear bomb factories while they were looking for biological warfare materiel and facilities. Tales from the desert by colleagues who were "lucky" enough to go to Iraq, tell of friendly Iraqis (not exactly cooperative, but nevertheless friendly, i.e., not belligerent). The strengthened system of nuclear safeguards evolved such concepts as indicators of diversion pathways with the help of the latest technology capable of detecting the presence of plutonium in mere atomic quantities, even long after the erring or illegal facility would have been dismantled. Advances in satellite technology, coupled with state-of-the-art analytical techniques, have moved up detection several notches in precision, specificity, and overall confidence and conclusiveness.

THE JOB THAT has allowed me a long list of "been there, done that" has also deprived me of a social life that would otherwise be very active in such an international milieu, where every national holiday is celebrated with an instant display of the alluring cultures of different countries, aside from visiting shows and parades of world-class artistes (after all, Vienna is the musical capital of the world, which every artiste aspires to conquer), plus the interminable celebrations of milestones and the hallowed tradition of hail-and-farewell parties among the UN staff and in the diplomatic circle. We are not even talking about the social calendar of the gregarious Filipino community, some 20,000-strong and still counting. My life has been greatly enriched by meaningful interactions with friends from diverse cultures and countries. Too bad it is a bit difficult to maintain contacts, e-mail notwithstanding, let alone relationships, given the lack of time when one is actually in Vienna. There are always many competing activities and so little time, though the spirit may be willing and the energy maddeningly exuberant.

A fringe benefit I treasure is my participation in the significant milestones in my own family. What joy to have been there during the precocious two's of my first niece Sandy, now a yuppie holding her own turf, cum BMW and all; the performance as a rather well-fed mouse and elegant snowflakes in the *Nutcracker Suite*, de rigueur at Christmas, of Chrissie and Melissa, now co-eds at exclusive Dayton U. That's my brother Armando's family: a daughter and two girls, he says when teased about the absence of a son, and adds, "one is in training bra while the others are in training pants."

I still chuckle when I recall the lively antics in the snow of Grace's frisky boys, Alan and Ben, the latter now on a full four-year scholarship at the University of North Carolina at Chapel Hill. How can one not hold dear to one's heart the privilege of sharing the angst of Orchid's first-born, dear sensitive Nath, in the throes of young love, now on his way to becoming a techie guru? One swells with pride at Wella's piano recitals and, more recently, at her topping the board exam over thousands of aspirants. Then, too, there was the pandemic grief at seeing beloved Nikko suffer during his short life, he who gave so much joy despite his pain.

We all rejoiced upon the appointment of Armando as chief pathologist at St. Luke's in Ohio and reveled in the fun when he and his doctor-wife Helen hosted the gathering of the clan from all over the world and from East Coast to West Coast USA in his gracious manor with tennis, pool, and nonstop food and entertainment galore. We vicariously suffered Grace and Ruben's uprooting from Ohio family and friends and their move to Charlotte, little knowing that it would also be our next nesting place. How well we applauded hesitant Orchid's entrepreneurial venture and Colonel Boyit's steady promotions in the air force hierarchy!

It is a life not counted in years or seasons, but rather in lives being lived to the full. Mama and Dad would have been proud, not so much of our achievements although, modesty aside, they are not to be pooh-poohed, but rather that we are happy and fulfilled in our lives. Speaking for myself, I owe that to the very supportive parents who allowed us to be ourselves, to the steadying influence of family and friends who care enough, especially my dear indulgent husband Manolo, who, atypical of the spoiled Spanish macho, demands so little of my time and attention, and lets me do what I have to do; and to my fiercely independent daughter Arancha (soon to start her own family in Spain) and my affectionate son Alvaro (now traveling extensively for a US-based multinational); to the unselfish mentors during my formative years and beyond; to the guidance and support of former bosses who believed in me, to the countless colleagues who curbed professional jealousy for sheer camaraderie. Most importantly, one has to believe that one can do almost anything as long as one is willing to work hard, is not afraid of committing mistakes, and is strong enough to get up after a fall and keep on walking that extra mile. It certainly got me places, literally!

The bottom line would be, were I to live life all over again, would I rather be somebody else doing something different? To my surprise, despite some gnawing anxieties and yearnings, I have come to the realization that hey, I wouldn't have changed anything, really, except perhaps that now, the wiser me, "the me nobody knows" would repeat this piece of advice succinctly put by Eleanor Roosevelt: "You cannot be hurt, unless you let them hurt you, so don't." Believe me, that will save you a lot of grief (and Kleenex!).

A story that begs to be told is of how love can be lovelier the second time around. Mine has not exactly been a nun's story — no one knows the whole story — but here's part of it. I met Manolo on the ski slopes of Navacerrada mountains near Madrid. No, we were not skiing. He was with his regular group of mountain hikers, and I was with Tita Nati and some friends trying to take in the winter scene. No, it was not love at first sight, either, because one of the ladies, a *viuda alegre,* was making a play for him and he was flirting back outrageously. But after a while we began dating tentatively, and before we knew it we had become a regular item. Our friends knew the relationship was serious when he introduced his family; in fact we double-dated with his sister Paquita and her fiancé Joaquin, and had regular dinners with his older sister Mari and her husband Antonio. (In his family I am known as the one to whom the first *sobrino*, Javier, gave his first smile. Baby Javier is now a doctor in economics, the Spanish equivalent of a yuppie but with a Mercedes 300SL instead of a BMW on account of a rich father whose business Manolo helped jumpstart.) An executive of Cyanamid, España named Jess, a Spanish mestizo, apparently convinced Manolo that it would be disastrous to the atomic energy program of the Philippines if I were to remain in Spain and marry him, so he sort of faded away. (Prior to this, he had no clue as to what I was studying.) He would call regularly at night but would not answer, but I carried on a conversation just the same, as if nothing happened.

In the meantime, I had other boyfriends and went on to finish my Ph.D. in nuclear chemistry and got a *sobresaliente cum laude* from the University of Madrid, the only Filipino woman to do so. The Instituto de Estudios Nucleares, especially the director, Prof. Dr. Duran of the Spanish Nuclear Energy Board where I did my thesis, was so delighted about the honor I received that it initiated a private investiture of my doctoral cap and academic gown (a vestige of the monks' hooded robes in which they would carry their rolled manuscripts) which they gifted me, together with a gold signet ring of the University of Madrid (henceforth I was authorized to seal all my works/manuscripts with the insignia of the University). The other significant appurtenances were white kid gloves so that all my works would be approached with the purest of intentions, and a huge book in which to record all my works. Dr. Dominguez, my thesis adviser, jokingly asked me if I felt any different after being awarded the doctorate. Jokingly I answered, "Why certainly, you breathe a little easier!" (since I didn't have to worry anymore about the results of my laboratory experiments going awry).

Upon coming back to the PAEC in fulfillment of my promise to General Medina, I concentrated on resuming my career and became chief of the Chemistry Research Division, garnering awards with my team of researchers in radiochemistry, nuclear chemistry, and the then emerging field of environmental chemistry. It was a proud moment when I received a national award for science and technology at the Cultural Center of the Philippines. I was the youngest awardee.

My active participation as an officer in various national scientific and professional organizations allowed me great opportunities to meet the decision makers and movers in scientific and technological circles. Together with Dr. M. Pasao of UP, I wrote *Me and My World*, the first book in science for preschool (now used as a textbook) which introduced the concepts of science through games and play, thus short-circuiting whatever aversion for science grown-ups might pass on to their young. During the book launching at the Philippine Science High School, we demonstrated to an auditorium full of eager preschool teachers the lesson-games with actual preschoolers who had great fun learning science while at play.

Once in a while, my mother or my sister Orchid would report that Manolo called from Madrid to say hello. On one of my trips back to the continent with Mom, I learned that he got married. He told me afterward that he saw me once in one of the major department stores, but that he was carrying baby Arancha in her "Moses" (portable baby crib) and I was too far away and gone before he could do anything. It seems that he told his family about me, though I never met his wife and his children.

After his wife died, he called up my home and asked where I was. Immediately, he called the Philippine Embassy in Vietnam and insisted that there was a Dr. Bautista assigned there. He had misheard Vietnam for Vienna! He called up my family again and this time he was given my phone number in Vienna. Since I was always on mission, when he finally reached me he asked *"¿Sabes quien soy?"* (Do you know who is calling?) He was so thrilled when I told him *"Claro que si"* (Of course). He asked me out to dinner and, thinking he was so far away in Madrid and I was always away, I replied, "Yeah, fat chance!" But he was determined. He arrived in Vienna the weekend that I had houseguests, Tia Puring and cousin Olive from Los Angeles, plus my sister-in-law Helen and my nieces Chrissie and Melissa, who were touring Europe. The Florist by Wire stocks must have risen quite a bit from the steady stream of red roses he would send from Spain. My neighbors on Am Krautgarten would excitedly deliver some of them because I was never home when the flowers came.

One Saturday in June, we finally met again and he couldn't believe it was me. I had long ago decided to have auburn brown hair instead of grey, and of course my contours were much fuller than they were the last time he saw me, and that instead of him driving me around everywhere, I was now chauffeuring him in Vienna in a Mercedes. Dinner was intimate – in a romantic garden restaurant called Sailer in the exclusive 19th district of Wien. And then it was as if the intervening years had never been. We fell madly in love all over again and would talk on the phone via long distance for hours. He regularly commuted between Madrid and Vienna since he was finishing a condominium project. We made the rounds of all the posh restaurants in Vienna – the Drei Hussaren, the Steierecke, the Vierjahreseit at the Intercon, the Hotel Sacher and the Imperial, the Bristol (Imelda Marcos's favorite, because it allowed her to just walk across to the Vienna Opera House) – and took in all the tourist sights and places. Then he asked if he could bring his best friends to Vienna. I said why not. His best friends turned out to be his children, Arancha and Alvaro, who were then in their early teens and wanted to meet me.

We were married in the US during a lull in my travel schedule. We wanted to get married in Vienna, but the paperwork needed by the Austrian bureacracy was quite daunting. So off we went to the US, destination Las Vegas, where there are supposedly hassle-free weddings. But my brother Armando in Ohio and our cardiologist friend Dr. Bernardo offered to expedite the formalities. So we were married by a justice of the peace, a patient of Dr. Bernardo's who looked like the ice-skating champion Katerina de Witt. Needless to say, when we came back to Vienna, our wedding made sensational news and created quite a furor among my friends at UNO City and in the Filipino community. Later we got married in a church in Cavite City, arranged by Orchid, Olive, and Tia Andy. We had an extended honeymoon from Hong Kong to Spain to Tokyo.

You might ask, is love really lovelier the second time around? You bet it is!

So, how about tackling that calculus or chemistry problem — not later, but right NOW?

Cecilia Manguerra Brainard

The Writer's Path in California

I USED TO THINK I was unique in the decisions I made, specifically those decisions that led me down the path to where I am now, a wife, mother, and writer living in California. Now I see that, like it or not, I'm part of a trend, that my thinking is part of a greater consciousness.

Take, for instance, my immigration to America: for years I thought I was so unusual for being the only member of my family to reside outside the Philippines. In fact, the attraction to America had already existed in my family as far back as the turn of the century, when my great-granduncle came to America as a *pensionado*, a student. As luck would have it, he became ill, almost died, and then heard God's call to the priesthood. He did become a priest, and, years later, archbishop of Jaro in Iloilo province. There, too, was my father, who stowed away on a liner and came to America to study engineering at Valparaiso University in Indiana. My oldest sister and my brother also came to America. The difference between all of them and me is this: all of them eventually returned to the Philippines, while I stayed on.

Sometimes I wonder about that 22-year-old girl who in 1969 left Manila with two suitcases, traveled half-way around the globe, and, bravely or unwittingly, carved out a life for herself in California.

The image is this: a girl-woman wearing a blue linen two-piece suit. Her hair is swept away from her face and twisted up in a fashionable bun. She is carrying a shiny black leather bag; under her arm is a large envelope containing her X-rays and immigration papers. She is traveling on an I-20 visa, a student visa. Trying to look smart as she clicks down the runway in her high heels, she glances upward, the

46

March sun shining on her face. As she looks at the plane, perhaps, or at the sky, or at her future, it is difficult to tell if her expression is one of excitement or apprehension.

I did not consciously decide to stay in America. My life script was to finish graduate work in filmmaking at the University of California in Los Angeles (UCLA), travel, then return to the Philippines. I suppose I expected to get married and live pretty much like the matrons in my family, that is, comfortably, with servants and pampered children. But as things turned out, I married the American Peace Corps volunteer who had once been stationed in Maasin, Leyte; after a brief stay in San Francisco, we settled in Santa Monica, California.

Funny, but in the early years, even when we had young children, the reality that I had "left home" never really hit me. I always felt as if I had just widened my concept of "home," simply extended my home to include California. Even now when I visit the Philippines, I don't feel that I had actually left it in the first place. I slide right into place with my Cebuano or my Taglish; I'm sure my friends think I've never learned to speak English properly. An American friend once looked at me and said, "You can take a Filipina out of the Philippines, but you can't take the Philippines out of a Filipina."

WHEN I ARRIVED in the United States, my brain was crammed full of media images of America. Starting with my Dick and Jane book, I had already formed images of snow, maple trees, and blue jays. Then there were the magazine and movie and television images of the Empire State Building, Disneyland, Hollywood, the Golden Gate Bridge, freeways, and numerous other ideas that pieced themselves together in my imagination as this enormous, tumultuous AMERICA.

I found it fun to match reality with the images in my head. Despite all the songs and poetry, the Golden Gate Bridge wasn't really golden; and despite the sense of largeness its huge skyscrapers gave it, New York City sat on a little island. I was positively enthralled by the famous art pieces in museums that I had only seen pictures of. Even now, I get a big kick out of visiting New Orleans, or Washington, D.C., or Alaska, or other parts of the United States, and seeing these places for what they really are, not just re-creations of my imagination or flickering celluloid images. One thing I've realized, after living in this country for three decades, is that America is huge and diverse; Hawaii, Alaska, and North Carolina could be countries in themselves.

The Satan in this garden of paradise is racism, because it does exist. At first I had no clue about racism and discrimination. I had lapped up the American ideas of democracy and equality; I thought Americans truly believed in these precepts. It completely threw me when I first experienced racism. As a young student, I had gone to a drugstore near UCLA and the salesclerk, an older woman, gave me static. I didn't know what that was all about; all I felt was her meanness. On another occasion, however, I heard a landlady comment that she would take in Biafran students but not American Blacks. I started to get the picture.

Let me tell you how I've handled racism. I assume that racists are ignorant, and when I come across someone who is sending me messages that I am inferior because I'm Filipino, I go out of my way to educate them about Filipinos, the Philippines, and myself. I may be wrong, but this approach seems to work. In fact I've integrated the idea of educating others in my writing projects. Whether I'm writing fiction or nonfiction, or editing books, I always keep in mind the importance of educating my readers.

As for the really nasty people, I've learned to dish it back to them. I rarely shout, but I am firm in giving them a piece of my mind. If necessary, I write letters of complaint to public relations officers, or for more serious matters, letters to newspaper editors. Even now, my sons cringe when someone has offended me because I can be relentless in exacting my pound of flesh.

WHEN MY FIRST son was a baby, I gave up the idea of becoming a filmmaker. I understood how difficult it was to break into the American film industry. Becoming an independent filmmaker was out of the question because of the high cost of doing films. There was a third and more important reason: I found filmmaking frustrating. There were so many people involved in a project and many ideas became integrated into the initial concept, that the end product could turn out to be quite different from that original idea.

Trying to make something out of myself, I went back to school and took pre-med classes. I thought I could be a doctor, but my test scores weren't that high. I gave up the idea.

By this time, my second son had been born. When he was young I worked part-time in a nonprofit foundation that was near my house. My hours were flexible and the people were good to me. I worked there for several years. When my third son came, I stayed home to take care of the three boys. It was around this time, at Christmas, when my husband gave me an electric typewriter. He had always known about my passion for writing and on many nights had seen me scratching away in my journal. He must have had an innate sense of my desire to have a career. I used to choke on the words "I'm just a housewife" when asked what I did.

Now that I had a typewriter, I contacted the editor of *Philippine American News* and arranged to write a bimonthly column which I called Filipina American Perspective. I also took creative writing classes at the Writers' Program at UCLA-Extension, where I now teach. Between driving the boys to and from school, to and from soccer games, to and from doctors and dental visits, I wrote. Bit by bit, I started to get my essays and stories published. Even then, I considered writing a pastime. I didn't take my writing seriously until my youngest son started kindergarten and I went job hunting. I immediately found work as a fund-raiser in a nonprofit foundation. Instead of being happy, though, I developed a splitting headache. It took a night of prayer and soul-searching before I realized I could not work full-time, take care of my family, and write. It was impossible. And so, with my husband's support, I chose writing. With that commitment I started book projects: first a collection of short stories, then a collection of essays, then a novel, several other books, and now I've branched out into editing, publishing, teaching, and book selling.

It hasn't been easy, let me clarify. It has been a slow climb up a steep cliff. It's been difficult, but fun too. Sometimes I complain about how hard it is to be a writer, and my husband says, "Nobody's holding a brick over your head." He's right, of course, so it must be something I want to do. Another thing I've discovered is that even though I've had my share of rejection slips, I've also come across some generous people who have believed in me and my work and have helped me. There was that phone call from the head of the Writers' Program at UCLA Extension inviting me to teach; there was that call from an English professor at UCLA to inquire if I would like to teach in her department; there was that call from a Stanford professor who directed me to his publisher so that my novel could be reprinted in paperback. There have been many other phone calls and letters, all unsolicited, all offering me some additional opportunity to grow.

I have not even mentioned my husband and his family who have welcomed me and accepted me as one of their own. When my husband's grandaunt died years ago, I was surprised to learn that she had written me into her will. My birthdays and Mother's Days are always remembered. I could not have been more fortunate in finding such a family in my adopted home.

SCANNING my 30 years in America, I see that I've picked my friends and tailored my work and lifestyle in a way that is comfortable and fulfilling to me. At home we speak English but eat rice and *adobo* and *pancit* along with pizza and burritos and roast beef. I visit Goldilocks restaurant twice a month to stock up on *pan de sal* and to have my *dinuguan*-fix. Our home is a two-story Spanish-style house with a red tile roof. Inside we have mahogany and oak furniture, but also a Santo Niño statue and some carved Chinese camphor trunks that came all the way from the Philippines. My day-to-day schedule consists of my literary work, interspersed with doing the laundry, running errands, and cooking. Even my garden combines East and West: I have camelias, roses, jasmine*, camia, bandera española*, dahlias, magnolia, *sampaguita*, and guavas.

Life goes on with a kind of ebb and flow. Now it is summer and almost as hot as the Philippines, then it will be fall and dreary, then it will be winter and chilly and hectic, then comes January with its gray loneliness, then spring when my rose garden goes wild with rainbow blooms, then summer will be back with its shimmering crystal blue sky.

That is how it is.

What was it my friend said? You can take a Filipina out of the Philippines, but you can't take the Philippines out of a Filipina.

I think she's right.

Dr. Violeta Centeno-Beltran

Doctor-Mom to Chicago's Unwed Mothers

I WAS INTRODUCED to Chicago through Carl Sandburg's famous poem.

Great was my delight when years later, in 1966, I found myself on a flight bound for the "Windy City." I was traveling with a group of young doctors recruited by South Chicago Community Hospital for its training program. Expectations ran high in the group as each of us wove a fantasy in his/her mind about life in America. Looking back to that memorable day at the airport, I think the spirit of the holiday season carried us through the pain of saying good-bye to our loved ones. The same spirit stayed with us throughout the journey as stories were told and jokes cracked, evoking a seemingly unending ring of laughter.

We were oblivious to the time until we saw and heard the "Fasten your seatbelts" sign. The dream had become a reality — we were in Chicago! When we stepped off the plane, the warmth of recalling the airport scene in Manila vanished into thin air. A very cold and crisp morning woke us from our reverie. I was freezing. I touched my nose to see if it was still there. All we could see were piles of snow, bare trees (trees back home always had leaves), and deserted streets (in the Philippines only fields in the barrios were without people). Did I make a big mistake in coming here? Oh, for the fleshpots of Egypt or India! O'Hare airport was a ghost town. But come to think of it, who would be awake at six o'clock in the morning on New Year's Day? People were still in bed nursing a hangover after last night's revelry.

The loneliness of the place gave me a heartache. Homesickness crept into my whole being, sending confusing signals to my brain.

Slowly the romantic picture I had of Carl Sandburg's city began to crumble, but somehow my faith in God took over. Although I felt like turning back, a voice within me said, "Stay." And so I stayed — for 33 years. But that's jumping ahead of my story.

Staying on in Chicago meant making a lot of adjustments and readjustments. I had to share a house with five other doctors. Cooking has never been in my books. I knew how to clean house, but with cooking it was a case of "give me liberty or give me death." Fortunately for me, the hospital cafeteria never ran out of food, so I was saved from starvation. But where were the rice and fish, the *pinakbet* and *bagoong* and *daing*? Oriental food could be bought only in Chinatown. That was a long bus ride from the hospital and we had no time to do any traveling. We relied on invitations to the homes of Filipino families to satisfy our craving for Filipino food. In return, we shared our cafeteria food with them.

If winter comes, could spring be far behind? We welcomed its coming. By spring, the doctors in the hospital got to know us better and as a result we got more invitations to dine at famous places like Palmer House and Drake Hotel or to go yachting or cruising on Lake Michigan. When I think about those gestures now, I believe they helped relieve the terrible homesickness gnawing at my heart. The long working hours at the hospital also helped to minimize my homesickness. I had no time to think about my family whom I missed very much.

Spoken English was another hurdle I had to make. Although English is spoken in the Philippines, we have our own way of speaking and expressing ourselves. It took me awhile to order hamburger because every time I said the word, it came out differently and the waiters could never understand me. Until I became wiser. I resorted to the "point system" — I pointed my finger at the food I wanted to buy. Thanks to Johnny Carson, whose talk show on television I watched every night, my skills in spoken English improved. My vowel sounds got better, and so did my listening skills. After a while, I was able to distinguish *cat* from *cot* and *pat* from *pot*.

AM I WHITE or am I brown? Which washroom should I go to — the one which says "For Whites Only," or do I have to look for another one? A disturbing and disconcerting situation, wouldn't you say so? This was the atmosphere in Chicago the year I arrived. It put me in a very embarrassing position every time my friends and I went shopping or ate in a restaurant or took a bus. The hospital assured us Filipinos that we were considered white. It was a great relief when in the Seventies these discriminating signs completely disappeared. Chicago gave me my first taste of social discrimination.

Obstetrics and gynecology is my field of medicine, but because I am a woman and an Asian I could not get a residency in many hospitals because this field happened to be dominated by men; in other words, male doctor applicants were preferred to females. I got a residency in general surgery at St. Elizabeth Hospital instead. As it turned out, I learned many skills during this transition period (1967) because doctors were in demand, and so I did nothing but work, work, and work. It was in this hospital that I was introduced to moonlighting. Jobs were for the asking. That year I learned and earned. I worked in the emergency room, in doctor's offices, in the medical records department, or wherever there was a demand for a doctor.

That same year proved the fallacy of the belief in the Philippines that America is paved with gold — the reality is you have to work hard to earn it. I was often assigned to the intensive care unit as well as to the head of the OB/Gyne department who happened to be a very busy man. I think his work ethic rubbed off on me because I got into his routine: breakfast at six o' clock, followed by hospital rounds, surgery at 7:30 a.m., more rounds or deliveries, and clinic hours all afternoon until 6:00 p.m. I still had night calls. The hectic schedule earned me his trust and confidence both as a person and as a doctor. Most of all, it helped me prepare for the licensing examination, which I passed with relatively good grades.

In February 1967 a great snowstorm buried Chicago in many inches of snow. Transport was at a standstill. The doctors who were not in the hospital could not report for duty, so everyone inside worked 24 hours for three straight days. Since my apartment was in the hospital compound, I became a part of the hospital brigade. We took short naps between shifts. My surgical skills were tested during this time. There was an emergency nephrectomy (removal of a kidney). I had never done one, nor had I aspired to do so, although I had assisted in several procedures. The urologist casually asked me to describe the procedure to him while we were scrubbing. Maybe I impressed him so much that he thought I could do it. To my surprise, when we got to the operating table where the patient was, he handed me the knife and told me to proceed. When the operative field was exposed he handed me the clamps, then the scissors, and finally the suture. As I held all the instruments in my hand, I leaned heavily against the operating table because my knees were shaking and I was perspiring profusely. That night after the surgery, I stayed up with the patient all night, my hand on her pulse. What if the suture were to come loose? She would hemorrhage to death! I was bathed in perspiration all night. I thought I would never see the light of dawn. As it turned out, the case went so well that the patient was able to go home after a short time. My confidence in my skills soared.

But an incident in a big department store in downtown Chicago nearly deflated my hard-earned self-confidence. I love listening to music, especially to classical and Spanish melodies. When I get home after a hard day's work, I turn on my stereo and listen to music. Anyway, I had an old stereo which I wanted to change to a newer model. I saw a certain model in this store which caught my fancy. I asked the clerk to let me see it. He refused me outright. When I asked him why, instead of giving me an answer, he said the model I wanted to see was a bit expensive. I got the message. I wasn't asking for the top-of-the-line model; all I wanted to see was a better model than what he was showing me. It was only after I showed him my hospital ID that he relented. I did eventually buy the model I wanted, and to remind me of leaner days and the feeling of being discriminated against, I have kept the stereo all these years.

In 1968 I found a slot in obstetrics/gynecology at the West Suburban Hospital in Oak Park. This was my last chance to get an interview in the Chicago area. I decided to be more assertive. By this time my extensive medical skills and my broader knowledge of American culture had given me the self-confidence I needed for the interview. I told the chairman that my age and experience were an advantage over the younger applicants. He must have agreed with me because when I finished talking he stood up, shook my hand and said, "You're in!"

After six months in this program I realized that the chairman of the OB/Gyne department was giving assignments comparable to those of the senior residents. After one year he was asking me to evaluate his consultations and letting me manage them too, so that I was able to focus on acquiring more technical skills and reading more literature related to the specialty. But even good things come to an end. Midway into the residency, we were notified that the program was targeted for closure because the specialty board believed that the field was saturated with specialists. This was a big drawback for me because most training programs do not give credit to the years done in previous programs. I was 40 years old and I dreaded the thought of starting all over again. Besides, I wanted to specialize in OB-Gyne. It was Christmastime when the news came. I had no one to turn to except St. Jude, the saint of the impossible. St. Jude has seen me through bad times and good. Surely, I thought, he would do something for me now.

And he did, by the grace of God. On January 2, 1971, the chairman asked me to go with him for an interview in another hospital, MacNeal Memorial Hospital in Berwyn, Illinois. There we met the chairman of the OB/Gyne department. I didn't do much talking. It was the two chairs who did, but the verdict was the same. There was no position available. Then the two disappeared for a few hours, leaving me to think dreadful thoughts. When they came back I was handed application forms to fill out. I started working the next day. Whose arm did they twist?

In 1972 I finished my residency. My training was finally over. When the late President Lyndon Johnson relaxed the immigration law, I was able to apply for an immigrant's visa without leaving the country. I asked myself, should I practice in Chicago or look elsewhere? Everything seemed uncertain. Again, I turned to St. Jude for guidance. The licensing and specialty board exams were the next hurdle after the residency training. The uncertainty of passing the exams became very real, especially when friends of mine could not get a passing mark. I decided I would review seriously while working full-time at the Salvation Army Hospital for Unwed Mothers. It was this hospital that applied for my temporary license while I waited for the results of the exams. In no time the results came out — I passed, with very good marks. I was now in a position to send for my children in the Philippines. Again, it was the Salvation Army that facilitated their coming to America. My joy was now complete, and a new phase in my life was about to begin.

WITH THE ARRIVAL of family and my involvement with the Salvation Army Hospital, I decided to stake my roots in Chicago. I applied for membership in different hospitals. At one time I was affiliated with three big ones. In time I learned that having too many affiliations was draining my energy, and so I chose to stay with Ravenswood Hospital as it was affiliated with the University of Illinois College of Medicine. I participated in the university's teaching program. In 1983 the university awarded me the Golden Apple Award for teaching excellence.

In 1986 I was elected secretary of the OB/Gyne department and when the department chairman retired, I assumed his position on a temporary basis while the search committee was on the lookout for a new chair. I was asked to apply after the committee had gone over 50 local and national applicants. After more than six months, the committee announced that I was the new chair. Accepting the job was a big challenge to me. I had a very busy practice. To help me cope with the demands of the new appointments, I took a crash course in budget planning, quality control, recruitment, leadership training, and even building construction as I had to know how to read floor plans for the new delivery suite.

I was on top of the world, so to speak. In medical circles people spoke highly of me. My fame as an excellent doctor had begun to travel far and wide. The Filipino community was proud to claim me as their own. The Filipinos in the hospital congratulated me for breaking into administration.

As chairperson, I introduced changes in the department: new delivery suites, implementation of the house physician program and surgical assistant program, active teaching, revision of policies, and regular departmental meetings. It was stressful to manage an active department, especially when one was "reminded" subtly about one's size and gender. I broke the glass ceiling, but it was lonely where I was. Somehow, though, hard work gets its reward. In March 1986, the Chicago Medical Society chose me for the Public Service Award, the highest recognition it can give its members. No other Filipino has received this award. Also, for the second time I was given the award for teaching excellence by the University of Illinois Family Practice Residency program.

After six years as chairperson of the OB/Gyne department at Ravenswood Hospital, I decided to step down and concentrate on my practice. Five years ago, upon recommendation of all the physicians at Ravenswood Hospital, I was named physician of the year.

RAISING A FAMILY in America is serious business. The lack of extended family may drive the younger member to seek attention and care outside the confines of the home. The time one should be spending with one's children is spent in the work place just to make ends meet. Oftentimes there is a breakdown in relationships because everyone is too tired to talk at the end of the day. Sometimes the parents are not there to listen to their children's tales of woe. Aware of these pitfalls, I tried to spend quality time with my children. I planned activities with them, no mater how hectic my schedule was. We ate out together, relaxed together, and in many other ways did things together. Perhaps what also kept us together was the fact that we spoke the same dialect, Pangasinan.

We always recalled stories that brought back good memories of life in the Philippines. Now that all my children are married, I can see that they are continuing the tradition with their own children. My 12 grandchildren were born in America (I delivered all of them) but they can speak and understand Pangasinan. Some, of course, speak it better than the others. Speaking the dialect has given them a strong sense of belonging to our family. They have become appreciative of their roots and the history of the Philippines. They are no strangers to Filipino culture, having made many visits home since they were children.

Our faith has also kept us together as a family. My parents' greatest legacy to us is a deep faith in a loving God. When we were growing up we never missed Sunday Mass and the daily evening angelus and rosary. My parents were God-fearing and their belief in God was unwavering. My siblings and I owe them our belief that God lives and is present in our lives. My children have inherited this faith and in turn have passed it on to their own children.

I AM NOW almost 70 and at the crossroads of my life. I have built a successful and enjoyable career. I have been blessed with a big family whom I adore. My grandchildren, whose ages range from eight to 21 years, are a joy to me in my old age. My health is relatively good and my mental faculties are still extremely sharp. Mind you, I am not thinking of retirement yet. Retirement is saying good-bye not only to the work I love most, obstetrics/gynecology, but also to the patients whom I have followed through from their reproductive years to menopause. These relationships span 20 to 45 years — from nurturing a seed and helping it to bring forth new life, to celebrating family events like graduations, weddings, birthdays, and all kinds of anniversaries. I have shared not only their joys but also their grief over the passing of loved ones. It is hard to say good-bye.

It is hard to say good-bye to those young faces I met years ago at the Salvation Army Hospital for Unwed Mothers. They have stable families now but they still come to see me because they are confident that we can keep the past a secret. Their own babies have become mothers and they tell them to see nobody else but me. A good number of patients at the Salvation Army Hospital have successfully turned their lives around. I am happy to know that I have made a difference in their future. I am proud of my award from the Chicago Medical Society in recognition of my work with these young unwed mothers. I think I must have delivered 600 patients a year during my 15 years in that facility. I was the only doctor there, and I made myself available 24 hours a day, attending not only to obstetrics cases but also to the women's personal problems. At every opportunity, I talked to them about education, self-respect, family relationships, and the dignity of work.

There is another group that does not want to hear my *adios*. They are my Hispanic patients. I was introduced to the Hispanic community when its leaders approached the Salvation Army for help with obstetrical cases that did not have any insurance and were not qualified for public aid. A Hispanic program was opened at a community house on Erie/Ashland. In the beginning, they were surprised to see an Asian, but the barriers fell when I was able to communicate with them in Spanish. Ravenswood Hospital continued that program after the Salvation Army Hospital closed in 1984. The program is alive and well, and I'm still a part of it as an obstetrician/gynecologist, friend, and counselor. I appreciate their loyalty.

Indeed it is hard to say good-bye. These years are bonus years for me. I still would like to use them well by joining medial missions, doing volunteer work in hospitals, teaching medical students and residents, or giving talks on subjects that fall within my area of expertise. Maybe I can even be a tour guide since I have traveled extensively to interesting places.

I hope you can visit this wonderful city. As a Filipino woman who has lived here more than 33 years, I am as proud of this city as I am of Manila. The Chicago today is very different from the Chicago of 1966. It is a world-class city, a center for political conventions, religious movements, and international events in arts and music, sports, and intellectual pursuits. In the world of sports the Chicago Bulls have put the city on the map, and in the world of entertainment "Taste of Chicago" has become a well-known annual event. Of the 80 restaurants invited to participate in it, one, the China Garden Restaurant, is owned by a Filipino family — mine. It serves Chinese cuisine (Mandarin).

I see the future as an open field beckoning me to come and walk around it. I feel drawn to it. There seem to be enough spaces for me to roam. I have been practicing medicine for the past 45 years and yet I feel I can begin again. The skills I have and the energy I feel come from loving my profession. It's a mutual feeling between my patients and myself. It is their trust and confidence in me that make me sense the future as an open field. I will walk around it as long as my heart and my mind tell me to do so.

Retirement at 70? Only when I hear the owl call my name.

Josie Opeña Disterhoft

Being
and Becoming
in America

I REMEMBER the early Sixties. I seem to have belonged to a small, very diverse group of young people who were being prepared for leadership. We were invited to act from a position of noblesse oblige, in recognition of life's gifts, an important one of which was that we were baptized Catholics and, therefore, among the chosen ones.

At this point I cannot discern how much of my participation sprang from a personal sense of conviction that this was a desirable or even appropriate role for me, Jopie, the teenage soul who liked poetry readings, film, and intense conversations. Or if my acceptance of the identity sprang from an inescapable feeling of obligation. There was, from this young and inexperienced group of friends, a tremendous and mostly enthusiastic sense of common and individual resolve to create futures that would include service.

Our group had more women than men. I loved knowing them and carry the experience of them to this day, almost 40 years later. They were out of the ordinary — they thought thoughts that were more than questions of personal survival, or issues of day to day which I recall were a major preoccupation then, dictated perhaps by the economic and political realities. That was a unique experience to have in the Philippines: where class lines did not matter too much in the interconnecting at the deep heart level, where different income levels, neighborhoods of origin, and schools attended did not prevent us from having our own versions of a shared resolve.

My being part of a striving Filipino family helped to shape me as well. In the years before the Depression, my father had come to the United

States from a farm in the far northern provinces of the Philippines to educate himself. He liked to tell the story of being a stowaway on a freighter from Manila to join some cousins and Ilocano townmates who were migrant workers on the coast of California, working in the vineyards and the sweet pea and strawberry farms around Hearst Castle. In Chicago he worked in restaurants as anything — busboy, waiter, chef assistant, janitor — to support himself through school and earn two engineering degrees. My mother was a schoolteacher who loved the gracious life as the daughter of the well-educated town philosopher and intellectual and also town treasurer, and a mother who was a small, exquisite, and self-schooled heiress of orchards and farmlands from her adoptive parents.

I think my parents were typical of families who wanted to improve their lot primarily by improving their economic situation. They thought education was the key to this success and so, in spite of great difficulty, they sent their five children to private schools. In addition they must have housed and educated two dozen relatives throughout my growing-up years. It was a value in our family, as it is in most Asian families and unlike in American families whom I have known, that one does not succeed, or plan for success, as an individual, but rather as a member of a family. You succeed or you bring shame as part of a family, never by yourself.

I was the firstborn to a family that eagerly awaited a son, who finally came after four girls. My father had a script for me, much like the ones handed to many eldest Filipino boys and girls then and even now. Go forth and succeed for the family, the script went. But I didn't, and still don't, know how to be programmed for success, or how to live by others' measures. At that time, I had an instinct for this, but now I am surer of it: the character structure I was born with needed the process and protection of knowing who I was and what I could do well, in order to shape a life.

IN AUGUST 1966 two friends and I left the Philippines for graduate studies, giddy with the thought of all the possibilities before us. Every relative and friend we had must have been at the Manila International Airport to send us off. The images from that first leavetaking are indelibly fixed in my memory, perhaps because I have come back for a visit only twice since then. In Hong Kong, we shopped for what we thought would be stylish protection from winter cold: beaded cashmere sweater twin sets, long mohair turtlenecks to coordinate with the dresses and pants that our personal dressmakers had painstakingly designed, sewn, and meticulously fitted, a luxury for which I would give anything now.

In Tokyo three students from Sophia University escorted us proudly around their sites, including their new Olympic-size swimming pool where we stood shoulder deep, wedged in our places in the water by half of the city's population. It turned out they were as grateful for the opportunity to practice their spoken English with us, as much as they were charmed by our company.

After the ritual visits to relatives and friends in Honolulu, San Francisco, and Chicago, I was to meet a friend, the chairman of the department of psychology at the Ateneo de Manila University, at Chicago's O'Hare International Airport, for the flight and introduction to New York City. We never connected. That Friday night, I hailed a cab at Kennedy International Airport and asked the driver to take me to an inexpensive lodging place in Manhattan for the weekend. I would contact the university which had given me a fellowship and a teaching assignment the following Monday. I had my passport and visa, a thousand dollars, two brown suitcases, no friends or contacts, and no fear. I had a room for four dollars and 50 cents a night for the next three nights at the YMCA beside the beautiful Seagram Building, the Four Seasons Restaurant, and three blocks from St. Patrick's Cathedral on Fifth Avenue. I walked that whole weekend, taking on the stride and staccato rhythm of the city, going fast and everywhere.

I wrote my family regularly, tried to tell them where I was. I was grateful to them for life, for the opportunity to be in America. To me, America represented the chance to be with more people who liked to think and to appreciate being, who were touched by film and beauty, who sought to create beauty in their lives. The first group of students I met, however, were quite the opposite of all that. They were insular, provincial. I had also set out to be a clinical child psychologist. I thought psychologists spent their days facilitating other people's ascent to freedom, connecting with them. That wasn't the experience I found in my first university.

Part of my adjustment was something efficient Americans find difficult to understand. I now had to take care of my physical and logistical needs when I never even had to find my own socks and shoes in the Philippines. But I have since mastered the activities and necessities of daily living. That took a while, for the notion of self-help needed major rewiring to incorporate into my system. But it is, I assure you, doable.

I loved the freedom that New York offered. I walked its streets far into the night and developed a sense of personal place in the nooks and crannies of the city, the theater matinees, the art galleries and museums, international house, the cafes of the west village where strangers were friendly, and the bookstalls. I learned how to nourish myself from attention to the here and now, to where my feet could take me. It was exhilarating freedom that carried the danger of cutting myself off too completely from earlier realities. Sometimes it led to living on the edge. Days or weeks spent disconnected in enjoyable melancholy gave rise to questions of meaninglessness and dark, paralyzing depression. That, too, I had to learn to monitor.

During the four years I lived in New York I moved house 12 times, and no, these were not upgrades. I thought it was what every young searching person with young existentialist pretensions did. One of the last apartments I had was actually a reasonably desirable one, an 800-square-foot first floor opening out to a garden on East 21st Street. But I inadvertently burned it down. I had left the apartment after a heated telephone argument with John, whom I would later marry. I did not notice that I had flicked onto the mattress a lighted cigarette ash head that slowly burned most of the room down. The next day I came back to see a notice posted on my apartment door saying I had been evicted. My landlord would have been happy to renegotiate my lease, provided I accepted his terms of accommodations. I marveled at the power of the body electric to pay for one's way through life, another reminder that I had to learn faster how to master the necessities of daily living. Was this what was meant by "starting to grow up"?

MY SEPARATION from the institutional Catholic Church began in the Philippines, where almost everybody is a Catholic. There was debilitating guilt in having done that, but no set of rituals or dispensations of sacraments can touch the soul that has lost its essence. That sounds so grandiose, if not obstruse. I think I needed to take myself to a place where I was freely and fully choosing to be part of organized religion. I wanted to know that the body, mind, emotion, and being in the world were as accepted by Catholicism as what is called the spirit or the soul as it is posited, for instance, in this version of the mission of Judaism as interpreted by the Talmud: to perfect this world in the image of God.

I had studied under American Jesuit priests and Belgian nuns who were among the first women graduates of the University of Louvain. My father had thought of America as a good place for him, and now for me, and so in many ways I was not so conscious of the difference in cultural expectations as I was of the process of individuating myself as a person and as a professional.

Early on in my professional life in New York City I was given a friendly little tip: I was told that to most people in America there were only two truly important measures of a person's worth. One was how much intelligence it requires that person to do what s/he was doing, and two, how much s/he was getting paid for doing the job. These measures were precisely what I had earlier rejected, but this time my response was to create the persona that was necessary to give me some authority in the workforce — the focus, competencies, and credentials for what I wanted to do. And then to find the company whose measures of life supported mine. This is no special dilemma or response; it is that of everyone who finally has to face an adult world s/he cannot yet change. It was noteworthy to me because it was mine, and I was pleased by my own rationality and ability to be commonsensical, if there is such a word.

John, too, had come to New York in search — that was the operant word then — of greater freedom and meaning. He tended to make friends from all walks of life, the more original and less postured, the better. He could switch from six consecutive Bunuel movies to Woody Allen to continuing the conversation of how ontogeny recapitulates phylogeny and why he wanted to study the cortical basis for learning and memory as his life's work. He was a highly kinetic, hazel-eyed midwestern American whose grandparents had recently immigrated from Belgium, Ireland, and Austria. The turbulence and the ecstasy of our developing relationship would not have been possible for us anywhere else but in New York because the milieu provided us the freedom to create our own expectations and the time and space to work them out.

We got married because it seemed to be the most natural thing to do. We chose to not have the wedding in Central Park only because it was a hot, muggy August, and so we crossed the street to the Ethical Culture Society where confession was not required before matrimony. After a noontime wedding, about 12 guests took the subway to Chinatown, then walked to Ferrarra's in Little Italy for dessert. The reception that afternoon was at John's sister's apartment in the East Eighties; we had prepared the whole menu by ourselves.

We moved to Pasadena shortly after the wedding. John was doing a postdoctoral fellowship in neurobiology at the California Institute of Technology. I worked as an organizational and staff development consultant for the State Department of Education and was assigned to two communities because I looked somewhat like the ethnic minorities: the Mexican-American community in the grape-growing valley in central California, and the Quechan Indians, a Colorado River tribe in San Pasqual. It was a heady assignment for a 24-year-old; an ego-gratifying life as a — what did they call me — change agent. I'd drive my gold Mustang at five o'clock in the morning, clocking 80 miles an hour on a five-lane highway from Los Angeles; or I'd fly into Yuma, Arizona, on a Hughes Airwest eight-seater plane once a week, for two days at a time, and think that I was making a difference in the quality of the — listen to this — compensatory education programs, and in the lives of the families and communities.

I have always been a quick reader of cultures and symbolic worlds, and have thrived on the consultancy framework. The clients were warm and accepting of me, but I soon realized the futility and the arrogance of change initiatives that were imposed from the outside. I soon switched to a deanship at a small college specializing in early childhood education where I felt the work was among more equal partners.

Among the board of directors of the college, and with the students and John's colleagues, many of whom came from universities and medical institutions from around the world, there was no hint of personal discrimination. Where a potential landlord thought I was Mexican, a rental lease was difficult to get; when I could not present an American passport at a Mexican border, I would be endlessly interrogated. In situations which assumed there was only one correct way of pronouncing words or articulating thoughts, I was corrected. Being short has presented a whole different set of complications; it strains the credulity of most Americans to think of the vertically challenged, as we are called now, as fully grown or able to be in authority.

I AM SOMETIMES asked if I feel lonely as a Filipino woman. I don't know exactly what that means. During my first year in California, whenever I'd long for some connection to the Philippines, John and I would fly up to San Francisco and walk around Chinatown. Being there among familiar sights and smells calmed me, in much the same way being at Kennedy International Airport did. As a graduate student, I would take the airport bus to the terminal and just be there, happy with the infinite variety of people, loving their looks and sounds, receiving the energy from their histories and hopes, and being reassured that there remain many different and valid symbolic worlds.

My son and my daughter have also asked that question and set about finding answers their own way. The summer before Jason's senior year of college, he arranged to write the introduction to Manila for his college's travel publication, Let's Go guides. For that project he made his first visit to Asia and the Philippines. His sister Judith intends to spend the latter part of her senior year in high school getting to know the Philippines. They might help me to answer that question better after the experience.

The next question I am asked usually is: Who are you now? How do I answer a question like that? With a recitation of facts, I guess. I am a citizen of Chicago, a city of eight million people in midwestern America that sits partly on a landfill of a lake. Chicago is one of the beautiful cities of the world, with a bike path that extends the 30-some miles of the lake's and the river's edges, with neighborhoods of varying grit and refinement, ethnicities and empowerment. I live in a very old house on a city lot which was built from oak and red-brown sandstone quarried more than a hundred years ago. The house was restored mostly by John's amazing will and endurance and some of the family's hard labor.

I work for a living as an early childhood educator in a major health system in the area. I administer, design, develop, and seek financing for programs and environments for children of working parents. We refer to them as day care services, and provide them for babies from six weeks of age in full-day, full-year programs. The work is deceptively simple and quite compelling to me. It is premised on the notion that both women and men have two basic rights, the right to work and the right to love, and should be supported in their exercise of both. Parents continue to have these rights, and where they need support, it is for the common good that the community or the government or the employer, or a combination of the three, provides superb quality educare. This provision enables adults to be productive at their jobs because the children are well cared for. Neither the adults' access to a productive work life nor the children's right to access of the best possible educare while their parents work is as yet constitutionally or effectively guaranteed in the US, so I devote a lot of thought and energy to these questions.

My two children are now aged 23 and 17. I did not become a US citizen until after Jason was born. Having children has been one of the most seductive, challenging, and absolutely joyful experiences both John and I have had in life. The decision to have children was a major shift of being for John. The eldest of 10 children, he had to act as a surrogate father to many of his siblings. When we met he felt that he had fulfilled his paternal obligation in life, if there is such a mandate. He knew, however, that there would have been a sense of incompleteness in me, in my notion of our life together, if we were not to have children. He thought, even before I had acknowledged or articulated it, that it was critical to my self identity to bear and raise children together. John has an instinct about me, an inner knowing of my essence, discernments, moods, and longings that is almost unerring.

It is humbling to be instrumental in the birth of whole other human beings. Both our children are such originals, splendid gifts who have forced from our depths unknown and untapped capacities to know and change and love. John and I have looked at the time and space in which we are together as the opportunity to create our individual selves, with the creation of the family being a large part of this life's work.

Jason is back in Cambridge for graduate studies. He wants to figure out for himself how humankind, we, are supposed to live our lives. We've just completed our first round of looking for colleges for Judith for the year 2000. Our social lives and activities and travel have been quite narrowly dictated by the needs of the children, of John's work as a brain researcher, and of my own as an early childhood educator.

CIVIC LEADERSHIP is an important way for me of giving something, an extension of the early incorporation of noblesse oblige. I have needed to be attuned to and to connect more fully with the underserved than I am formally able to do in my job. I come from a country and a family that know poverty. I also seem to have a gift for seeing what seems to be useful to organizations. I am able to join a group of people responsible for decision making and to assist in illuminating the process; I discern quite easily and effectively the interplay between character structure and organizational leadership and function, and I am comfortable with change and want to participate in those processes. I also enjoy the intellectual challenge of the involvement.

I have few friends, but now that the children are older I have entered the stage of wanting to connect with new friends, or to reconnect with the old ones whose warmth and images I have carried with me all along. I have so many questions to ask, so many stories I want to hear from them. The idea for this project started with a gift from a friend who sent me a book about Filipino women going through midlife dilemmas. I loved reading it - it seemed like I was connecting to their essential selves, and I was hungry for more friends to connect with.

I have been told that in my role as a mentor, I help people to acknowledge their uniqueness and individuality. I do that very naturally, meaning, I invite people to reach points of freedom in their lives and to discover their gifts — which is why I like working with children — and to provide support so they are free to develop them. But I would rather call that networking. Mentoring seems to me to be so important.

Recently, I did something quite uncharacteristic, something I didn't tell my scientist husband about, or my children, for fear of being accused of having become a spiritualist. I had my aura read at a body/soul conference. A small Polaroid photograph captured on film a halo of intense reds and golds around my head, colors that my reader of auras interpreted as evidence that "you are constantly thinking, you are highly intuitive and see through what people say to note what they really mean. You create extraordinary energy and expend it, as though the mind does not want to stop making new connections. You are able to get others motivated and interested, but your energy needs to be replenished. You need physical exercise to supply the use of energy and thought, preferably aerobic. Slow down your thoughts to match your available energy supply."

I have never believed what sound like quasi-scientific approaches and claims, but this psychologist echoed both my internist's judgment and my own of my current physical score card and the state of my inner work. And so I have taken this reading seriously. I will at least renew my membership in the health club and await what the next year will bring as a clue to the next phase of my life.

Ching L. Escaler

A Front-Row Seat
to World Events

THE SAYING "Life begins at 40" is an inevitable cliché that crops up when that milestone is reached, but in my case, turning 40 was special because of what the occasion revealed to me about my life and about myself.

As I approached my 40th birthday, I had been widowed for almost three years and I found myself amidst a growing political turbulence sparked by the assassination of Benigno Aquino, Jr. the previous year. I was increasingly becoming part of an awakened citizenry that was openly fighting for radical change in the country. Careerwise, it was also a restless time for me. I was involved in the full-time management of a tourism-related business which had to continue collaborating with a government I could no longer support. But as a widow with three teenage children and with no other work possibilities, I could not easily discard the job. There was also a personal relationship that had to be resolved in ways that were still not clear to me at that point.

Given all the questions swirling in my mind, and my hectic pace as a neophyte political activist, I decided to mark my 40th birthday in the Cenacle convent. I went on a closed retreat. There, alone for two days and two nights and guided by a spiritual counselor, I prayed and reflected on the past 40 years, slowly retracing many events in my life, from early childhood to the more recent years of widowhood. I tried to focus on many of the major decisions I had taken, especially those with life-changing consequences: the good, the bad, the "right" as well as the "wrong." I attempted to discern some pattern that could give me a better understanding of where the present was taking me.

I was struck by what this process of introspection revealed to me. It became apparent during my reflection that my entire life until then had been mostly a series of unplanned events and decisions, each one leading to the next, seemingly unconnected, but all taking me to where I was at that very moment. It was as if whenever I tried to consciously take control of my life by setting clear goals and directions, carefully mapping out well-crafted routes to get to them, my efforts were almost always sidetracked by unexpected events. These events provoked an almost instinctive but firm decision from me, and moved me into something I had not previously planned for. At the same time, I saw how each of these separate events was like a building block of a larger picture, a distinct signpost amidst the twists and turns of a dizzying roadway, adding still another enriching dimension to my life and helping shape the person, the woman, that I had become.

It felt like some unseen hands were gently yet firmly directing my life in ways that differed radically from where I thought I wanted to go. The seemingly impulsive decisions which resulted from such an irresistible "pull," in spite of the obstacles encountered, would inevitably lead me to something infinitely more challenging and fulfilling. A few years later, I would connect this Cenacle experience to a quotation from Matthew Arnold which has since become central to my life: "For the creation of the masterwork two powers must concur: the power of man and the power of the moment, and the man is not enough without the moment."

That retreat did not fully resolve some of the questions of the moment. But it helped to give me a better understanding of some of the unexplainable forces at work in my life. I came to appreciate better that historical moments are not of our making. We simply find them, and they find us. We sink or swim in them according to our capacity to cope. Moreover, we do not freeze moments. We accept them, find our points in them, and if they are not to our liking, we seek to revolutionize them.

It is important for me to share this 40th birthday insight at the very outset so that the main subject of this essay, the past 10 years of my life as a Filipino woman diplomat, can be seen, and hopefully appreciated, from this very personal perspective.

So much has happened since I turned 40, and now, 15 years later and way past midlife, I have the opportunity to reflect on how this "woman" has responded to her many "moments." It is particularly significant to me, since 10 of the past 15 years have been devoted to a life I never planned or prepared for, that of a diplomat taking on three of the most exciting positions in any diplomatic career — as ambassador to the United Nations in Geneva and then in New York, and as deputy director general of the International Organization for Migration (IOM).

I welcomed the invitation to contribute to this book, coming as it did at a time when I was preparing to close another chapter in my life and to return home after 10 years of living and working abroad.

I HAD BEEN OUT of the Office of the President in Malacañang for almost a year and a half and was being happily challenged by the work I was doing as head of a large corporate foundation. Sometime in late 1988, as I sat next to then secretary of foreign affairs Raul Manglapus at a wedding dinner, he asked whether I had ever considered serving as an ambassador. I was floored by his question, but for some unknown reason found myself pursuing the conversation. Why not, I replied, and did he have anything specific in mind? To which he responded: "Would you consider Geneva?" I felt directly challenged by the firmness in his voice and so responded positively. Shortly after that exchange, the secretary's attention was diverted, and that was that for the rest of the evening.

Soon enough I was to find out that shortly after that brief dinner conversation, Secretary Manglapus spoke with President Corazon Aquino. When I saw her a few days later, she told me how pleased she was that I would accept an appointment as the next Philippine ambassador to the United Nations in Geneva. It began to dawn on me that I had just made a major decision in my life that would have a great impact on my family and my professional career. Going back to public life after almost two years of cherished privacy in a corporate setting was a rather frightening prospect, but things began to move swiftly, and I was soon caught up in the official appointment process.

What seemed, however, like such a straightforward offer and acceptance of a presidential appointment resulted in a flurry of controversy, much of which I understood and accepted as I recognized my lack of experience for such an important diplomatic post. There were some difficult moments when criticism was loudest, but there was always an equal determination to rise above these which led me to stay the course and persevere. The rest is history, as they say. In June 1989 I found myself embarking on my first diplomatic experience as the ambassador and Philippine permanent representative to the United Nations in Geneva.

Geneva is the European headquarters of the UN and hosts the main headquarters of most of the UN's specialized agencies, and technical and humanitarian international organizations. As ambassador, I was expected to promote and protect, within a multilateral system, Philippine interests that spanned a wide-ranging array — human rights, natural disasters and complex emergencies, labor, health, meteorology, aviation, refugees and migration, telecommunications, and trade and development, among others. It was a daunting task, especially for a newcomer like myself, and one that required long hours of meetings and conferences and poring over voluminous documents. It meant endless rounds of informal and formal meetings with fellow diplomats honed in the art of multilateral negotiations and at home in the labyrinthine ways of the UN system. I was, however, determined to learn as much and as quickly as I could.

As head of the Philippine Mission, I had a front-row seat to world events as they happened, like the fall of the Berlin Wall and the consequent reunification of the two Germanys, the Gulf War, Nelson Mandela's release and the beginning of a post-apartheid South Africa, Chairman Yasser Arafat and the Palestinian Liberation Organization's first appearance in a UN conference, the collapse of Communism and the breakup of the Soviet Union and Yugoslavia, the failed Uruguay Round trade negotiations. More than the front-row seat, however, I was an active participant in negotiating international decisions that impacted on such world events. While the big powers obviously held sway in many major decisions, multilateral negotiations allowed the smaller, less powerful countries like the Philippines to make their contributions through the strength of their individual representations.

There were a number of issues, especially those related to human rights and refugees, that I came to understand more easily than others. The situation of the Vietnamese boat people was something I was familiar with. I was aware of the generous and humane policy of the Philippine government in providing care for all those who had found their way to our shores. I appreciated the importance to the Philippines of helping to find durable solutions to providing a better life for these refugees, as well as to easing the burden on the countries of first asylum. I arrived in Geneva in time to witness the signing of the UN Comprehensive Plan of Action (CPA) which would provide the legal multilateral framework for a more orderly management of the refugee issue in the region in the years to come. I would remain engaged in this issue throughout my years as Philippine ambassador in Geneva and in New York. This continued even when I joined the IOM long after the end of the CPA, when I had to make a decision to keep the IOM engaged in helping the Philippine government find solutions to the last remaining group of Vietnamese long-stayers in the country.

The same was true for human rights. The struggle against the Marcos dictatorship exposed me to many of the issues I now faced in the UN Commission on Human Rights and other UN human rights committees. This time I found myself on the other side of the negotiating table, being confronted in different UN meetings by many former fellow street parliamentarians who were now denouncing the continuing human rights violations in the Philippines during the post-Marcos era. The NGOs were as predictable and strident as the government representatives were in the positions we would take in formal and official meetings. The formal exchanges would inevitably result in the usual rhetorical and ideological debate. But perhaps because many of the NGO representatives were my friends from the anti-Marcos struggle, there was much more openness and honesty between us whenever we met in more informal settings. I felt that, given my previous involvement with human rights groups in the Philippines, I was more readily accepted by many of them and that there were genuine efforts on both our parts to understand the issues from each one's perspective. At the same time, while continuing to toe the official government line, I could at least temper such positions with an honest recognition of the gap that still existed between the government's honest intentions to address such violations and the sorry state of actual implementation.

The Gulf War and its impact on thousands of Filipino migrant workers in the Middle East happened on my second year in Geneva. The Philippine Mission had its hands full liaising with the relevant international organizations, notably the UN High Commission for Refugees (UNHCR) and the IOM to ensure the protection, care, and eventual repatriation of our nationals during and after the conflict period. It was a heartwarming experience for me and my colleagues in the Mission to see our efforts in the multilateral arena quickly translated into concrete actions which directly benefited our displaced *kababayans.* I would carry this on throughout my stay in Geneva by successfully negotiating an enhanced compensation package for our Filipino migrant workers.

One area where I had very limited experience or expertise was in trade issues, especially in the highly technical work required by the ongoing Uruguay Round of trade negotiations under the General Agreement on Tariffs and Trade (GATT). As soon as I started work, it was clear to me that this particular area was critical to Philippine trade interests and that I would have to work hard in order to be accepted and to be effective as a key player in the negotiations. Having an edge in such negotiations depended a lot on being able to access reliable and relevant information through the informal system of "corridor diplomacy" outside the more structured and formal conferences and meetings. The initial entry was perhaps easier for me, being one of only a handful of female diplomats in Geneva at that time. But it also required a solid technical knowledge of the issues, which I had to learn on the spot.

Aside from diligently reading and studying each and every document and being briefed regularly and thoroughly by my staff on every issue at hand, I disregarded diplomatic protocol and participated in numerous informal working-level meetings of the different delegations. I discovered that the technical issues were often hammered out by trade experts at the working level and then submitted to their ambassadors. Attendance at these working meetings greatly facilitated my understanding and grasp of the complex issues and gave me more self-confidence whenever I faced my peers in the negotiations. In time I found myself being invited to small closed-door meetings at the ambassadorial level and being taken on as a serious representative not only of the Philippines and ASEAN but even of the group of developing countries. Oftentimes I would be the only female ambassador in smoke-filled rooms engaging in tedious negotiations with my male colleagues. The biggest tribute to all these efforts was my election as head of the GATT Committee of Trade and Development, the very first woman to hold this post in its almost 50-year history!

How did all this hard work affect my family life? My three children came with me to Geneva and enthusiastically welcomed all the wonderful experiences and opportunities that living in the heart of Europe had to offer. When they first arrived in Geneva, Johnny was 23; Mark, 21; and Margarita, 17. They learned French quickly and soon had friends from all over the world. While I was busy most of the time, they each pursued their own interests at work and in school and learned to appreciate a bigger, wider world than what they had known in the Philippines. They began to be more interested in international issues, and family dinners would be an occasion for lively exchanges on topical issues.

We had a lovely home close to the Vieille Ville (Geneva's Old Town) which regularly and warmly welcomed both my diplomatic colleagues and my children's friends. We looked forward to weekends when we would travel to the neighboring countries, many times with other friends. Those three years were among the happiest of our lives, and the bond among the four of us, which had grown stronger after my husband's death eight years earlier, deepened even further during this period. Now, whenever we think of Geneva and those three years, we all look back with much affection and nostalgia.

I LEFT GENEVA prematurely and abruptly to join the Ramos presidential campaign in March 1992. It was a decision that came to me quickly and naturally, but one which even my children could not understand and found hard to accept. For me, however, there was no agonizing over the decision, only an instinctive, unequivocal response as soon as I learned of President Aquino's decision to anoint then defense secretary Fidel Ramos as her successor. I was convinced that in 1992, as in 1983 and again in 1986, we were faced with a critical battle to defend and uphold our fledgling democracy. It was clear that I could not be a mere onlooker to the struggle from faraway Geneva.

I left Geneva convinced that while I had served the country well during those three years, that was the end of my diplomatic "career." I plunged into the Ramos campaign with no other future plan than to find my life again in the Philippines. There was much to do back home and I planned to join the family business after the elections, including setting up a foundation to honor the memory of my grandmother.

But my plans to settle back home would again be redirected, this time to New York. Soon after his election, President Ramos appointed me as the first Filipino woman ambassador and permanent representative to the United Nations in New York. I accepted the appointment without hesitation, happy that I would be engaged again in multilateral diplomacy, this time at the very heart of the UN in New York.

The appointment, however, like the Geneva posting, would have its initial share of political and media controversy. This time, largely due to a better appreciation of the work I had accomplished in Geneva, the main issue was not my competence. The controversy came from the unexpected unhappiness of some women legislators based on an unfortunate misunderstanding. I would eventually get the appointment, but only after I was given a good public lesson in humility.

New York ambassadors like to make a distinction between Geneva and New York by saying that while the European city focuses more on humanitarian and technical issues, New York is *the* political center of the United Nations and, therefore, definitely more important, if not more prestigious.

I have some serious doubts about this neat differentiation between New York and Geneva, but it was immediately obvious to me that, given the worldwide political attention accorded the UN in New York, my work took on a more exciting and higher level than what I had experienced in Geneva. This was particularly evident when one saw the impact on world affairs resulting especially from the decisions of the UN Security Council.

It became equally clear to me, however, that the post-Soviet era had created a real power imbalance in multilateral diplomacy, and the United Nations was — and still is — reeling from this lopsided political situation. In spite of the international attention which the UN in New York generates, one cannot help but feel uneasy that outside the Security Council, perhaps more specifically outside the permanent five of the Security Council, where many of the *real* decisions are made, a great deal of frustrating rhetorical debate and posturing goes on among the rest of the UN's 180 member states.

But I will be the first to admit that the New York experience was a politically exciting and heady one, even if not quite so technically challenging as Geneva was for me.

The New York international environment is perhaps a good starting point in itself. New York brings together with ease the "movers and the shakers" who interact freely with the diplomatic community in ways quite unheard of in Geneva. New York society is most welcoming to the UN and its ambassadors, and offers endless opportunities to meet fascinating people of varying interests and professions, distinctly apart from the UN community. It was, and continues to be, a highly stimulating place politically, intellectually, and professionally.

My being a woman diplomat in Geneva brought with it unique experiences, but nothing quite like what I experienced as one of only seven female ambassadors in the United Nations in New York (out of 185 member states). Madeleine Albright, the US's celebrated first female secretary of state, became the seventh female ambassador in the UN shortly after I assumed office, and her first official social function broke all UN protocol precedents. Instead of the customary lunch with the ambassadors of the permanent five members of the Security Council which she was expected to host, she invited the six other female ambassadors, drawing the attention of the American and international media to this unprecedented event.

Besides Madeleine and myself, the other female diplomats were from Canada (Louise Frechette is now the deputy secretary-general of the UN), Liechtenstein, Trinidad and Tobago, Jamaica, and Kazakhstan. It was to be the first of a series of monthly luncheons, rotated among the seven of us, for which we were dubbed by our male colleagues the "G-7" ("Girls-Seven," as many of them condescendingly muttered on the side). The men were actually annoyed that while Mrs. Albright remained rather inaccessible to many in New York due to her regular weekly trips to Washington for cabinet meetings, she was always most accommodating to her female colleagues for our monthly get- togethers.

I thoroughly enjoyed those regular luncheons with the "G-7". There was a lot of UN business to attend to, and it was great exchanging views on many of the burning issues on the UN agenda while at the same time feeling completely at ease with one another and relating first and foremost as professional women. The group expanded further to include other high-ranking women in the UN Secretariat, as well as visiting female ministers from many countries. Our male colleagues would always inform us of a visiting female dignitary and immediately one of us would host a lunch for the occasion. It was quite a network of interesting and dynamic women leaders which definitely enriched my New York experience as a diplomat and as a woman. This group continues to be an active force within the UN system in New York.

New York was a beehive of activity throughout the brief two years that I was there. The first multiracial post-apartheid presidential election in South Africa touched me more directly. The Philippines was a member of the Committee against Apartheid and a vocal and consistent advocate of an end to apartheid. I was invited to join the ambassadors of Ghana and Nigeria on a UN mission to South Africa a few weeks before the election in 1994. Tension was high, given the violence going on in the country, especially in the Kwazulu Natal province, and there were strong fears of more violence in the coming election. The UN team was requested by the General Assembly to visit South Africa to assess the situation and the status of preparations for the election. The three of us fanned out to various cities of South Africa for a week and met with all the leaders of the different political parties, NGOs, and UN officials monitoring the election process. Much to our disappointment, our meeting with Nelson Mandela was cancelled when he fell ill, but Thabo Mbeki, his eventual successor to the presidency, gave the team an incisive and comprehensive briefing which impressed us very much.

Months later, I would meet Mr. Mandela when he addressed the UN General Assembly in New York as the first president of a free and multiracial South Africa. He warmly thanked me for the consistent and active role the Philippines had played in the fight against apartheid in the United Nations. Meeting Mr. Mandela was most certainly one of the major highlights of my diplomatic life.

Throughout my stay in New York, conflict and emergencies were almost a daily item on the international agenda. To mention only a few: the continuing tension between the international community and Iraq and between Israel and the Palestinians, Haiti, the failed UN efforts in Somalia, the Cambodian election, the uneasy coexistence of the two Koreas, the threat of nuclear disaster within a disintegrating Soviet Union, the increasing violence in the Balkans and in many parts of Africa. There were bright points, too, and the historic handshake between PLO Chairman Arafat and Israel's Prime Minister Rabin was certainly a moment to remember.

There were also the endless conferences and informal meetings on politically charged issues relating to the reform of the Security Council, and the acrimonious debate that went on for weeks and months on the issue of reproductive rights during the preparatory meetings leading to the Cairo Conference on Population and Development. The preparations for the Beijing Conference on Women were also starting and the "G-7" was highly supportive of the newly appointed secretary general of the Conference, Gertrude Mongella from Tanzania. It was fascinating to meet and work with so many women NGOs from all over the world and to witness their tremendous dynamism and commitment to women's causes. Ambassador Albright hosted an exclusively female working lunch at her Waldorf Towers apartment where I had the unique experience of sitting between Mrs. Mongella and Barbra Streisand discussing and denouncing the atrocities and human rights violations being committed against women, particularly at that time against the Bosnian women.

Two years later, in 1995, wearing now my IOM hat, I addressed the plenary session of the Fourth International Conference on Women in Beijing on the issue of women migrants. It was quite an exciting experience when I shared the speakers' list on the second morning of the conference with Hillary Rodham Clinton and the prime ministers of Pakistan and Bangladesh, Benazir Bhutto and Hasina Wazed. Even more thrilling was the unique experience of being reunited in Beijing with four distinguished Filipino women who had served as chairpersons in the four international UN conferences on women: Senators Helen Benitez and Leticia Shahani, Undersecretary of Foreign Affairs

Rosario Manalo, and the chairperson then, Dr. Patricia Licuanan. That was a reunion to remember.

Aside from the heavy workload and hectic pace I had to keep, New York presented a different kind of challenge to me on a personal level. For the first time in my family life, I found myself without any of my children. Johnny had gotten married and was working in Geneva; Mark was back in the Philippines teaching at the Ateneo; and Margarita had decided to pursue her university studies in London. The umbilical cords had been severed in one fell swoop, and I was confronted with the realization that my life would now have to adjust accordingly. All the children were pursuing their own lives and finding their own worlds. We had wonderful and happy reunions whenever these were possible — in Geneva, New York, London, and Manila — but it was in New York where I came to love and enjoy being alone once again.

While the UN work kept me occupied during the week, the weekends offered a new experience. Whenever I was not traveling, I rediscovered and delighted in the pleasures which solitude brought about: long walks in Central Park which made me more acutely aware and appreciative of the changes in the seasons; leisurely strolls through Manhattan's museums and art galleries; catching up on my non-UN reading while listening to favorite operas and string concertos in my 33rd-floor apartment with its breathtaking view of the East River; reestablishing and renewing friendships and making new ones outside my UN world; discovering the joys of watching movies and attending afternoon concerts by myself, something I could never get myself to do before; and simply relishing a new sense of personal freedom and cherishing what I now call my "alone time." It was a wonderful and exhilarating feeling, and I felt whole, happy, and at peace with myself and with my life.

I HAD BEEN in New York for only four months when an unexpected call came from Ambassador Lilia Bautista who succeeded me in Geneva. My name had surfaced among many delegations in Geneva as a possible candidate for the position of deputy director general of the International Organization for Migration. She was requested to find out whether I would be interested. She did this perfunctorily, thinking that having just arrived in New York, I would not even consider the idea.

Again, something prompted me to instinctively respond positively. Lilia and I consulted then secretary of foreign affairs Roberto Romulo, who, after informing President Ramos, gave us the go ahead. The Philippine government nominated me in February 1993 and the IOM election was scheduled in May of the same year.

Soon after my candidature was launched, our ambassador in Washington, Blyke Suarez, suddenly passed away. Once again, I faced an unexpected crossroad. President Ramos, upon the recommendation of Secretary Romulo, offered me the Washington job, clearly the most important diplomatic appointment in the Philippine foreign service. I was deeply honored and overwhelmed by this vote of confidence, but for some unexplained reason it was very clear to me that I could not accept, and preferred to take my chances with the IOM election, or failing that, to stay on in New York.

What we expected to be a three-month campaign turned out to be the longest and most controversial election in the IOM's 43-year history. It took three council sessions interspersed over almost a year to get a consensus vote which elected me in May 1994 to a five-year term. It had nothing to do with my credentials. The main issue was the insistence of the Latin American bloc, which had a controlling vote, that the position of deputy director general historically and traditionally belonged to their region, a stance which disregarded the growth in IOM's membership from the Asian and African regions. My eventual election to the position by consensus as the first Asian and first woman broke this tradition in the IOM and opened up the possibility for geographical rotation, a practice that governs most international organizations. I am delighted that my successor is another woman, who is a distinguished leader from Africa.

I was therefore back in Geneva at the end of August 1994, after a fun-filled 50th birthday celebration with friends and family in Manila. By some uncanny twist of fate, I was also back in the same apartment near the Vieille Ville that had been home to me and my children during those first three happy years in Geneva. It really felt like I was coming home.

The IOM is an intergovernmental body whose mandate is to promote orderly migration. It was founded in 1951 outside the UN system by 15 governments in order to assist, together with the UNHCR, the orderly transfer of migrants and refugees displaced at the end of the

Second World War and, shortly after, the beginning of the Cold War. The IOM now has 70 member states and over 50 observer states with over 1500 staff members located in 65 missions all over the world. Like many international humanitarian organizations, its main headquarters is in Geneva. It started as, and continues to be, a highly effective service and humanitarian organization, especially in transport and migration health services. In more recent years, with the growing importance of migration on the international agenda, the IOM has strengthened its work in other relevant areas, like technical cooperation and capacity building in migration management and in countertrafficking measures, especially those involving women and children.

Once again I found myself a participant, this time even more directly, in a series of world-shaking events like the conflicts in the Great Lakes, Haiti, Angola, Chechnya, Bosnia, Afghanistan, and more recently, in Kosovo; in the massive population displacements in Rwanda and the two Congos, in the countries of ex-Yugoslavia, and in post-Hurricane Mitch Central America; and in the uneasy postwar democratization efforts in the CIS countries, Guatemala, Mozambique, Cambodia, Ethiopia, and again more recently, in East Timor. The past five years also saw the dramatic increase in clandestine population movements all over the world, fueled by the demise of Communism and the collapse of traditional borders, the growing social and economic gaps among countries, and a more sophisticated global criminal system preying on more vulnerable migrants like women and children. The growing feminization of migration continued to challenge traditional understanding of the issue and required more innovative responses. The IOM was increasingly confronted by all these developments and, like many of our international partners, attempted to find better and more creative ways to address the problems. As deputy, I found myself directly and actively engaged in helping the IOM respond to such challenges.

It would be difficult to cover everything here and do justice to the past five years I worked with IOM. After serving in two multilateral posts as a government representative, the IOM offered me the opportunity to see the other side and to address many new as well as familiar international issues, this time from the perspective of an international civil servant working in the service of its member states. I also joined the IOM at a critical point in its history, amidst an international environment of diminishing resources, which demanded radical management reforms and greater accountability from the donor community.

As the IOM's deputy director general, I was expected to focus on the day-to-day internal management of the organization, overseeing an annual program budget of almost US$300 million and over 1500 staff members from around 40 countries, while the director general was supposed to be more active in external and diplomatic affairs. This clear division of work was never really possible, given the complex nature of our programs as well as the precarious state of health of the director general during the last five years. I often had to balance my time between staying on top of daily affairs in Geneva and traveling to faraway, unfamiliar places like Sarajevo and Vukovar, Mozambique and Addis Ababa, Kiev and L'viv, Guatemala, Panama, and the Dominican Republic, to deal with many of the issues where they were actually taking place.

Jim Purcell was an outstanding director general who, at the start of his 10-year term, had the vision to recognize the changing migration landscape and to see the important role that the IOM was increasingly being asked to play. At the same time, he had the courage and the determination to take the necessary steps to modernize and move the organization into the next century. He took me in as a full partner and together we embarked on an internal management review process that led to radical reforms in the IOM's structure and in its budgetary, human resources, and information technology systems. It was not an easy undertaking, especially when I had to face a restless and sometimes hostile multicultural staff, as well as governments expecting more from the organization with much less resources.

In addition, Jim relied on my previous work at the UN to rapidly move the IOM closer to the United Nations system. Five years ago when I started, the IOM had just been accorded observer status in the UN and was virtually an unknown entity in UN circles. Today, the IOM enjoys an almost de facto specialized agency status and is regarded in the UN community as the only international organization dealing exclusively in migration issues.

As a woman, I feel particularly proud to have contributed to the introduction and institutionalization of the IOM's gender policy in both program and staff development. There is much more gender sensitivity now among the IOM staff worldwide and a strengthened awareness of the need to address the specific needs of migrant women in its programs and projects. But much more work remains to be done. I am certainly pleased to have contributed in laying the groundwork for this important task and feel confident that the many IOM men and women committed to this cause will continue to build on what we have accomplished so far.

I was well on my way to being elected, this time by acclamation, to another five-year term when I decided to withdraw in March 1999. Various extraneous factors had again converged, to a point where it became personally clear to me that I could not stay on. I ended my term as the IOM's deputy director general at the end of August 1999, more than 10 years after I first arrived in Geneva.

GENEVA the second time around was an extremely fulfilling experience for me. The professional opportunities and challenges in the international arena that the IOM presented to me these past years gave me a sense of personal accomplishment which I never thought possible. At the same time, encountering Geneva again and my Vieille Ville home, this time without the continued presence of my children, strengthened my appreciation of all the blessings I have received in my life, not the least of which was the unique experience of my life abroad these past 10 years. It gave me a much stronger sense of who I am as a woman at the midpoint of her life and a greater faith in my ability to handle the future. It deepened my understanding of a global multicultural work environment and allowed me to thrive in it. I have come to relish and treasure in more profound ways the wonders of solitude, and to be more accepting, more comfortable, even more forgiving, of my weaknesses as a human being.

Johnny and Charlene have given me two beautiful grandchildren, Max and Claudia, and all of them will soon be heading home to Manila from New York. I look forward to spending more time with my grandchildren and having them get to know their "Nana" better. Mark and Barni, married for over a year now, are settled in Manila and pursuing their respective careers in academe and in the environmental field. There is much catching up to do when I go home to build and nurture a renewed relationship with them as a married couple.

Margarita has just completed a doctorate in biotechnology and will be doing three months of volunteer work with the Assumption sisters in Tanzania. We continue to share a special relationship beyond that of mother-daughter and it has grown deeper and more solid, especially these past two years. She has found a warm and loving friend in Stuart, a fellow scientist. I thank God every day for the wonderful gift of family and for these children with whom I have intimately shared these past 10 happy years.

As I end this chapter in my life as a Filipino woman diplomat abroad, and move toward reconnecting with family and friends in the Philippines, I am often asked the question: What next? I will not venture a response right now. There will definitely be more twists and turns on the road ahead, probably more difficulties and perhaps heartaches. But, as I have always done these past 55 years, I am determined to do my best to meet and seize my moment, with brilliance, with heart, and with faith.

Ofelia Gelvezón-Téqui

Life and Art in the City of Lights

WE HAD JUST taken Mama and my sister Milagros to Kai Tak Airport after they had spent a week with us in Hong Kong. Milagros was checking in their luggage while Marc and I stood nearby chatting with Mama. Then a gossamer film seemed to pass over Mama's eyes and she gently fainted into Marc's surprised arms.

Everything that followed seemed like a blur. Mama recovering from her swoon, the wheelchair, the ambulance to Queen Elizabeth Hospital, the doctors' exploratory questions, vague reassurances, and Mama feeling so tired she just wanted to go to sleep. Milagros and I reluctantly left her and went back home across the harbor, figuring out how to break the news softly to the family waiting in the Philippines, especially to Papa who, we knew, had a heart condition.

We had spent almost three years in Hong Kong and this was the first time Mama had come to visit us in spite of repeated invitations to the family. There were advantages to living on the Island as we were spared the onslaught of countrymen who were more interested in shopping in Kowloon. Close friends, though, took the trouble to cross over on the ferry and we would often go out to dinner in Lamma on the bank's slow junk or eat French home-cooked meals.

Life in Hong Kong was leisurely. The children were happy in the more relaxed atmosphere of the French International School and were performing very well. Their free time was filled with a host of interests and activities. The bank provided a live-in maid and a driver who gave me valuable time to paint, continue my *tai chi,* and attend the orchid society's meetings. On the surface, existence seemed to be more genteel, but I suppose it was quite demanding for Marc whose days started early, ended late, and all whizzed by on meetings and trips and deals.

It was different from life in Paris where we had been living since the beginning of our marriage. Much as my family loved Marc, they had to accept the fact that he would take me away to live thousands of kilometers and several time zones away. But I was eager to live in the City of Lights and savored in advance seeing my art history books come to life. And so, one late September evening, Marc and I debarked at Orly airport with two pieces of baggage in tow and a seven-month-old baby in my belly, to meet a small crowd of his waiting family.

I knew he had a large family, with a dozen brothers and sisters and equally numerous cousins. Although Marc's mother is half-English, she is basically French, and I was the first " foreigner " to come into the family. We were received and welcomed by his family and friends who were all regaled by his descriptions and tales of life in those faraway Pacific islands and certainly curious about the indigenous wife he had brought back with him.

I was probably not the exotic tropical flower I was supposed to be. I was more familiar with Bach and Palladio than with the *kundiman* or the rice terraces. My Western art education would prove to be a faithful ally in social circles, but at the same time it silently reproached me for the shaky foundations in my own culture.

So there I was, inarticulate in everyday French in spite of my fourth-year diploma from the Alliance Française. I was perplexed by my babies whose cries and colic couldn't be explained by Dr. Spock. The horizons offered by a promising art career were now reduced to the walls of our small apartment by the Jardin des Plantes. Like most career-oriented women of my generation, I had no previous experience in cooking or cleaning and now resented the plates and pots that had to be washed, the bathroom and toilet that had to be scrubbed and kept sweet-smelling. I was angry when all my diplomas did not help me master the knobs of the washing machine and all the laundry turned mysteriously and unexpectedly pink or blue or green. I never understood how sudsy water flooded the kitchen floor and on all fours we would have to frantically pull out all the plugs and wipe the floor dry. How I hated being Martha when I had been used to leading the life of carefree, insouciant Mary!

I wished a giant hand would break through the clouds in thunder and lightning and in Gustave Mahler crescendo to whisk me away deus ex machina. But revelations do come, slowly, quietly, almost imperceptibly. I started to look forward to the reappearances of asparagus and girolles in the market. Greengages were my favorites, called Reine Claude plums by the French after the queen of François I. They tasted like pure sugar, and any excess of gustatory pleasures was checked by their trusty laxative effect. I became very familiar with kitchen jargon and cooking processes. I was getting kitchen cultured. It helped that we lived near the excellent market of rue Mouffetard. Marc's expansive gregariousness extended to his table, and so we had friends around for dinner very often. I would serve Asian dishes to our French friends and French food to visiting Filipinos on the pretext of culinary cultural exchange. That was also because if my *pato tim* was not up to par, the French would have no basis for comparison. And I could safely pass the veal blanquette which I ordinarily serve as a festive dish to Pinoy friends.

Household machines no longer held secrets for me. At my fingertips I could command dazzling white washes or equally brilliant plates and crystal-like glasses, just like in the commercials. I had at my beck and call a microwave, a juicer, a sauce-maker, an all-purpose mixer, a blender, a grinder which could serve me at all hours, uncomplaining and tirelessly. Aided by them, I became more daring in the composition of my menus, with mousses and terrines and soufflés in the unusual or surprising combinations of the current nouvelle cuisine. I tried to emulate Paul Bocuse's principle of taking advantage of the best the market had to offer that day of a given season. But I was also determined to leave my children more than just recipes.

With Yann-Philippe, the youngest, now going to kindergarten, Marc and our then-neighbor, Pandy Aviado, encouraged me to go back to printmaking. I looked for a workshop that would teach color viscosity printing, intimidated into not wanting to learn directly from the master himself, S.W. Hayter. It was just as well, as I found out later how the Hayter workshop was quite orthodox and could have discouraged my experiments with the possibilities color viscosity printing had to offer. I learned to divide my days. Martha's part was the morning: making beds, going to the market or the grocery, and cooking the day's meals while the machines washed and dried. The afternoons belonged to Mary, and as each metro station took me farther away from home, I would shed the preoccupations of home and begin to tackle the again familiar problems of composition and iconography.

I took up my old images of the Apocalypse rendered in the pinball machine framework of my shaped zinc plates. I was not that far away to ignore the lamentations of a country sucked dry by a dictator. These found their way into my etchings. This "exile" has somehow heightened my thirst for knowledge of the Philippines. Marc and I wanted to go beyond the nostalgia. He started to collect French books, maps, prints, postcards, and even comic books that touched on the Philippines. He was equally at ease on the ship Astrolabe with La Perouse or on the hacienda with La Gironière in Jala-Jala or in Intramuros with Antonio de Morga. He found a translation of an early 17th-century travel account of a Dominican priest named Gabriel Quiroga de San Antonio, and now he is translating it into English. I would look over his shoulder and slowly satiate the hunger and thirst for my historical roots.

THE DAY AFTER Mama's fainting spell, Milagros and I apprehensively went to the Queen Elizabeth Hospital and were pleasantly surprised to find Mama all smiles and rosy-cheeked. She wanted her rosary, her night clothes, something to read. She spoke with the kind of wonderment of someone who rarely visits hospitals, of the machines buzzing by her bed, of the x-ray wheeled in to scan her chest, of the Chinese nurses whom she could understand only by their smiles. She tolerated all those tubes dripping liquid in and out of her body, but was quite vehement about the food, which she found oily. Aha, Milagros and I winked to each other, if she complains about the food, then she must really be getting well. Mama said she felt so much better and we should ask the doctor to let her go home.

While her doctor was not brimming with enthusiasm over Mama's progress, she prudently asked that Mama be kept in the hospital a few more days for observation. In the meantime, I called the family back home in Pasig, reassuring them that Mama was fine and in fact had started to criticize the hospital menu. To calm their apprehensions, I borrowed Girlie's portable phone so that Mama could talk directly to

Papa. Later, Papa told me that Mama's voice came through strong and not at all that of someone who was sick.

Milagros and I now organized how we should keep her company. Milagros would go to the hospital in the morning with Mama's lunch and I would go in the afternoon with whatever she requested for dinner. With the warm lunch box, I walked sprightly past the nurses' station when a Filipino helper, who had been keeping an old Chinese lady company, ran toward me with the world's distress written on her face. "Your mother!" she cried.

Attendants hastily pulled screens around Mama's bed. More machines were rolled in. Doctors rushed in and out, their gloved hands holding ampules and syringes. For a short while, I watched numbly as everything was happening just like in the movies, and then slumped down in a chair, helpless. After a while, the activity behind the screen perceptibly went on a diminuendo. Mama's young, fresh-faced doctor noticed me and approached. Like in the movies, I had hoped she would announce a happy ending. But, we tried our best. Did all we could. Her heart gave way. Too weak.

I found my way to her bed as the machines were wheeled out one by one. A respirator that was pumping air into her lungs was still on. Mama's heartbeats, reflected as green waves on a screen at first, had high pointy peaks but gradually changed to what looked like nervous scribblings, and finally flattened out. I tried to arrange her mussed-up hair, held her in my arms, and whispered prayers in her ear. Strange, I thought, it is now I saying those prayers exactly the way she taught them to me when I was small. Milagros arrived, having been alerted by the hospital, and Marc a few minutes later. And there we were, the three of us, engulfed in grief, trying to palliate our pain with prayer.

I THINK I succeeded in harmonizing Martha's and Mary's activities without too much dissonance in a relatively simple life in Paris. With the birth of each child, we moved into a bigger apartment. The moving van seemed to increase in volume too. But there was time and place for the quiet joys of seeing our children grow and evolve. There were weekend mushroom hunting expeditions, ski and kung fu lessons, ping-pong or swimming competitions, pottery, and yoga. There were parents-teachers meetings and catechism lessons. It was a calm, ordinary life in which we would savor the not-quite-ordinary events.

The two summer months we spent in the Philippines were full of pleasures and discoveries. The children learned to eat watermelon seeds and chew sugarcane, grimaced at *kare-kare*, played with their cousins, and greeted their grandparents by taking their hand and bringing it to their foreheads. From their cousins and playmates they picked up the words for bodily functions in Tagalog, sometimes in Ilonggo or even in Kapampangan. While they looked forward to running and swimming in white beaches, I thought that here were circumstances favorable to letting them know and be proud of the tropical half of the culture they were born into. Somehow at their young age, the beaches, the swimming pools, the shopping malls made a greater impression. One day, they asked me how come practically every place in Manila was named Rizal. Taking that as a cue, Marc and I took them to the national hero's house and birthplace in Calamba. Upon arriving at Rizal's house, they eagerly ran up the stairs and into all the rooms, then ran down and made a quick tour of the garden. So where's the swimming pool, they asked, puzzled. History lessons would have to wait until they were older.

But I guess their pride in being half Filipino is a living experience. In school or with their playmates, the children took note of their difference in experiences and heritage as we surrounded them in Paris with things Philippine. In the meantime, collecting Filipiniana had become a passion with Marc and my worst rival for his attention. Scouring the weekend flea markets became as mandatory as going to Sunday Mass. I started to grow tamarind, avocado, and *pitogo* (a cycad) from seeds and now they are a couple of decades old. I also brought back orchid species and ficus that the French customs just waved off, and these turned our east-facing dining room almost into a jungle but it looked appropriately tropical with our then fashionable rattan furniture. There are days when the scents of cooking *adobo* or *sinigang* linger in the vestibule. Pot-au-feu is inevitably eaten with lemon juice and *patis,* and not only with Dijon mustard.

When Marc was assigned in Hong Kong, I thought it would be difficult for us to remain the exotic hybrid creatures that we had become in this vibrant city that is a blend of East and West. It turned out we would have the best of both worlds and an opportunity to enrich ourselves with another culture. And we did so, avidly. The interest in Chinese ceramics, stirred in the early Seventies by archeological diggings in the Philippines, was rekindled. With each trip to the mainland, we would bring back a pot, a plate, a bowl, shrugging off the possibility that these could have been made yesterday as the Chinese have never lost their pottery technology. All we sought was a delight in the harmony of simple forms, in the unctuosity or crackle of the glaze. It was touching to discover fingerprints or marks left by a potter whose hands had long ago turned to dust. I became more involved in the slow-motion world of *tai chi*, learning also elegant choreographies with the sword and the dagger. I was becoming fluent in market, taxi, and restaurant Cantonese. While proud of my French cuisine, I never exerted any effort to master Chinese cooking. There were greasy spoons in Wan Chai where a mere bowl of noodles with beef innards could put all my expenditures of energy to shame.

HONG KONG has the reputation of being the rudest city in Asia, but in our grief my sister and I were thankful for the many wordless and anonymous gestures of kindness. We needed the reassurances as it seemed to me those still raw moments were the hardest part of going on living. We had to file Mama's death certificate in the Registry Office where the clerk received us with the usual Hong Kong efficiency but with unfamiliar kindness. Then, with the papers, we had to go back to the funeral parlor as we were to be taken to the hospital to retrieve Mama's body from the morgue. The funeral parlor director asked us to go one floor down where their vehicles were parked. As we descended, the air grew heavier with the odor of probably a thousand faded flowers and burnt-out candles. It seemed like the very walls of the stairwell were smeared with the pain of countless mourners before us.

As we waited for the van's chauffeur, another van drove up and stopped at street level. From below, we could see the silhouette of the driver go around to the back. He opened the door and unloaded a long wicker basket with a completely wrapped body inside. In the morning heat, fumes of something stored in the cold were rising out of the basket. Milagros and I could not accept the idea of seeing Mama again, not in those conditions.

I was not any stronger nor braver, but someone had to identify her. Mercifully, the hospital employees gestured for me to wait outside while they went in and rolled out a stretcher. When they uncovered Mama's head, my apprehensions subsided. She looked like she was still sleeping, her face peaceful, her skin surprisingly pink. I suppressed the urge to smooth down her hair and simply nodded at the attendants. Milagros was sitting outside and I reassured her of how Mama looked. I felt as close to my sister then as we had been as little girls playing in the unfinished back veranda in Iloilo. That night Marc slept in Mama's room while Milagros and I fell asleep holding hands.

I had been working for a number of years at Françoise Bricaut's printmaking atelier and she gave me the keys so I could come and go at my convenience. This was where I bit my zinc plates in nitric acid and printed my etchings series on the Apocalypse, the allegories of good and bad government, and Tony's garden. While the first two series were my commentaries on the Philippine political landscape, I delighted in recreating Tony Padilla's rooftop orchid garden, this time on copper plates. The Sta. Ofelia cycle evolved from Estampitas, the small prints of religious images for which I invented a Sta. Ofelia, *virgen y martir*, for lack of a real saint carrying that name. My Sta. Ofelia rose resurrected from a tomb of nitric acid with martyrdom instruments of burin, scraper, and etching needles in her hands. Milagros, identifying me with Martha, said I should have put a vacuum cleaner and kitchen utensils instead.

In Hong Kong, I did not find a printmaking workshop right away, and so I did acrylic paintings for my exhibits. The large dining room table served as easel and my instantly dry canvases would simply be rolled or tucked away in the kitchen. No fuss, no odors, no trace of the creative birthing pains that had taken place earlier. I painted the joyful and the sorrowful mysteries, transposing biblical images into contemporary Filipino. My intention, as friends had gently chided me when I portrayed "suffering peasants," was to elevate and sanctify the ordinary. Had the Holy Family lived in the Philippines of today, I suppose we could have easily participated in the party they would give after finding Jesus in the temple, or shared in the joys of welcoming Mary's visitation laden with *pasalubong*.

While following in the footsteps of Rizal in Paris, I once wondered why Valentin Ventura is not hailed as a national hero in the Philippines. He never wrote a book that changed the course of history, nor did he lead an army to victory. But Ventura did welcome and shelter many of the 19th-century Filipino expatriates in his home in Paris. He bankrolled the publication of Rizal's *El Filibusterismo* after the original financier backed out. It was also Ventura who took home the remains of the artist Felix Resurreccion Hidalgo who died in Spain. In my view, Ventura was like most of us who are often in the background but doing our share of the task in our small, limited ways. Then and there, the Valentin Ventura Fans Club of Paris was founded. On another dimension, I suppose this is why St. Therese of the Child Jesus, who never left her convent in Lisieux, became the patron saint of missionaries.

I think that in my art exalting the little ordinary everyday things has become one of the recurrent themes since Martha seems to take precedence over Mary in much of my life. My recent exhibits have revolved around still lifes, around objects of the home which are there for the pure, quiet pleasures of forms and colors, evoking also what is placeless and timeless. In my canvases I have managed to merge two of my passions: epiphytes and ceramics. Like a true Gemini, I am attracted both to the ephemeral and to the permanent. I am familiar with the transient seasonal blooms of my orchids, and my daughter Beatrice, who is a student of archeology, has pointed out to me that pottery is one of the artifacts that undergo the least deterioration.

WHEN MARC, Milagros, and I arrived in Manila with Mama's casket, I was relieved to see the family quite composed, and we were reassured that Papa was taking things well. My other brothers and sister took over the tedious and painful preparations for the wake and the burial, assisted by Angeling, our faithful maid who had been practically Mama's right hand for over 40 years. Well-meaning friends and relatives kept asking us to recount what happened, how Mama died in the hospital. As we relived the pain over and over, we found that articulating our grief also became therapeutic. The open casket which revealed Mama's body forced those of us who had not been with her during her last moments to accept the reality of her death.

But as we lived our pain, we were made to feel strongly the warm and comforting bonds of solidarity. We were particularly touched by the visit of an old lady who introduced herself as Mama's childhood playmate and who said she and Mama had not seen each other since their grade school days. Our own childhood playmates and neighbors came too, still recognizable though graying, balding, or paunched, and they greeted us with hugs or handshakes that soothed and helped us heal. Eleven months later, we would go through the same rituals again as we suffered another bereavement. Wounds not fully healed reopened with the sudden death of Papa.

It was just as well that we had to leave Hong Kong when Marc was reassigned to Hanoi. The experience of Hong Kong had been bittersweet. We left for different destinations — Marc to Vietnam, Beatrice and I to Paris to join François, our eldest child, and Yann-Philippe was to stay behind in Hong Kong. François had spent only a year in Hong Kong and gone on to studies in microbiology in Paris. Yann-Philippe had one more year to go at the French International School. Beatrice had been having panic attacks the year before and because of her fragility, we decided it was best I stay with her in Paris and just come to Hanoi during the university breaks.

As with orchid blooms, one can never accurately predict the development of children, though each has received the same nurturing and care. We are parents only once in our lives, as children move rapidly into different stages and we learn and evolve with them. As we walk along with them, we have to learn to balance discipline with affection, when to slacken the hold and when to rein in. It is a constant listening to, and dialogue with, each child's particularity. François was a difficult, unruly, hard-headed boy, the intention of a thousand novenas. He has grown into a young man on the threshold of independence, conscious of his capacities and goals. Beatrice was the model little girl and was probably secretly persecuted by her brothers for being such. Her last year in Hong Kong was marred by anxieties that surfaced in alarming manifestations. We were perplexed, as among our children it is she who articulates most her thoughts, problems, and needs. We put our confidence in professional help, constant presence and love, and a thousand more novenas and Masses. Beatrice is now on her second master's degree, the first having been in archeology and this one in cultural management. And she is still madly in love with Walter, her dog. Yann-Philippe, always self-confident and charming as most youngest children are, seems to have escaped life's adversities. As he juggles his economics studies with being a part-time bartender at a trendy joint in the Bastille, he too has become the object of a thousand novenas, that he may not lose sight of his more important inner life. I suppose that at 22, one can still afford to stray along the way.

Though I never lived in Hanoi for very long stretches, I felt a kind of homecoming each time I landed at Noi Bai airport. It was something close to nostalgia for a world I have not experienced but of which I have imprecise memories. I was reminded so much of Manila's dusty streets, our playground in the Fifties. Here Vietnamese boys would throw wooden tops on the ground, proudly admiring the spinning toy as their playmates wound the string around their own tops, impatient for their turn to show off, very much like my playmates in Pasaje Rosario. They also played a game I vaguely remember, where they aimed slippers at a line drawn in the dust a few meters away. I loved the unique yellow-green of young rice growing in flooded fields on both sides of the highway from the airport. At other months in the year, the rice emitted a perfume that took me back to my childhood in Iloilo. Marcel Proust was wrong. It is not the taste of madeleines but the odors that bring back remembrances. Hanoi was not only another place, it was also another time.

WITH THE WHOLE family now back in France, life has shifted tonality, like a totally new movement in a major key. We are back to the effervescence of Paris. I peer more closely again at paintings of the masters at the Grand Palais or at the Musée d'Orsay, noting their techniques or color sensibilities, wishing I could have learned the craft at their feet. It is I now who goes on regular pilgrimages to the flea markets with fervent hopes of discovering an Hildalgo painting or a Pardo de Tavera sculpture. My expeditions so far have been rewarded only with Baccarat coasters unearthed from decades of grime and dust.

Just before leaving for Hong Kong, we bought an old house in a tiny fortified village in the southwest of France. Most of our time and energy now are concentrated on its restoration. Marc and I fell in love with its yellow ochre stone walls over a meter thick at the basement and never meeting at right angles. The kitchen floor is made up of beige wedge-shaped stones driven into the earth and trampled smooth over years and years. Like the proverbial blind lovers, we did not see the holes in the orange canal tiles of the roof that allowed the rain to seep in and create insidious hole traps in the floor boards. We were just ecstatic over the pegged wooden beams in the attic and intrigued by the Roman numbers carpenters had chiseled on them once upon a time. We now jokingly refer to the house as the ruin that is our ruin.

It was a rare opportunity to have been able to acquire, along with the house, all the contents its former owners had left behind. That was much better than rummaging through the flea market, and we felt like children let loose in a toy store. We were eager to salvage and bring back to life furniture and other objects in the house that had been forgotten. We sanded and treated and waxed chairs, tables, and cupboards, killing millions of wood worms in the process. It was sensuous pleasure to touch wood that had been polished until it felt silky. We sorted out objects and mended them. Marc must have made scores of trips to the public discharge, with the car loaded with disemboweled horsehair mattresses, rusted and gaping pots, assorted paper, and plastic that had accumulated through the years. We once came across gleaming pitchers and basins never used for washing, as well as toilet accessories, which the owners must have found too pretty for daily ablutions. And there was a mummified cat which merited theories from everyone as to how it got to be that way — tucked in the shelves of an oak cabinet.

There was no real garden to speak of. After probably half a century of neglect, hazel trees had forced their roots into the stone fences, causing the fences to heave and undulate. An iron gazebo covered with wisteria had gone mad, twisting the metal bars and shooting out frenzied growths even on the ground. The brambles were as thick and vigorous as those that covered Sleeping Beauty's castle. We had the most luxuriant nettles in the whole village, growing as tall as me and certainly more stinging. Through this jungle poked out a century-old yew tree whose majesty was being overshadowed by a couple of faster growing ash trees. Here and there were a mirabelle plum tree and old-fashioned rose bushes, and a jasmine vine struggled to hoist itself up above the mesh of vegetation.

Marc had hired a team of workers for the Herculean task of clearing the garden. One Easter weekend, we drove down to see the job that had been done. And there it was, one long stretch of land stripped of weeds and ugly trees, sloping down to the country road and gracefully leveling off under the giant yew tree. Since the terrain had been unkempt and wild for generations and now was clear of bushes, it gave up assorted scrap metal which we gathered into a pile worthy of any avant-garde installation. There were a couple of rusting car fenders, an almost complete skeleton of a bicycle, the frame of a toy pram with one wheel missing, rolls of barbed wire, pierced tin buckets. They all seemed to have been thrown there since the last world war.

The workers had spared and even pruned the walnut trees whose sticky buds were now a tender green. There was a faint perfume of spring flowers in the air. Probably the wisteria. Probably the white cherry blossoms. It is Easter.

Sr. Emma de Guzman, ICM

Rebirth in Mini-Africa

MVAA IS CARVED from the forest. A single road winds through the main street and leads to the other villages and towns. Trees cover the horizon, but that does not keep the exploding sunset from dancing in the sky in brilliant red and orange. This was how Nature welcomed me when I arrived in Cameroon two days after leaving cold Brussels.

The trip from Belgium to Cameroon involved a one-night stopover in Douala, business capital and seaport. I was alone, just as I had left the Philippines alone the year before. That first night on African soil was unforgettable. I was met at the airport by a fellow sister who was on her way home to Belgium. We had to sleep in a military base as there was no room available in the Mission Procure. My co-sister was offered a room by a French officer who knew her as a missionary. We were taken to the military base, to a house being rented for transient French pilots, and ushered into a comfortable room with two beds. As we slept that night, we were awakened by a drunk French pilot who demanded to be let in, insisting it was his room and he wanted to sleep there too. The lock was not working, so we stacked our suitcases behind the door and kept watch the rest of the night. The man quieted down only toward dawn, and went to sleep in the room across his, which was empty.

I will always remember the next day. I took another plane for my destination: Yaounde, capital of Cameroon.

"J'ai faim!" (I'm hungry!) Those were my first words to my superior when she met me at the airport. I had had nothing to eat since the flight from Brussels to Douala the night before. It was 12 noon when the plane landed at Yaounde airport. I had finally arrived at my first destina-

tion. After a brief lunch, we drove by car to the first mission place of our ICM sisters in Mvaa, where the Catholic mission compound is. It was almost surprising to see a clearing in the mission compound after long, winding roads in what seemed to be a virgin forest. There, clusters of low buildings housed the high school, the sisters' convent, the presbyter, the elementary school, the dispensary, and the maternity clinic. I felt as though I had entered the pages of the books of Dr. Albert Schweitzer in Lambarene and Dr. Tom Dooley in Laos.

As a welcome for me, we had supper with the CICM priests, who kept the light generator on until nine that evening. Then it was bedtime. That first night in Mvaa, my second in Africa, was a sleepless one again. I discovered that the forest comes alive at night. It seemed as if it had prepared a concert to welcome me. A cacophony of sounds and shrieks and whistles filled the air. I was able to distinguish only one sound, like a baby crying in the dark. I wondered why it was screaming. I was not scared, but I could not sleep. I had to keep telling myself that I was in Cameroon at last. I was happy to be in a tropical country like the Philippines.

The next morning I was told that the shrieking baby was actually a bird that makes such sounds at night. After a few days, I got used to the unusual bird sounds, like a lullaby putting me to sleep.

EVERYTHING WAS new to me. Like a child, I babbled as I struggled to speak in Cameroonian French. I accepted correction, listened, drank in the words, and learned everything from speaking French in an Ewondo environment to getting acquainted with the people to recognizing faces and names and tasting new food. I was amazed and enthusiastic about everything. A whole new world was being opened to me.

Cameroon is in West Africa. Its name was derived from a Portuguese explorer who arrived in the Wouri river in Douala in the 14th century. The river was full of shrimps and so he called it *Rio dos camaroes,* river of shrimps. In the age of colonization, Cameroon (Kamerun) became a German protectorate. When the Germans lost the war, the country was ceded to France and England. Thus, the country has two official languages, English and French, and the people have unique European and Bantu names.

"Africa in miniature" is another name given to Cameroon. This country of 475,000 square kilometers has all the geographical contours of the vast African continent: dense forest, desert, seacoast, savanna, and mountains. Compared to war-torn African countries like Angola, Rwanda and Burundi, Cameroon is lucky to be enjoying relative peace. Its forests are still abundant despite the presence of logging companies that cut down an alarming 200 trees a day, at least. The question is, for how long they can do that? The inhabitants of these forests have been rendered homeless, their natural surroundings turned into wasteland.

It took me some time to remember the smiling blank faces and to pronounce their Ewondo names. At first they all looked alike to me, so I tried to remember them by their clothes. When they changed their clothes I had a difficult time remembering which name belonged to whose face. It was easier to remember their French names, but it was more acceptable to call them by their Ewondo names. Memorizing these was a real challenge at first, but I learned. I had to give up my usual memory aids and create new ones. Let me give you a few of my friends' names: Jean-Claude Mbassi, Dieudonné Messanga, Théophile Tagne, Jean-Galbert Kougoum, Nicole Kwata, Marie-Thérèse Awanda.

I discovered an effective technique for remembering names. When I met someone whose name I couldn't remember, I would say enthusiastically while shaking his or her hand, *"Bonjour, Julienne"* (or some other name that came to my mind), and instantly he or she would correct me: "No, it's Francoise, Sister. Julienne is my neighbor." It was an ingenious guessing game I often succeeded in playing.

After some time, I noticed the different hues and shades of their skin. Truly, black is beautiful. It ranges from dark to pale to light brown, from hazy to striking. But what impressed me most about them were their beautiful eyes and curly eyelashes. Their light brown and blue eyes, though, were particularly charming.

In time the names of the towns also found their way into my heart: Okola, Mvolye, Messa, Mvele, Kumbo, Nkambe. These are the places in Cameroon where the ICM sisters live. This is the country of my second birth.

It is not only Nature but also the animal kingdom that welcomes the newcomer to Cameroon. There are varieties of butterflies, dragonflies, birds, and insects I've never seen before, among them *salagubang* (beetle) thrice the size of a matchbox. Strangers to Africa often associate the continent only with lions and tigers and elephants, but sometimes there are tiny insects even more dangerous than these.

One of these insects is the *"mout-mout"* which is so small it cannot be seen by the naked eye but it leaves traces on your skin like small red dots. On my second day in Mvaa, I got scared when I saw the marks on my face, arms, legs, and body. My first thought was leprosy because I did not feel anything. My fellow sisters laughed and explained that it was part of the forest's welcome for newcomers. It seems the *mout-mout* bite newcomers more since they have not yet tasted the new blood. In time the red dots on my skin became patches that started to itch. Since I had to explain to everyone the 7,100 islands of my country, I pointed to the numerous "islands," big and small, on my arms and legs.

The Cameroonians are a happy and hard-working people who love the earth. They call her mother provider because it is from her womb that food is given to all.

Vegetation in Cameroon is very similar to that in the Philippines. What I like most is the *saluyot* which varies in length from six to 10 inches. Cameroonians prepare it almost like we do our *dinengdeng,* but without *bagoong* or *patis.* Palm wine is a local drink extracted from the top trunk of the palm tree. Every morning the men climb the tree to get their day's drink, even if the global market has successfully introduced beer and other bottled drinks in the remotest village. There are no roads, no electricity, no water, very few vehicles, but there are small bars selling bottled drinks. Buying, drinking, or serving them has become a status symbol among the people.

I LEFT THE Philippines for the first time in August 1974. I did not choose Cameroon; it chose me. Africa was not even part of my dream as an aspiring missionary.

When I entered the ICM (Immaculate Heart of Mary) congregation in 1969, I wanted to become a missionary in faraway lands. To me at the time, that meant Brazil, where our ICM sisters were doing pastoral non-institutional work.

I arrived in Cameroon after a short stint in France and Belgium. As a member of an international missionary congregation, I lived with our Belgian and Congolese (Zairian) co-sisters. I was the first Filipino ICM there. I worked with the Cameroonians, lived with Belgians and Congolese, and we all spoke French while trying to learn Ewondo. How I survived is a question I am often asked. I really don't know. It is only when people ask me about life in Cameroon that I realize 25 years have passed.

When we were in the novitiate, the sisters told us that a good missionary must have three qualities. The first is patience, the second is patience, and the third is patience. I added a fourth: a good sense of humor. When the first, second, and third do not work, a good laugh is healthy. We cannot change the world, nor can we change cultures and people. It is the height of ambition to believe that we can make a difference in their lives. People everywhere need happy, good-humored human beings who can laugh at themselves and at others. This means not taking oneself too seriously and accepting one another's riches and differences. I am lucky to have this gift. I seem to find the right words to blurt out when a situation is becoming too tense; then everyone laughs and we all go home feeling light and happy. These are for normal daily events that would otherwise become very painful.

In the cycle of life, however, we know that there are desperate situations which cannot be settled by a sense of humor. This is the domain of God and it calls for deep faith and prayer. My own "Internet" to the Heavenly Father, a satellite-free, wireless network, is always on, and He never turns me down. This was what kept me alive as a person and as a missionary in Cameroon. Then, too, my hobbies are simple and I can pursue them everywhere: reading and writing. Reading energizes me much, even if it is a two-year-old *Time, Newsweek, National Geographic,* or *Reader's Digest,* or any other magazine or book I have at the moment. I got "updated" on world events, new products, and the electronic world even if we did not have electricity or water or a telephone line. Now there's water and power, but the telephone might take longer.

I still cannot grasp situations that call for the use of fetishes, sorcery, and voodoo magic, more so if these are meant to eliminate people who are beginning to succeed in life. Like people dying because a witch doctor cast an evil spell on them. Young people are afraid to return to their hometowns because of this. Instead, they go to the cities to work or to study — anything that will help them improve their lot in life.

A rich minority in Cameroon (merchants, politicians, high government officials) enjoy the luxuries that globalization offers. They send their children abroad for the best education and drink French wine with their meals. Cameroon is the world's fifth biggest consumer of champagne. It also has a football team that has become famous in the World Cup competitions.

The majority of the people, however, are poor. They subsist on almost nothing. At four in the morning, the women in the villages set out to walk five to 15 kilometers just for a pail of water for their cooking needs. They spend the rest of the day in the fields planting what the family will eat: root crops, bananas, peanuts, vegetables. At three in the afternoon they go home with the day's harvest and firewood which they carry in a big basket on their backs. They cook their only meal for the day at about four or five, when their husbands arrive from the cacao plantations and the children from the town school.

The houses in the middle of cacao plantations are made of mud and contain minimal furnishings: a bamboo bed, a table, a few chairs. The dirt floor is swept clean and sprinkled with water to keep the dust down. The cacao is exported to Europe and comes to our grocery shelves as delicious chocolates or pralines. The farmer who works from day to day has no say in the buying price of cacao. Neither can he influence the nonstop rise in the prices of commodities. While the rest of the world enjoys delicious chocolate bars, the farmers who plant and harvest the cacao live in subhuman conditions. The women in the remote villages do not even figure in the political and economic scenes. Government and foreign markets take care of that. Good roads, water, electricity, health services, and schools are still unreachable dreams.

We work for people empowerment, women's issues, health services, awareness of HIV/AIDS, religious education, a better life for all economically, socially, culturally. The Word of God takes flesh when people are able to live decent human lives. But governments enter into alliances for profit-earning ventures that enrich only those in power. Meanwhile, life in the villages is as before. The world approaches the third millennium with its problems of Y2K, but most women in Cameroon and the rest of Africa still walk several kilometers to the nearest spring to fetch water for their families.

My adjustment to Cameroonian food — *cuisine a la camerounais* — was an exciting culinary experience. The Cameroonian diet is hot and spicy, but I still cannot eat *"pili-pili"* (hot pepper). The women I worked with understood this and learned to set aside a plate without the usual hot pepper sauce. But I have tasted rich exotic delicacies, and liked them. Do you know that viper meat tastes like a cross between fish and rabbit meat? Prepared with tomatoes and onions or peanut sauce, viper meat is very delicious. Or how would you like roasted or grilled crunchies? This is not junk food, mind you. Depending on the season, you can have roasted crunchy termites or small grasshoppers. There is a delicacy I call "aborted butterflies" — edible caterpillars — and eating them is like having chunks of butter, real fat. The dish is prepared with a special sauce wrapped in banana leaves and then boiled. My favorite, though, is *nnam ngon*. These are big squash seeds (similar to our *butong pakwan*) which are individually shelled and crushed to make paste the size of a casserole. It is mixed with spices, onions, tomatoes and fish, shrimps, or chicken (your choice), wrapped in banana leaves, then steamed over boiling water. It is a yummy and healthful protein-rich dish found only in south Cameroon.

I WENT AROUND the country giving training seminars to women. Where the sisters live, in the central south of the country, I worked mainly with Etons and Ewondos who belonged to the Bantu tribe. Their hospitality is unbeatable. Visitors to their homes always leave with their hands full of bananas or cassavas from their hosts' back gardens. Strangers are always welcomed as a brother or sister. This sense of family extends to the whole clan. As missionaries, we have a special place in their hearts and are considered their own. If you speak their language or even only a semblance of it, you are deeply appreciated even if it is badly spoken. They are so polite that they will not even correct your pronunciation but will strain to understand what you really mean.

Let me tell you about a hilarious experience I had. In one of the live-in training seminars for the mother catechists, I gave a closing talk before some 65 women at the end of the three days. As parting words I wanted to tell them in Ewondo "not to forget to meet once a month and study very well your lessons before teaching the children. Try also to bring a younger woman as apprentice." I noticed that the women were straining not to laugh. My close collaborator nudged me and whispered that she could continue for me. I was grateful to her because, after three days, I could feel fatigue setting in, especially since I had to speak French and Ewondo at the same time. I also thought the women must be eager to go home. So I let my colleague take over. Everybody waited until the final prayers, and when the good-byes were being said all the women started laughing and embraced me warmly. Only then did I find out what I had actually said: "Before teaching the children, you must meet once a month during your monthly period and study the moon. Take a young girl with you who also has her period and study the moon together."

Since the women lived in different villages which were accessible only by foot, they jested that they would have to walk 20 to 30 kilometers, only to find out how they would study the moon together. More laughter. Ewondo, you see, has seven tones. One can say the same word in seven different tones and it will have seven different meanings. *Ngon* can mean month, moon, young woman, and monthly periods, or a special food menu. I found myself laughing outrageously with them and gradually my Ewondo improved.

For a start, I worked with the women who were mother catechists. Later we had complete training seminars that included analyzing the signs of the times (*Gaudium et Spes*, Vatican II); discussing the role of women in the family, the village and Ewondo society; learning the uses of herbal medicines: identifying medicinal plants, making cough syrup for children and pomade for rheumatism. The herbal medicine seminar was actually started by another Filipino ICM, Sr. Loreto Jamelarin. The people called her "herbal doctor."

Because soap and medicines were so expensive, we also learned to make soap and skin creams, as well as yogurts to supplement the people's meager diet. We tried to improve their health and the sanitary conditions in the village, and we taught the women how to hold a participatory meeting and pass on to others what they had learned during the seminar.

In 1977 the bishop made me a member of the diocesan pastoral team of the Archdiocese of Yaounde. The team gave training seminars on the Bible and the training of catechists. With a Canadian La Salle brother, we made catechism books for children with accompanying posters. Later I began the long and tedious work of translating the books into Ewondo. I worked with the women and an experienced American linguist who guided us in the art of translating the word of God.

In 1979 I became part of a Rome-based Pastoral Animation Team called Service Monde Meilleur (known then as the Better World Movement) when it started in Cameroon. Our main work was to conscienticize the parish leaders toward the renewal of the parish according to the spirit of Vatican II. In 1983 I was elected as its national coordinator. Then, in another election in 1991, I was promoted to membership in the coordinating team for French-speaking Africa of the Africa Francophone des Iles et du Continent / Service Monde Meilleur.

The work took me to other countries where the team conducted training seminars for church leaders: bishops, priests, religious, and lay persons involved in the renewal of the parish and the diocese. I was the only woman, the other members of the team having been priests — Congolese, Burkinabe, French, German, and Cameroonian. I enjoyed my work and learned a lot. My co-workers appreciated my contribution as a woman religious missionary from the Philippines. I often told them that growing up with five brothers and numerous male cousins actually prepared me for the work. They also appreciated the fact that we could work together without making one another feel "oppressed" or "depressed."

As I worked in the different dioceses from north to south, I learned to get along not only with Cameroonians but with other nationalities as well: Europeans (Belgians, Poles, Swiss, French, Germans, Spaniards, Irish, Portuguese, Dutch, Italians), North and South Americans (Canadians and Americans, Brazilians, Colombians, Peruvians), and Africans (from South Africa, Congo, Malawi, Burkina Faso, Ivory Coast, Senegal, Burundi, Rwanda, Mauritius, and Reunion Islands).

Among ourselves we often joked that our meetings resembled the United Nations in miniature. As the only Asian and Filipino most of the time, I discovered the joy of living with other people and learning from them.

But outside of these pastoral seminars, which actually took up only half of my time, the work I enjoyed most was baby-sitting. The first baby I took care of is now in university and several inches taller than I am. In Cameroonian terms, I'm actually a grandmother. Cameroonian children are fun. They taught me a lot about simplicity and laughter. One two-year-old once challenged my creativity on how to keep her busy without the usual toys and dolls. I learned that domestic ant houses caught and kept in matchboxes make for inexpensive and utterly interesting toys for toddlers. Even as the dazed ants easily scamper away, there's always a long line coming up to keep the game going.

Another form of compliment among the Ewondo is giving your name to a baby. As a policy, I always refused when asked to become godmother or homonym to a child. I would explain that as a missionary I would not be staying forever in one place. A former student of mine, though, did not bother to ask me. One day she came to our convent with a baby in her arms, her firstborn. Her name is Emma, the mother told me, and she's been baptized. I took pictures of the cute child to send home and gave her a present. She's now five years old and I call her my homonym.

THERE WERE MORE interesting sides to my being Filipino and brown. It placed me in the middle of the white and black races into which Europe and Africa are polarized. Being Filipino and brown-skinned had its advantages and disadvantages. The Africans didn't consider me white (because I'm not black). Neither did the Europeans. Sometimes, when a discussion touched deep-seated pains due to history (like the black slave trade and colonization), I could listen with detachment and be objective. I didn't exactly get myself caught in the middle, but sometimes I could be pulled aside during the breaks by a black national looking for a sympathetic ear or by the European on the other side explaining the errors of history. Since I did not belong to the race of either the oppressor or the oppressed, I was sympathetic to both sides.

In all this I learned a basic truth. Color is only skin deep. The blood that flows through our veins is red. We feel the same emotions, are hurt by the same painful words. We all exult at being loved and appreciated. Only water really quenches our thirst. We are all brothers and sisters.

My best friends are multicolored and multicultured. I've been embraced by men and women of countless races. I'm happy to be a Filipino woman. They are happy to have me in their midst.

My former bishop, Monsignor Jean Zoa, the first Cameroonian archbishop of Yaounde, called me "my daughter from faraway islands." My first parish priest introduced me as *"Mininga* Toyota" or Lady Toyota. Let me tell you why. I was just beginning to go with him on visits to the various faraway villages. He didn't know how to introduce a missionary sister from the Philippines. It was the early Seventies and most missionaries used Toyota pick-ups. The priest figured out a way to introduce my country. He would ask the whole village gathered in the church, "Do you see the Toyota cars that pass in the village? Do you know where those cars are made? In Japan, a very far country in Asia. Sister Emma comes from the country not far from Japan where those cars are made. It is called the Philippines." One catechist exclaimed, *"Mininga* Toyota" and somehow the name stuck. (*Mininga* is the Ewondo word for woman or lady.)

The women I worked with called me their *co-épouse* (co-spouse). This was actually a compliment as co-spouses are supposed to be closely working with one another. The women showered me with the harvest from their fields: bananas, oranges, corn root crops, peanuts. I in turn shared my knowledge with them and taught them how to teach it to others.

They were incredible women. Some of them could not read or write, but their memory was very good. From what they themselves memorized during the training seminars, they were able to tell the gospel stories to the children and teach the children to pray. They would go home with their religion guidebook and their children who had been to school would read it to them.

At the start they asked me, "Tell us the story of St. Paul's letter to your people. You are the first Philippian we know." To them I was a Philippian.

Another priest-collaborator nicknamed me Mama. I could not hide my surprise because I had always thought he was much older than I. I learned later that when one calls you Mama, it is meant as a compliment and in fact is the highest form of respect.

WHEN I LEFT the Philippines in 1974, I had absolutely no idea about Cameroon. I only knew I had to pass by France to learn French. Nothing had prepared me for either experience, but I was young, adventurous, and full of missionary enthusiasm. Nothing, I told myself, could go wrong.

Lille, France, in autumn 1974 looked bleak, dreary, and cold. And it was. My first experience of autumn and winter almost gave me a depression. I missed the daily rising and setting of the sun. Just thinking of the blue skies back home made me homesick. One night I couldn't sleep because of the cold, and so I imagined myself at high noon in one of the Philippine beaches where the sand is so hot it almost burns your feet. I drew a picture of a big sun and placed it on one wall of my room.

After six months in Lille, I was sent to Auvillar in the south of France where we had a convent. A sister gave me more French lessons, after which I could talk to more people with the strong accent of the Midi. The superior then was Sr. Trinitas Valdés, a Filipino. It was the first time since coming to Europe I found myself with another Filipino woman. Being with her helped my transition period. I also found the weather in southern France more to my liking. Besides, winter was over by then. It had given way to spring and summer. Alas, just when I was beginning to appreciate the four seasons, it was time to leave, time to move to Cameroon. It was August 1975.

As I write this, it is August 6, 1999.

Twenty-five years is not really long, but long enough to make anyone at home in her adopted country. Now my heart is in Cameroon even if, in the beginning, it was not even part of my dreams.

In the novitiate we were asked to write our letter of application. After a year, our general superiors in Rome gave me my mission assignment: Cameroon, Africa. I remembered going to the library to find out where it was. My obedience opened my horizon and my world-view. The words of our foundress, Marie Louise de Meester, became real: "Let your heart be like His, so generous and so great that the whole world may find room in it."

Now I have been "Cameroonized." I had to shed some of my Filipino-ness in order to gain new habits. I learned to say things frankly and honestly, as the Cameroonians would say. With them there is no guessing or anticipating. If you don't say it, no one else will guess because the body signals are not the same.

I was liberated from the habit of crunching something in my mouth practically the whole day. In Cameroon one or two big meals a day are sufficient. I can survive even if I don't eat rice every day. There is a variety of staple food in Africa: yams, sweet potatoes, boiled or fried bananas, boiled cassava, cassava flour made into couscous.

But there was one Filipino habit I did not give up, even as I got used to shaking hands to say hello and good-bye. This is our habit of smiling as a way of greeting. Smiling is a beautiful universal language. And when I was on home leave, I still touched my father's and other elders' hands to my forehead. I did not lose my sense of humor, even if there were moments that could not be solved by humor. Such as when I had to drive through rough, rugged roads where the only space on the road without holes, during the rainy season, had to be enough for the size of my tires. Or when I had to cross swamps and rivers on two wooden planks or over the uncut trunks of trees. I would get nervous when two lines of cars would be waiting at both ends of the road for their turn. In the end I learned my lesson — I simply stepped out and signaled to the drivers of waiting vehicles to help my vehicle across. I would give the driver the keys and sit on the sides while he maneuvered my car to the other side. Then I had the luxury of closing my eyes so as not to see how deep the river was.

That was one of the "survival techniques" I discovered. People were happy to help, and the story went around of the sister who was afraid to cross the river on a wooden bridge. Luckily, nobody ever ran away with my car. People recognized me as a missionary who needed help and they gave it wholeheartedly.

My experiences in Cameroon transformed me. The cross-cultural encounters and exchanges were very enriching experiences. They made me a better person. I saw the relativity of cultures and behaviors and realized that we are all humans with capacities to learn from one another. No culture or language or habit is better than another. We all hold a piece of the secret of the universe, a part of God's divinity. Each piece is a marvel, an expression of the limitless beauty of man and the rest of God's creation. Color is only skin deep. We are all the same inside and we all have something to learn and enrich one another with. Besides, I am now colorblind.

Life in Cameroon enriched me. The people's respect for Mother Earth is something other, more civilized cultures are relearning now. The Cameroonians have not lost it yet. Before a Cameroon woman digs her hoe into the ground, she says a prayer and apologizes to the earth for hurting her, explaining that she needs to feed her family. The trees in the forest are considered alive. Their ancestors are part of their past and their future. The water spring is sacred.

I developed an acute awareness of what is not said but rather spoken in their body language, as well as a sensitivity to what is said when the real meaning is not spoken. One learns this when one gives up one's world and enters the universe of the other. The universe of the Cameroonian is complex. I do not pretend to understand it fully. I only know that in having been allowed to enter it, I have become a better person.

I HAD MY DAYS of exploding sunshine and days of darkest gloom. Gloom was a day in 1996, on a trip to northwest Cameroon in the English-speaking region. Our district superior, a Belgian sister named Louisette Vanryckeghem, was taking our newly arrived young Congolese (Zairian) Sister, Marie Josée, to her new mission post in Nkambe. I was to accompany Sister Louisette. Nkambe was more than 10 hours' drive from Yaounde. I suggested that we take a driver for such a long trip, but Sister Louisette considered both of us good enough and said we would take turns at the wheel. She had been to that newly founded ICM mission several times, while Marie Josée and I were going there for the first time. We left at five o'clock on a Sunday morning. I drove the first lap of the trip, till almost noon. We made several stopovers, the last at the bishop's house in Kumbo where we had lunch with the bishop.

At about 2:30 p.m. we continued our trip. The northwest province is mountainous and has beautiful, breathtaking sights, like Baguio in the Philippines. It was Sister Louisette's turn to drive and I sat in the back seat with a pocketbook. I normally avoid taking the front seat when I am not driving, and on long trips I read a book to take my eyes off the road.

The northwest province is entirely different from the densely forested southern part of Cameroon. Africa in miniature offers a different view and landscape on this side: tea plantations, rolling hills and valleys, eucalyptus trees growing everywhere. It is a feast for the eyes. The houses are also built differently: red bricks made of mud for the walls, interspersed with big enclosures called the Chefferie, akin to a small village surrounded by walls where the traditional local chief lives.

The Ring Road highway winds up and down the hills and valleys. At about 3:30 that afternoon, after passing a small village in what is called Upper Mbot in Tabenkem, something happened. There was a lull in our conversation and I was about to doze off. At a certain point I opened my eyes and saw tall grasses in front of the car. Before I could react, I saw Sister Louisette trying to veer the wheels to the right. The tall grasses were growing on the side of the cliff. We were in mid-air. We had fallen on a sharp cliff about 90 meters deep before the ravine rolled down the valley. In a flash I thought: "Now is my turn to see God face to face." I felt a thud, then a turn, and another thud. It felt as though we were in a can being bowled down the valley from a high point. None of us screamed. We were so shocked we could not utter a word.

I looked out of the car. I couldn't open the door. Peeping through the windshield, I saw that I had to maneuver a jump to get out of the vehicle. By then I was screaming, "Help! Help!" I smelled gasoline. Instinct told me I had to get out of the car as fast as I could. But I couldn't find a flat space, for we were suspended over the ravine and surrounded by trees. Looking up, I realized how far down we had fallen from the road. The four wheels of the car pointed skyward and were still running. I didn't realize that I was the only one still left inside the car. Amidst my own screams, I heard Marie Josée also screaming, "Where is Louisette?"

I started crawling, looking for a way out, first through the back window, but it was too high to jump out and the doors could not be opened. Finally, I crawled out through the broken front shield. There was no flat space to jump out to. Searching for something to hold on to, I focused on a small branch of a tree and jumped. I didn't know where my step-ins were, but at that moment they were unimportant. All I could think of was that we had to get out of that ravine as fast as possible and that we could not do so alone. "Lord! Help! Please, help us! Help!" I screamed again and again.

Marie Josée was crying her heart out in the typical African way, "Louisette, Louisette!" I crawled to where she was, wondering myself where Louisette was. Holding on to grasses and the branches of trees, I reached Marie Josée and saw the reason for her wailing. Louisette lay near a tree, seemingly inert. Quickly and slowly I crawled upward to reach her. I shook her body, thinking she needed first aid or artificial resuscitation. Shaking her legs, I called out her name. I looked into her face and saw her eyes. They were open, and blood was oozing from her nose and mouth. I understood right away that the Lord had taken her. She had died instantly after being thrown out of the car and hitting her head against the tree. Her body was about five meters away from the car.

I remember screaming and wailing, "God, no! Lord, help!" I knew I had to take charge and get us out of there. I was afraid the car would explode any minute. And Marie Josée did not speak English.

I knelt beside Louisette's body, closed her eyes, made the sign of the cross on her forehead, and did a semblance of the rituals of Extreme Unction. My prayer was, "Go in peace, Louisette. Go and meet Jesus, He is waiting for you. We love you, go in peace. Forgive us, we forgive you. Go and meet Jesus, He is waiting for you. Go! Go in peace!" At the back of my mind I knew we had to help the dead leave. This was the same prayer I told my mother at her deathbed in 1986. Ten years later, in the ravines of Africa, I found myself repeating the prayer to Louisette. Marie Josée and I were wailing, screaming, praying, crying.

I took my handkerchief out of my pants pocket and wiped the blood off Louisette's face. Flies were already hovering above her. By the time people started arriving, my voice was hoarse from screaming. I told them we were ICM sisters, that they had to inform the bishop that our superior was dead. I asked them to take us back to the road. They told me we should go down instead because we were too high. They all said, "*Asya, Asya.*" It was their way of expressing their condolences. But nobody moved to touch the body.

Then I thought of the blankets we had in the car. I requested the people to get them and to please take us back to the road. Darkness was setting in and our chances of finding another car on the road that might take us back to the bishop's house were very slim. When the people came back with the blankets, I was like a madwoman giving orders left and right.

"Please wrap her body. Please carry her up. We are ICM sisters. We are going to Nkambe. Help us. Tell the bishop. Call the parish priest. Our superior is dead." I knew they would do all that by foot and that the longest part of our journey was only just beginning.

Then, like in a slow motion picture, they started moving. They wrapped Louisette's body. An old woman gave me a pair of rubber slippers. I realized then that I was barefoot and my blouse and pants were full of blood — Louisette's. The men carried her body wrapped in the blanket. Marie Josée and I followed, walking slowly. In the end, two young men had to carry us on their backs for the climb up. I could no longer walk. The cliff was very steep.

Louisette's body was laid on the side of the road. Then all our things were slowly brought up. It seemed as if the whole village was now with us, helping and consoling. They placed Marie Josée's suitcases, our boxes, and all the contents of the car on the side of the road near Louisette's body. They looked at the body, some of them crying, and I just kept repeating who we were. We looked like refugees crying for our dead. Then I requested them to pray or to sing. They sang their old English songs for the dead, and made me cry even more: "Lord Jesus, open the gates of heaven, accept our sister's soul..."

After what seemed an eternity, a pick-up car going to Nkambe stopped. It was full of people, bananas, and sacks. The driver was very kind. I asked if he could turn around to take us back to the bishop's house. But I myself saw it was impossible. The people crammed inside that car had paid for their trip up to Nkambe and unloading half-way with all the pieces of luggage would take more than an hour. The driver decided to continue on his way and promised to get our ICM sisters, whom he knew. They could get a car and come for us. We could only wait. As we did I changed my prayer to: "Lord send us a car, get us out of here before it gets dark." The singing and praying continued. More people came. More *Asyas*. It was Marie Josée's first word in pidgin English. She will never forget it.

The parish priest of Tabenkin himself came before dark in his small Suzuki jeep. He placed Louisette's body in it and drove us to the bishop's house about an hour away. The prayers of a Cameroonian sister who was with us calmed me down. The priest seemed to me to be driving so fast I could no longer look at the turns or the ravines, and I kept telling him to slow down because I didn't want to have a second accident. I couldn't believe that only a few hours ago, we had been on this same road, and now we were back with a dead sister.

The mission hospital in Shisong run by the Franciscan sisters lovingly took care of everything. By evening, Louisette's body was in the hospital chapel and the nuns were singing and praying. A doctor examined Josée and me, x-rayed us and put us to bed. But we had a sleepless night. I kept seeing Louisette's face full of blood. The bishop came to console us. He took us to the chapel to see Louisette's body. She seemed to be sleeping on the bed in front of the altar. We prayed with the nuns, and I kissed Louisette good-bye.

The next day, we returned to Yaounde in a cortège: the ambulance with Louisette's coffin, the bishop's car, and four other cars carrying priests and sisters. The days that followed were intense with grief and sadness for the ICM sisters in Cameroon. But we also had deep moments when we felt God closer than ever through our Cameroonian family.

We buried Louisette in the Catholic cemetery in Mvolye, Yaounde, surrounded by caring Cameroonians and our fellow missionaries. Death had brought us all closer to one another.

God has given me new life. I am deeply grateful for my Cameroonian brothers and sisters and countless co-spouses. They accepted me as their own. In both joy and grief we were one. I owe them a return trip to forever.

Yes, a return trip to forever.

Betty L. King

Healing
with My Dogs

"When the soul of a man is born in this country, there are nets flung at it to hold it back from flight... nationality, language, religion... I shall try to fly by those nets."

- James Joyce

UNLIKE JOYCE, I could not always fly by the nets flung at me to hold me back from flight. There were just too many of them, and they came in many forms and guises.

Growing up a girl in a Chinese family in Manila meant having nets flung at me from the day I was born. When I went to live abroad, I thought I had put them all behind me. Abroad, I thought I could be whatever I wanted to be, free to shape and reshape who I was and where I was going. I was unfettered, free to pursue limitless possibilities.

I traversed the world from Asia to Europe before finally settling down in America with my husband and our "children" with four paws. After an electric interlude in Paris, we moved to America to build a home and a new life. But there I realized something of my old life had tracked me down; the nets had caught up with me. They came like flashbacks in real time, ghosts from the past.

The flashbacks brought back an ambiguous sense of identity that early in life had caused me to falter, ever unsure of myself. I underwent bouts of inner conflict growing up a Filipino-Chinese in the Philippines. Immersing myself in the multicultures of the world abroad did not alleviate this insecurity until a mysterious dog, ugly as sin but irresistible as French dark chocolate, waylaid me on the streets of Paris and took over my life. He became my best friend just as I became his sidekick, his *copain*. With this French mutt beside me, I began to build up my self-confidence. Somehow he completed me. To the French I was more human and worthy of attention when I came with a pet. Without him, I was just another foreigner to despise or to ignore — another barbarian. He was the key to a new identity and a new existence.

America endowed me with a succession of equally insouciant friends. They came to me as though preordained, as if somewhere it had been decided that my fate was to be linked with this other species. Some literally knocked at my door, there in my neck of the woods in North Carolina. Whenever one did, I welcomed him or her as gratefully as the one before. To the Chinese a dog that comes to you is a bearer of good fortune, and must never be turned away. Each of them, singly and severally, guided me around, or over, those nets.

It was in America where one day a tragic, totally unexpected experience, involving one of these beloved companions, led to a decisive turning point in my life. It was a nightmarish event that singed my mind with a crippling memory. Ultimately it led me to refurbish my outlook on life. Whenever I came up against a racist net, such as minorities like myself often have to endure in America, my four-pawed wards were there to heal and salve my stricken spirit. They always empowered me and gave me the strength to transcend the hurt and bitterness. They gave me wings to soar above the malice and the hatred.

MY PARENTS were already in America when I arrived. They had fled the encroaching tide of war in China, just before the Communists took over. Leaving Xiamen on the mainland, they started the family in Binondo, Manila, where the *kongsi,* the clan center, was located. My grandfather had built a thriving pharmaceutical empire that stretched across Southeast Asia and Hong Kong. I was born into this clan, the second of five girls. On the same day 56 years earlier, The Great Helmsman, Mao Zedong, was born. His own exultant flight began when, as a young boy, he rebelled against his own father.

On the day I was born, 30 minutes into the day after Christmas night, a net was already lying in wait, as if to snag me early within a paradox about my identity. Anticipating the birth of a son because I weighed so heavily in her belly, Mother cried for days after I was born. I was *merely* a girl, another daughter. Father's mother cursed, because I was one more worthless female mouth to feed. Better that I be dumped between the graves at La Loma Cemetery, or thrown into a baby tower for the vultures (although there were no vultures in the Philippines and no baby towers). On my second birthday (a Chinese baby is one year old the day she is born) there were no red-dyed eggs to insure my fertility, no strings of noodles to wish me a long life.

In an expatriate Chinese family, to be a girl was to go through life with a dead albatross around one's neck, adrift on a lonely sea. I was told that my being a girl disgraced my parents, making them lose face. We girls were acne on our parents' faces. All of us sisters felt shame and guilt. To hide an uncertain Self and cover a shameful face, I started wearing a figurative mask.

Apart from being shrouded by a nebulous self-identity, I was caught fast in a taut and unyielding Confucian hierarchy. It was a pecking order that brooked no dissent. Children obey parents without question, wife submits to husband, women kowtow to men, the young to the old, subordinates to superiors, the poor to the rich. This was how Chinese tradition defined relationships, how it preserved harmony in family and society, how it produced a sense of duty and obligation in people. For centuries the Confucian order was singularly successful in creating social and economic order. So successful was it that today its smaller clones, China's neighbors in Northeast Asia — as well as Taiwan and Singapore in Southeast Asia — are called the Tigers of Asia.

I was growing up in a society that was not Confucian, not rigidly structured, in which authoritarian ways were not the rule. The Philippines was then dubbed the showcase of democracy in Asia. Freedom, the individual, mattered, not subservience to the collective. I was constantly exposed, by school, peers, and the media, to the ways of democracy and the ideal of equality. Girls were far from being devalued; they were desired. Sympathetic to my quandary, my Filipino friends and classmates (I had no Chinese friends) encouraged me to stand up and add my voice to the clamor for self-expression and equal time.

To overfly the Confucian net was for traditional Chinese a supremely unfilial act. It was to commit the Chinese version of original sin. But I could not always suppress the desire to spring free. Suppressed, the desire was often too much for me to bear. Like a tightly swaddled Russian *babushka*, I was conditioned to acquiesce in silence. The contradiction between desire and obedience nagged at me and threatened my sanity. The burden became the monkey on my back. I could not shake it off, and still cannot to this day.

My parents dealt with the complex demands of the outside world in the only way they knew: through their five daughters. To prepare us for this task, they had the perspicacity to pack us off to the *crème de la crème* of Philippine schools – a private Catholic school for girls. At St.

Theresa's College we had to abide by stringent rules designed to keep us from lapsing into the heathen worship of Buddha, Lao Tzu, Kuan Yin. From the age of four to 20, I embraced with passion the religious culture of the straitlaced Flemish nuns. Immersion in Roman Catholicism made me feel awash in sin, destined for an eternity of roasting in hell. I was convinced that unless I became a perfect Christian and thoroughly West-ernized, I would not be saved. The thought filled me with angst. To cope with this religious net, I made piety a mask. Besides, I had no intention of regressing into Chinese ways — I wanted a ticket to heaven. Religion exacerbated the ambivalence I suffered about my self-identity. To my sense of shame was added a nagging sense of guilt.

The death of my grandfather, the clan's patriarch, and the presence of much wealth led to acrimonious wrangling among the nine brothers. Finally the clan splintered. Members left the *kongsi* and scattered to Canada, Australia, Europe, and the United States. Even today we sisters have no clue as to where our kin are. Our parents were always tight-lipped about them.

The breaking up of the clan took us out of Chinatown and to a new home in Quezon City, an affluent, middle-class suburb of Manila. There I spent many happy hours with my Filipino peers and neigh-bors. But in this environment my sisters and I, along with other young Filipino-Chinese, lived on the margins of the two cultures. To the Chinatown Chinese — those whom my family had left behind in Chinatown, who spoke only Chinese, and sent their children only to Chinese schools — I was called, with contempt, a "banana barbar-ian" — yellow on the outside, white inside. To them, though I was a full-blooded Chinese, not *a mestiza*, I spoke Hokkien but with the accent of the Filipino, my ways were too *huan-na*, and I had never attended a Chinese school. On the other hand, to Filipinos I was not quite "with it," not really one of them, even if I talked and thought like a typical *colegiala*. I was neither completely in nor out of any culture, Filipino or Chinese. I always had to tread a pencil-thin line between the two. Being marginal was agonizing, at times gut-wrench-ing. Contrary pressures from inside and outside of my family over-whelmed me. A cultural net pulling me from both sides in two different directions dragged me dangerously close to the brink.

I disliked my half-existence. Dislike turned to hate at having to be a shadow. I hated being a chameleon, having to slip a mask on and off, switching faces like Janus. It was punishing — being Chinese one time, Filipino another time. I was Chinese by race and ethnicity, yet I was a Filipino national. I wanted desperately to completely, unequivocally belong. But where? Always on the sidelines, teetering on the edge, as it were, was not the answer. I was tired of having to prove myself all the time and trying to win acceptance. Behind a carefree mask I was crashing. Seemingly unconcerned, I felt the dead weight of the incubus on my shoulder inexorably pressing me down.

This was the time of the Cold War. McCarthyism and the anti-Communist hysteria in the United States were creating havoc at all levels of American society. The Vietnam War began, sucking up American participation and escalating. Student and populist backlash in the Sixties was causing one upheaval after another on campuses and in cities in the United States. Non-Communist Asia echoed the paranoia and fear. It was a reverse form of the domino theory in the so-called democratic countries. The ethnic Chinese within these countries, historically treated as scapegoats and as convenient targets of blame for domestic failures and corrupt regimes, were caught in the frenzy. When the Cold War was coldest, even rich Chinese capitalists were suspected of being Communists or Communist spies. Material success had its price. Not only were they despised and envied, now they had become a dangerous Fifth Column.

The overseas Chinese were in a peculiarly oxymoronic bind. As Communist suspects, they were a menace, if a helpless one. Neither Beijing nor Taipei was in a position, or was inclined, to succor them. I was caught in that mesh. A Filipino-Chinese like me, second-generation Chinese, no matter how well assimilated, was also a threat, if even more helpless. I was a red *kapre* — an evil spirit among the Filipinos – but one that was scared and timid. I walked in fear because I had relatives in mainland China, the evil empire. That was a mortal sin. The Flemish nuns and Irish priests pronounced Communists to be sinners destined for hell. I was more afraid of hell than of any government on earth. Growing up a Filipino-Chinese girl in Southeast Asia during the Cold War was, for me, sliding down a precipitous slope toward a yawning abyss.

MY GROWING-UP pains were not just adolescent hormones kicking in. Real slam-bang battles raged within me: I was modernized, yet expected to be traditional; I was female, yet pressured to assume the male role; I was young, yet forced to be mature; I was an unwanted daughter, yet to earn the right to exist, I had to take on the responsibilities of a filial son, as my sisters also had to do; I was told I was an equal, yet treated as an inferior; I could express myself, yet when I tried, was quickly suppressed; I was an individual, yet the collective was more important. I could not reconcile *yin* and *yang*. It was always a no-win, Catch-22 trap. Unlike the Dutch boy holding back the North Sea successfully with his finger in a hole in the dike, I could not dam the waters rushing through the floodgates of my mind.

I was too young and clueless to evade every net. Thrashing about, twisting and turning, I often found myself even more entangled. Everyone kept telling me what to do, what not to do, but nobody could tell me how to avoid becoming enmeshed. All grew angrier and angrier with me. And I grew angrier and angrier with everyone.

Marrying a Harvard-educated Filipino intellectual and going abroad made life begin to effloresce into a myriad scintillant points of light. Academic life offered new paths to explore in my search for identity. At the outset the ivory tower was a safe and serene place to escape the nets. But even academe could not be a haven for long, as the rapacious conjugal Marcos dictatorship left no corner of the Philippines unravaged. Upon the advice of Carlos P. Romulo, former president of the University of the Philippines, friend and benefactor to us both, we reluctantly pulled up stakes and moved to England. I had won a scholarship to study at the University of Manchester. It was particularly ironic for my husband to be forced out of the Philippines this way. In the Fifties, after getting his degree from Harvard, he had turned down a prestigious teaching post at Smith College in Massachusetts to return to the Philippines "to serve [my] country." Now, in the Seventies, he had been cast adrift instead of topping off an academic career in the Philippines. Like many expatriate Filipinos, we had become virtual refugees.

After my studies in Manchester, we moved to New York City and from there to Paris, where my husband took up a post as a divisional director at the UNESCO. Our life had taken a different turn. Living abroad had begun to have a momentum of its own.

Life in the City of Lights presented too many stimulating events for me to stagnate in the same familiar grooves. The dizzying diplomatic partying, the forays into Faubourg St. Honoré, the shopping sprees at Galeries Lafayette, the *dégustations* at the Loire, the *calvados*-tasting in Normandy, bargain-hunting at the Pigalle, the *Bateaux Mouche* canal rides down the Samaritaine, the picnics at Fontainebleau, the trail walks at Barbizon forest, cruising for a quick look at amorous couples at the Bois de Boulogne, sun-tanning on the naturiste beaches of Les Landes — were a partial list of the merry adventuring in which we indulged.

In all these high adventures —— and misadventures —— I had a man Friday with which to unlock gates and open doors into the secret recesses of French society. He was the Parisian mongrel with the puckish streak. He quickly took center stage in my affairs, pulling me into situations I never imagined I would ever enter. He had a *"je ne sais quoi"* stance that could extract a smile from the dourest Parisian. He was a whiz at getting things done for me as well as for himself. Without him, I could not have gotten as far as I did in the French cultural scene.

He made me aware of what it meant to be alive in Paris. He taught me existential happiness — to be happy with just being happy. Unlike the French, his world-view was not suffused with angst. Unlike me, he had no inner conflict about his own true Self. He was comfortable in his own skin. Though he did not look like much, he always demanded, and was given, star billing. In no time he had begun to bloat like a pot-bellied pig, but he continued to gorge on delicacies he conned from the neighborhood *bouchers, fromagers,* and *boulangers.* He wasn't at all daunted by taunts and gales of laughter at being called a *petit cochon* because of his ludicrous shape and his corkscrew of a tail. He did not take a back seat to anyone, human or canine. No one knew what breed he was, or what hybrid. Nor did he care. He was deliriously, uninhibitedly, insanely happy. He could not be held back from flight by any net set out his way. Life was a bowl of cherries.

EIGHT YEARS went by and soon it was all over. Upon my husband's retirement, we moved back to America together with our two four-pawed children, to live near my parents, sisters and their families. But returning to the filial cocoon was like stepping back in time, a sustained flashback. We resumed where we had left off, as if nothing had happened in the interval.

My family, like countless other Filipino families, had uprooted themselves to begin life in this brave new world. The tyranny, corruption, and violence under the arbitrary iron rule of Ferdinand Marcos's martial law was starting to spread its poison. America, on the other hand, was the land where, if you played by the rules of the game, you had a fair chance of attaining the American Dream, Everyman's Dream. America was a vast gaming table which held many prizes for the winning. We were confident the odds were in our favor; the dice was loaded with seven medical doctors in the family. Three of my sisters graduated with medical degrees from the University of the Philippines College of Medicine, the best in Asia, and did their residencies in Chicago. Four sisters in all were married to physicians from the United States and England.

Unfortunately, the safety net that cradled us in the Philippines soon began tattering into shreds. Living in America was reactivating old nets and activating new ones. Interracial marriages unraveled the interpersonal fabric of the original nuclear family. The extended family became a multicultural Tower of Babel. The diversity in origins — an English-Irish Protestant microbiologist from Limerick, Ireland, an agnostic Filipino scholar, a New York Jewish anesthesiologist, a Taiwanese Chinese anesthesiologist, a Dutch-German Lutheran orthopedic surgeon from Minnesota — each one brought differing world-views, values, perceptions, lifeways, church affiliations, and habits that made for cacophony rather than symphony. We were always talking past each other. It was a captious babble, sans any dispute-resolving mechanisms of any sort.

Each of us sisters had become a woman of independent means. But the fevered climb up Gold Mountain, strewn as it was with boulders and jagged rocks, was taking its toll. Money and success had a disquieting, demoralizing effect, as if achieving them were not enough. To fill the vacuum in our new lives in America, we started to play games with one another. Adrift in America, the family had lost whatever anchor it had. Half in and half out of both American and Asian communities, we were misfits in the culture from which we came, and misfits in the culture into which we had ventured.

To be sure, keeping out of mainstream American life was not entirely voluntary on our part. There were, and still are, too many insurmountable barriers to full entry. The melting pot that America was supposed to be, especially the South where most us had located, never really happened. Like equality, it was an ideal, not the reality. The playing field for nonwhite minorities was still not level. Racial and ethnic divides were still too wide.

Even in the extended family, those of us who were not of the dominant culture were always being subtly reminded we were interlopers. Despite its growing multiculturalism, America was still the exclusive birthright of a few, which did not even include the nonwhite Native Americans.

Living on the margins of the dominant culture, bereft of a viable support system, without even a community to connect to except ourselves, we leaned on each other more than it was safe and sane to do so. Far too often, we gnawed on each other, as if in frustration. Even as we achieved the American dream of luxurious houses, lake properties, jet skis, sailboats, European holidays, equestrian hobbies and show horses, German luxury cars, none of these brought a sense of fulfillment, nor did they strengthen family solidarity. Even as the family stayed together, it did not stay well together. We were one, big unhappy family in the land of plenty.

Compared to my sisters, I was far behind in the rat race. Deliberately being a maverick in the family made me a deviant in the American scale of values. Presumably, I did not have what it took. As a consequence, I was consigned to the bottom rung of the pecking order. Estranged and banished, I turned to a kindred soul who himself needed succoring. Chornley (we nicknamed him *Chewbacca*) came into my life at my most vulnerable moment. Like many pets, he was slated to be thrown away as a worn-out toy and discarded as an inconvenience. I would look into his expressive eyes, and he would stare right back. When our eyes met, I knew I could not let this Borzoi (Russian wolfhound) be "put away." He joined my pack of three. Needing help, he gave me help. Giving comfort, I received comfort. Mutualism took seed. His trust, in turn, empowered me. His makeover was my success story.

Whenever he curled up beside me, it did not seem to matter how much or how little money I earned, how well — or how dowdily — I dressed or looked. All that mattered was the chance to be up close and personal, his magnificent silken body snuggling up to me, aquiline snout on my lap, hazel eyes half-lidded over, feathered ears cocked to my endless chatter. At that moment nothing else mattered to either of us. He did not patronize my self-doubt, self-pity, low self-esteem. Even at my most insufferable moments, he was there, unconditionally, unambiguously. No put-ons, no questions, no commentaries, no criticisms, no recriminations, no judgment, no guilt, no punishment. Just blind devotion, a wagging tail, and a wet tongue. Asking nothing in return.

With him by my side, I learned to take things in stride, to fully appreciate every moment, to see the true and ignore the false. He taught me to rejoice in simple things, to exult in the vitality of nature, to respect every living creature. And as I learned to value all forms of life, my mind turned to Eastern philosophies — Buddhism, Taoism, and Hinduism. Becoming a vegetarian was a natural step in my ascent to a new plane of existence. It did not come easy. As a Chinese gourmand, as the saying goes, I used to eat everything with four legs except tables, everything that flew except airplanes, and everything that swam except submarines. Turning vegetarian made me more alive. It was if all creation had conspired to enlighten me. Life became more meaningful, existence more tranquil. My world did not become more constricted; on the contrary, it expanded beyond the limits of perception. A lost sense of wonder and a more profound awareness of the Creator's hand in every manifestation of life returned. I began to find unalloyed happiness in the simple things of life, where before I had little.

Then one day Chornley was brutally murdered. At first I believed he was a victim of another random act of the violence that had become as American as apple pie. Anguished sorrow shortly turned to rage when I realized it had been an insidious hate crime. The cowardly perpetrators had maliciously disposed of his body as part of a cover-up, a conspiracy of silence, a pact in the night among hooded conspirators to aggress against those who were different. I did not fit into the stereotype of Asians in the South, i.e. mail-order brides, military service wives, laundry, grocery, restaurant owners. Neither was I one of the good ol' boys. These made me a target, an easy moving target. Owning a rare, classy dog like Chornley made me stick out like a sore thumb. I was being the tallest tree in the proverbial forest, the first to be toppled by a hurricane. Since they did not dare harm me physically, someone very dear and precious to me had to be the "sacrificial lamb." I was told, "Ya knaw, girl, ef a neigger waulked up da hill wid his dawg, we cain't kill him, but we shore cud kill his dawg." It was a classic "down-boy" message. The evidence was clear: the killing was as deliberate as it was symbolic. I was painfully reminded of the signs in Chinese parks at the Western enclaves in old China that read: NO DOGS OR CHINESE ALLOWED.

To make matters worse, the justice system was equally helpless. Justice was not served despite all the earmarks of crime and its perpetrators.

Thus, I became a victim twice over. I was convinced American justice was not blind, after all. In fact, institutional racism was alive and well in America, especially in many communities in the South. Again, I was told that my only recourse was to follow the biblical "law of the talon," an eye for an eye, that is, go and do the same thing to the perpetrator's cat or dog. I don't even have a gun, and how in God's name could I hurt another living creature?

It was clear that violence toward animals was covert racism disguised and symbolic. No one who has never been a victim of racism can ever imagine how crushing such a message is on human dignity and integrity, what an assault it commits on the human spirit, how hopeless one feels in the face of such depravity and callousness, how resentful and bitter one gets to be.

In my unspeakable sorrow I turned for solace to my remaining dogs. Once again I drew strength from their unconditional love and unwavering trust that I would find meaning in what happened. They, too, had been unwanted, neglected, and even abused before I rescued them. But no matter how much pain they had suffered from humans, they had given me back only love. How superior they are, how much better they can teach our species to be more human. I saw in them what many humans lack: total acceptance of other humans, regardless of color, creed, or nationality. My race, ethnicity, religion, age, gender, and politics never mattered one bit. What mattered was me. Without masks.

This shattering experience opened my eyes to the realities of America. I became acutely conscious of the racial undertones underneath the surface cordiality, the pervasive control by the white, male-dominated culture on so many aspects of American life, including the criminal justice system, legal and cultural attitudes that treat children, spouses, and animals as chattel and "property," toward whom any act of violence could be dismissed as a mere misdemeanor. Child and spousal abuse in this view is just a domestic quarrel and nobody else's business. Similarly, animal abuse, no matter how heinous and brutal, is also casually treated and rarely prosecuted in court. In the American system of laws and scale of values, life as property is less valuable than material property itself. Shooting a dog, no matter how priceless he is to her human companion, is just a misdemeanor; slashing an automobile tire is a felony.

The perpetrator of this hate crime knew his way around the law. He reflected the dominant culture and its ways. He expressed his racism in a culturally accepted way, "It's just an animal." If society shrugs off violence to women, children, the handicapped, homosexuals, the elderly, AIDS victims, why should anyone be concerned with a victim that is, after all, "just another animal"? In all this, the victim is consigned to an inferior status. But because animals are supposedly without rational souls – no feelings, no emotions, no self-consciousness, no mind, just instincts and reflexes – their right to life is even less important. To such people, in fact, their right to life does not exist at all.

That was what they used to say of African slaves and Chinese coolies. Many of whom were stripped naked and branded like cattle, beaten and hung up by their thumbs, chained and kept in bamboo cages, in ships bound for America to help build the great railroads, or to labor in plantations. Many died in transit, or were burned alive when their ships caught fire. Extremist views among the dominant white culture went so far as to say that "the nerve endings of a Chinaman or a Negro were not as fully developed and could not feel as much pain" as the white man's. To them, the color of one's skin was a gauge of the complexity of one's nervous system. Today, they say the same thing about animals – that their nervous systems are not as developed as those of humans and therefore their pain is very much less than that of humans.

In this sense there was a clear parallelism between racism and violence to animals. I saw a link between violence to animals and violence to humans, a cycle of abuse that starts with devaluing what is vulnerable and helpless. Jeffrey Dahmer, the white serial killer who butchered and even cannibalized his victims – African- and Asian-Americans – started torturing animals at an early age. Debasing those who are different from us excuses violence in all its forms. Despising the victim justifies prejudice and exploitation. Not too long ago, slavery, the Chinese coolie trade, child labor, medical experimentation on the mentally ill, were all legal. Today, medical experimentation on healthy animals, including primates, is legal. In addition, abuse of women, children, and animals is still just a misdemeanor under the law.

Chornley's killing made me look for other killing fields, such as animal shelters. Here I saw dogs, some purebred and healthy, cowering in corners of cages that were on death row. From the extermination chambers that were just boxes I could hear their frantic screams. They were to me exactly like human screams for help, panicked howls gradually dying down into moans and whimpers until I could hear no more. These dogs wanted to live. They were there through no fault of their own. Eleven thousand years ago, their ancestors, the wolves, began to trust man too much and voluntarily domesticated themselves. Little did they know that they would someday become nothing more than a statistic, numbers to be added to the 10 million dogs annually "put to sleep" in America's five thousand animal shelters.

It was my wake-up call. I could not cover my ears with my hands, shut my eyes, and walk away. I had to do something, if only to honor Chornley's memory. The steadfast, trusting stares of my remaining dogs, Chornley's faithful gang, unleashed my mind. As I reexamined the purposes of my life, I emerged from this crucible of loss and its painful message with a clearer sense of what I had to do. I must turn a bad thing into a good thing. But how could I, a woman and an ethnic minority in the American South, be a voice for the voiceless? Do I have the necessary *chutzpah* to speak out and make a difference?

As I looked back to the past, it dawned on me that all the nets had been cast for a purpose. The persnickety, morally upright teaching nuns at St. Theresa's had laid a strong moral base on which to launch myself onto the high road in my later years. It provided the backbone I needed to become proactive, an un-Asian thing to do in the American South.

I decided to strike at the root of many of society's contemporary problems. For a starter I organized a rally to stimulate public awareness and discussion about racism, violence, and the vicious cycle of abuse. With this I began a campaign to enlighten people about the sociocultural origins of violence, for example, by pointing to the wooden inability of many to empathize with those who are different, the insensitivity to the needs, feelings, and intrinsic value of other life forms. I tried to identify, along with many activists who thought and felt like I do, the fatal consequences of violent acts for perpetrators and for society at large. Animal cruelty at an early age, usually dismissed as a childish prank or sport, could very well be the early signs of a syndrome that would have explosive consequences at a later stage. Fourteen-year old Eric Smith, who killed four-year-old Robie in Savona, New York, said that when he was eight and felt rage, he strangled a puppy. Similarly, Klebold and Harris mutilated animals prior to the rampage of killings at their Columbine high school.

I looked into the county's animal shelter and was appalled to see the abominable and cruel conditions there. If I were to mount a crusade, it had to begin here. Forthwith, I launched a reform agenda and agitated, tooth and nail, for much needed changes. After a bruising campaign in which I was personally attacked as a liberal minority, my persistence paid off. Like my feisty Jack Russell terrier, I hung on and never let go, until, perhaps in exasperation, the county commissioners threw in the towel, if only to stop me from getting up on their backs. The day of triumph came. Single-handedly, acting like a prosecutor with every piece of evidence and proof I could adduce, such as a well-researched white paper and a compelling video presentation, I persuaded the county commissioners to put aside $300,000 for a spacious, modern facility with better equipment than the old one, a more caring staff, better adoption policies, new spaying-and-neutering programs, and a more humane way of putting down unwanted pets.

Of course, my ultimate task is to set up no-kill animal sanctuaries. As for the crusade to reform people's attitudes toward animals, nowadays when animal control officers in my county investigate animal abuse cases, they recognize such abuses to be red flags signaling the probable existence of other forms of abuse — against women, children, the elderly, the disabled.

Plumbing the symbiotic relationship between humans and animals, I turned my own dogs into pet therapists for nursing and retirement homes, and to help children with ADHD (attention-deficit hyperactive disorder) by helping them to focus. In turn, the joy and laughter my dogs brought to the old and lonely, the young and restless, gave them a new lease on life.

My home today is a sanctuary for dogs with damaged personalities, as well as an improvised animal behavioral clinic, to help disturbed dogs become whole again. The process involves reintegrating dogs into the human community by giving them a purpose vis-à-vis such a community, i.e., as life companions, therapists, moral teachers, spiritual healers. *Missy*, a pregnant bitch let out into the cold on an icy gray night on New Year's Eve, spent time in my sanctuary, after which she became a partner to a bachelor disk jockey, becoming his portal to a more sociable life with other human beings. *Scruffy*, a backwoods breed of indeterminate ancestry, became a boy's protector from a neurotic, petulant mother. *Maddie*, a tiny black puppy thrown out of a pickup truck, became a 12-year-old girl's best friend. *Bandit*, a feisty, long-haired Jack Russell abandoned in a horse show, teaches children responsibilities and lessons in commitment. *Jackie*, who had lived at the end of a chain for two years, became a spiritual companion to a depressed divorcee. Just four months ago, I rescued a dachshund from Paris from being "put down" as a result of a persistent biting misbehavior. *Noelle*, born in New Delhi and purchased in India by a US State Department family seven years ago, now lives with me. She is still undergoing therapy and a makeover under my constant, loving supervision.

Being proactive has taken me far afield. In the campaign to effect legislative changes concerning the ethical treatment of animals, North Carolina has recently changed the law to make animal abuse a felony when malice is proven. In addition, state laws now allow resident pets in hospitals and nursing and retirement homes.

As an activist in America, I have added a new dimension to my existence. Having taken up a cause, I no longer have a problem of identity. I have become sure of what I am and what I want to do. I think this is what is meant by "when God closes a door, He opens a window."

I have taken the first step in the journey of a thousand miles. By trying to increase awareness of the link between racism, prejudice, and violence to animals, I hope to help achieve the critical mass of people and of votes needed to effect social and legal changes. In this process I hope to involve more minorities. While animal issues are still the exclusive domain of the dominant majority, I am determined that this will not long be the case, in this and with many other issues.

We may all look different from one another, but together we, humans as well as nonhumans, make up one existential continuity. Some of us might be wise, others foolish; some noble, others base. But in the democracy of existence we are all the same. No one escapes the inevitable.

By identifying with creatures, great and small, wise and wonderful, I can fly by all the human nets set out to hold me back in flight. With them beside me, I can fly into the light of day, without masks.

Marietta Enriquez de La Haye Jousselin

Le Ciel Est a Moi
Heaven Within

ONCE UPON A TIME, Paris was my great fantasy, my fairy tale city of light and magic. When barely in my teens, I would languish in the living room, listening to my mother's long-playing record of Delibes' tender *Lakmé*. At 16, after one year of academic French at the university, I read Françoise Sagan's *Bonjour tristesse* while collecting French records and memorizing the lyrics of songs like *La Vie en Rose* and *Feuilles mortes*.

Paris came alive to me through writers from Flaubert to Hemingway, who showed me through its streets, squares, and buildings. They fired my imagination as they took me through St. Germain des Prés, the elegant Marais of Madame de Sevigné, and down the now discreet arcades of the once gaudy Palais Royale. It was a delight to follow Hemingway through Montparnasse and the Left Bank, or to visualize Scott Fitzgerald's account of his Paris sojourn, and to imagine Marcel Proust playing in the gardens of the Champs Elysées.

When I arrived in the city one sunstruck morning in early spring, I was a young woman dazzled by the most beautiful city in the world. I was struck by her beauty, although it was not the first time I had seen her. Strangely enough, even while still on the plane looking down at Paris, I felt as though I were coming home.

Coming down the Champs Elysées from the Arc de Triomphe at the top toward the Tuileries at the bottom, the Louvre right in front of me and Paris spread on either side and beyond, I closed my eyes and pretended that the city was all mine.

Armed with all my preconceptions, plus what I thought was sufficient knowledge of the language, I prepared for new adventure in the city by the Seine. I looked forward to experiencing life here, this time not as a tourist but as a resident, really feeling the people, the culture, and the streets, enjoying their elegance, glamour, and *joie de vivre*. Little did I realize that just reading about its *savoir faire* and *savoir vivre* would not be enough.

Arriving as a foreigner, I observed the country and its people without getting very far, since the French are by nature secretive, reserved, and above all, suspicious. Although I have never felt intimidated by Paris nor by the French, trying to decipher the dynamics and idiosyncracies of the society can be frustrating and difficult. The superficial aspects of the culture are delightful to behold, but unless you have lived here since your youth, or are one of them, trying to probe deeply into what Frenchness means can be a colossal task.

MY PROBLEMS in those first years were not essentially related to the French, but were quite basic, such as learning the rudiments of cooking, cleaning, and shopping for essentials —seemingly menial tasks, but necessary for sheer survival. It was the beginning of my life as a very well-educated unskilled worker abroad. I used to think that every idiot could do household chores, and quickly concluded that anyone who spent all her time on them must be an idiot. Not anymore.

Worse still, seeking advice from the French on how to solve simple problems around the house is next to impossible. They are far from the do-it-yourself world. If the floor sags, call the carpenter; if a faucet leaks, let it go until a flood starts. Handicapped I certainly was in the beginning, in a city with which I was not familiar, and it took some time before small hard-earned triumphs began to make my daily life easier, as I grunted and stammered in my academic French.

The French are very special, and are interestingly different. Gertrude Stein once said, "How can foreigners say they like France but not the French? It is the French who made France — and keep it that way." So be it! To live in this country, and to enjoy and appreciate its people, an open-mindedness to their modes of behavior, their attitudes, and their ways of thought is necessary.

The French have a culture of contrasts and oppositions, with everything a confrontation and a conflict, be it in politics, the social context, or religion. Unlike Asians, who smile first, then try to understand, and thus achieve peace and harmony, eternal conflict has earned for the

French the reputation of being *râleurs* or whiners, an essential character ingredient which renders the social structure complicated. Living in daily combat, where every aspect of everyday life is a challenge, the Frenchman first opposes, then waits and sees, and only then negotiates.

Nothing is simple for the French. They abhor this century for its simplification and minimalism. One French student in my art class once explained to me, "Only those objects which are complicated can be considered beautiful. How can you compare a gothic church to the pyramid of Louvre, the chateau of Versailles to the Bastille Opera House, or Louise XIV to Pompidou?"

The bedrock trait of these basically conservative people seems to be a resistance to change. This almost primordial aspect of their nature, I feel, is the explanation for their being xenophobic, basically suspicious, and prone to adhere rigidly to the old order. Change disturbs them since it seems to endanger their well-defined place in the cosmic world.

Superficially, there never seems to be a problem, until one gets into situations that are *unFrench* — meaning anything from high-tech gadgets that surpass the imagination to the juxtaposition of ultramodern buildings against their city. Until he understands, the Frenchman defends himself against an unknown world and reacts cautiously, even negatively, as he observes and analyzes the foreign elements. His mind remains always the real agent that governs his actions and decisions.

La raison toujours is the Frenchman, who is in his element when he is going about some intellectual activity which stimulates his mental faculties. It is important for him to be clear and logical in what he is doing, because the worst thing that could befall him is to face an awkward situation in which he becomes the object of ridicule due to personal misjudgment.

When you present an initially incomprehensible subject which he finds difficult to understand, be prepared to enlighten him. You may first get a categorical "No" for an answer or, with some luck, he may ask: *Pourriez-vous me preciser* ..., in which case you must be ready with a clear and logical explanation.

Even in his pleasures, the Frenchman maintains a rational and balanced approach. Wine, for example, he seldom takes in excess. What really counts for him is the vintage, the region, and the occasion on which he feels drinking is appropriate.

As for the general reputation of the French as great lovers, their Latin nature aflame with uncontrollable passion — maybe so. The older generations were raised to kiss hands, but the younger population seem to love to demonstrate their seductive powers to the world. This is no secret. Walk along the streets in the middle of the day, and witness young or middle-aged couples engrossed in kisses lasting several minutes, unmindful of people passing by. I have often wondered if they really prefer to have the public watch their private passions.

IT WAS PURE chance that I came to Paris, and pure chance that I had the opportunity to work here for a while before getting married and now living here permanently. For a real *citadine* like me, who has never lived outside the city, what better place to settle in than a house with its own inner garden, tucked away behind a portal right off the busy and constant bustle of the Avenue des Champs Elysées? Since I have never planted a garden nor done much in the kitchen except to plan menus, it has been such a joy to live *en plein Paris* surrounded by food shops, the cinema, museums, and elegant streets.

Everything changed after I got married; I have since become almost one of them. Doors started to open for me: my French circle has expanded through activity in some organizations, and more especially, by my becoming part of a complex and interlocking network of new relatives and friends.

Slowly, my fuzzy, unfocused images of France started to clarify. I used to view the entire fabric of French society as a clear, structured system. My mistake was not understanding the invisible network of subclasses, which made society seem confusing. After much probing, I would say that in its most subjective aspect, one's social place remains a matter of birth, background, and whom you associate with. It is amusing to find French snobbery, with its touching simplicity, still obsessed with kinship in its most anthropological form, which is: who married, marries, and will marry whom.

One of my first blunders, for example, was asking a count if he considered himself part of the grand bourgeoisie. He ignored my question and looked at me with suspicion. My previous notions, full of rectitude about equality, human rights, and such, have since been shattered. I have had to open my eyes to the realities of a social system with subtle medieval overtones and diffused layers of the élite class.

As I moved through my husband's various circles, I found the opportunity to become a participant-observer at close range. Initially, friends, family, and associates would talk very fast and sometimes all at once, completely oblivious to the fact that someone in the group was non-French. Being Asian, I dared not talk too much nor sound too aggressive. Neither did I consider it courteous to argue in polite society. One quickly realizes, however, that audacity and quick wit are needed to survive in the waters of the Parisian social and cultural mainstream. I have also learned to keep my head above water by not taking myself too seriously nor taking everything others say personally.

Perhaps it would be best to look at Paris through the eyes of an artist and of a humorist. Once this viewpoint is established, one can then appreciate its humaneness, enjoy its various faces, and overlook its warts.

My eyes, having been confronted with the other realities of life in this enchanting city, now see not only its beauty but its problems as well. Still, I must admit that the spell cast over me remains, and that the realities around me never quite triumph over my romantic notions.

Paris is a visual feast. No other old city in the world can compare with this paradise, with its river meandering through, and the many bridges to cross. The buildings do not rise in vertical arrogance, crushing you with their height, as they do in most modern cities, except for the few 20th-century buildings which disfigure the skyline. On the whole, the scale of the city is quite human; its harmonious façades and rooftops are awesome.

On the other hand, automobiles have multiplied, making traffic almost impossible most of the year. Derelicts, the French *clochards*, are seen increasingly on park benches or in metro stations, and bands of thieving gypsies promenade, looking for unguarded tourists. They distract you by waving a piece of paper or a newspaper before your eyes, while they take your money without your realizing it until it is too late. Once burned, I have become the soul of caution. Anything important I now put in an inner pocket or money belt.

Violence also exists, it is true, but it is less common here than in other cities of comparable size. One does not hear of people being pushed off the platform in a metro station. You find many annoyances, of course, such as *dragueurs*, who try to pick you up in the streets, or vehicles belching smoke in heavy traffic. Except for a few areas which are not recommended, however, I find that I can walk practically everywhere without fear.

For Paris is a real walking city. It belongs to the pedestrian who journeys through the various neighborhoods, through the *quais*, observing the scenery as the people in turn observe him. The city is one grand spectacle in which everyone plays a part. As the seasons change, the scenery and the characters change as well.

This is especially true in the café, the Frenchman's decompression chamber. As he drinks his coffee and reads his newspaper, he watches the world go by. Sitting in the café relieves him of the high pressures of the day. The most delightful quarter for this is St. Germain des Près, with its cafés full of young people and tourists of all nations.

My favorite walks take me all the way to the *rive gauche*, up to the Café Deux Magots facing the Romanesque church of St. Germain des Près, or around the Cathedral of Notre Dame with its book stands along the *quais*, and the Quai aux Fleurs where in the 12th century France's most celebrated lovers, Héloïse and Abelard, would meet. Paris streets, churches, and museums are my refuge, especially when things go wrong and people around me become nervous and tense. Standing in the middle of a room in the Louvre and gazing at paintings and statues transpose me into another world of power and animated vigor.

In a *vieux monde* culture like that of the French, where modes of behavior and thought processes are transferred from generation to generation, perceiving their soul is no easy task, unless you know the codes. For instance, one has to know when to use *vous*, and when *tu* is acceptable. I shall never forget my first French professor, who told the class to forget that *tu* existed. You have to know when and with whom to shake hands when you say *Bonjour, Monsieur,* or *Madame.* The average Filipino, who finds it difficult to erase the smile from his face, may find himself in a compromising situation in this city where one does not, should not, smile except in certain situations and in familiar gatherings.

There are numerous codes of behavior one has to know so that one does not put one's foot in one's mouth, such as the dress code, the code at receptions, the code on the telephone. "I knew the language and the culture but not the codes," noted an authority on culture-crossing. "The codes are the most important thing for feeling well in France. That's when you find out how extraordinary and wonderful the French are."

The perils, pitfalls, and pleasures of speaking another language, especially if it is French, are not only that you say things differently, but that sometimes you end up saying something quite different from what you really mean. There are words called *faux amis* — false friends — which exist in both English and French but do not have the same meaning. Thus, someone who is *spirituel* is not necessarily holy, but rather funny and witty. When you have *confidence* in someone, it means that you want to share a secret, and this has nothing to do with trust, for which the word used is *confiance*. A person who is *precieux* is not a gem, but someone affected or pretentious. Sometimes not even the dictionary is sufficient to explain the nuances words have developed through time and usage. As you master the language, a new world opens up and you suddenly realize that you are seeing the world with French eyes, with your thought process evolving at the same time.

When you are not used to the French, they may seem difficult to get along with. But this, I have discovered, is the result of the high standard of their quality of life, which is not necessarily equated with material aspects. Their sometimes impossible demands have created the pleasures of the French table, which is hardly ever bad, and the Parisian woman's eternal obsession with remaining slim and glamorous.

The *Parisienne* is conscious of the fact that her success depends on the quality of her physical attraction. But behind this chic and femininity, she generally has both feet on the ground and her world under control. Her *élan de vie* is actually one of common sense and logic. How did she get this way? Through contact with the Frenchman? Is it part of the psychological warfare in this land of misogynes? Or is it perhaps linked to her social emancipation, the political consequence of her economic independence? And then again, maybe she has always been like that?

I have come to the conclusion that the Parisian holds three things sacred: *le pain*, his holidays, and the quality of the air he breathes. His bread, the *baguette*, in all its variants and shapes, has to be baked three times a day so that he can buy it fresh just before a meal. Eating frozen bread or day-old bread is unheard of here. The simple pleasure of good bread is his birthright.

The August and winter vacations are also sacrosanct. For man does not live by bread alone. At first I could not understand how important this was to the French, since I find August especially relaxing in the city. Now I realize that it is, in fact, the ultimate compensation for everything that goes wrong the rest of the year. Thus for the whole month he is free as a lord, no matter how subservient he may be the rest of the year in his work. In the winter, *bien entendu*, parents take their children off to the mountains to ski.

When he is back in the city, the Parisian's favorite distraction is to *prendre l'air*, literally to breathe fresh air, but with a completely different connotation. Here it means a yearning for space away from the noise and pollution that aggravate the city dweller, an escape from the apartment way of life. The vast majority stretch out in the sun to add color to their otherwise pale skin, or spend hours strolling in the many parks like the Bois de Boulogne. This is contagious, and I now find myself often looking for bits of space or scraps of untrammeled greenery.

I HAVE BEEN ASKED if, after living here for almost 20 years, I feel French. Joseph Conrad most aptly put it when he wrote, "My nationality is the language I write in." I can honestly say that I now speak and write adequately in French, but I am far from being absolutely fluent. My first language remains English, even if at moments I feel a weakening of my sentence structures and a dwindling of vocabulary. There are times when I wonder if I do have a mother tongue. It is difficult to avoid feeling a duality when one's pattern of life revolves around two countries.

I can be quite sure, however, that although I may occasionally feel Parisian, I shall never feel French. Nor can my reactions be French. In a restaurant, for example, when the food or the service is not up to my expectations, my breeding tells me not to offend the chef or the waiter. The French, on the other hand, will show their total dissatisfaction to all concerned, and depart in a huff without leaving the usual *pourboire* or tip.

If I seem to fluctuate between praising the French and putting them down, it is because in France both feelings do coexist, more or less peacefully, even among the French themselves. In fact, the French critic, when he is criticizing his country and his people, is unbeatable. For my part, whenever I am exasperated by the French, which is rare, they turn around, say something funny, or joke about themselves, and I end up laughing and liking them all over again.

Nothing is more relaxing than living in a city where you can be by yourself, not because the people want to do you a favor, but because they want the same privilege for themselves. I have found both solitude and anonymity here, where the people are much more private than in my own country, and therefore respect your privacy in return for respecting

145

theirs. In this context one can readily understand their natural preoccupation with any possible threat to their obstinate individuality. *Chacun pour soi* — each man for himself — has made the country almost impossible to govern. And yet they have produced Paris, still the most civilized of all cities, and a second home for me.

The paradox of my existence in Paris is that I do not think I can live alone, and have never had any intention of renouncing the world like a hermit. On the other hand, I cannot imagine myself being constantly surrounded by people, the mere thought of which gives me a feeling of claustrophobia. I have always needed space in which to think things out, to quietly appreciate private joys like watching the sun set over the Seine, or enjoying the minute details of a landscape by Cezanne.

After much reflection, I have come to the conclusion that the point is to be at peace with oneself and thus be happy. It sounds so obvious that it actually seems trivial. It may seem an impossible task in this maddening world, but I have found that one can come close to it by merely simplifying one's life and doing what one honestly wants to do.

I know I shall never be completely happy in this world because of the absence of my children. When they are with me, it is pure joy. Whenever I am with them, I find myself learning as they share with me their views and their world. I, in turn, share with them my values and my ideas, which in their present world of various shades of gray, are not that easy to delineate. Between my children and myself there is now an unstated assurance that though disasters have passed and will pass, our mutual sympathy for each other will always remain.

Some problems of my real world, I must admit, took time to resolve. It took me a while to finally find a clear perspective of what I wanted to do, and what I could do away from home without having to go to work at a standard job. I have asked myself of what use was all of my education if I were just going to keep house, which I did not really find fulfilling, and not put into practice everything I learned. As it happens, I am married to an old-fashioned, traditional man who is totally against my involvement in any enterprise or profession. The day-to-day life was wearing down my strength in daily challenges and situations which demanded analysis in order to make an honest and authentic statement. Could I muster enough imagination and courage to apply to menial tasks around the house? At first I found myself suffering from work paralysis and emotional exhaustion. I was unable to read, much less to write on anything. I felt myself drifting. What surprised me, though, was that in learning to be creative and resourceful at home I started to discover other facets of myself as yet unrecognized.

Although the fundamental conflict between my sense of myself as a woman and my identity as a professional lingers, I have set aside the latter and have finally transcended stereotypical definitions of self and success. I have managed to carve out of my life an identity I can live with, and which I can love and enjoy, although it is completely different from my previous self. I have learned to pursue my various interests — art, antiquities, travel, history, literature, spirituality — on my own terms. Most of all, I have found the courage to seek both the motives and the rewards for my intellectual and artistic efforts within myself and for myself, regardless of what the rest of the world values.

Gradually, I have realized that the reason I was constantly flirting with personal anarchy was that everything in my life overlapped. I was moving from one activity to another without definite boundaries. Every part of what I was trying to do or to be was centered within the house. I told myself that I should forget about wondering what I thought I was good at, and instead ask myself what I most wanted to do as a whole person. The question is not whether one becomes a successful or unsuccessful writer, artist, or craftsman, but rather what personal satisfaction one earns. Would I prepare myself for a totally immersed home life and perhaps take courses in homemaking in order to assume my feminine role with flying colors? Or rather listen to voices from within, and stop confusing life filled with mere activity, with one meaningful because self-fulfilling?

It took discipline to make time to work on my translations from French to English, but I felt a strong need for some intellectual and artistic activity. Writing short articles occasionally for the Filipino community in Paris and going to art classes give my life new dimensions. I began gaining a sense of purpose, and a few years later my first translation was published by the National Historical Institute in Manila. Thus began a change from passive to engrossing activity, which has brought much satisfaction as well as added meaning to my life.

My prayers were eventually answered by other mixed blessings. Now I have two work spaces: an atelier for painting when I am not at art class, and a work room-office where I have all my books, files, and computer. I also have a wonderfully supportive husband who encourages me to finish my projects, knowing I have problems completing ventures unless pressured by deadlines. Another blessing is my unstructured time with hardly any domestic demands, which is essential for me to concentrate on whatever I am doing. I used to feel that at the end of the day I had not accomplished anything, that time had just gone by without any activity or development taking place. Now these definite activities became the beginning of the change from a passive to a full, happy life.

It is here in Paris that I have reached an age of tranquility, won a sense of peace, and found time to look within my true self. My greatest fear had been the lack of activity, and the inability to work and use my brains was in itself an assault to me. Now I no longer try to solve the enigmas which used to torture me in my younger years, and I have resolved the problems which used to keep me awake. I have found enlightenment from the powers above and in moral principles. I have found peace of heart and also the strength to accept and cope with pain and fear as they come along.

Here in Paris I have been able to come to terms with myself. Here I have been able to seriously consider and understand my existence and God's design for me. Here I have had innumerable moments of happiness, meaningful friendships, and deep reflections — more than enough to thank God for.

Linda R. Layosa

Anywhere, Everywhere: The DH's Saga

MY STORY BEGINS 10 months after the outbreak of the celebrated people power revolution in 1986, an event that made Corazon C. Aquino the first Filipino woman president. It was her husband Ninoy's assassination upon his return from exile in the United States in 1983 that stoked the people's outrage and eventually led to the revolution.

The event gave hope to our sagging economy. A great number of the masses were jubilant, expecting the change of power to bring about progress. They were wrong. That year and the years that followed made life even more difficult for them. This was understandable. Anyone who came after Marcos would have faced the same problems in running the country.

I soon became one of the thousands of Filipino women who fled to Hong Kong as economic refugees, particularly as domestic helpers. DH for short.

I had been a private school teacher for 14 long years. They were good and fulfilling years, and I never entertained any thought of leaving the profession. I enjoyed teaching young children and training them to be good declaimers and spellers who inevitably emerged as gold medalists in school competitions. For a time, I also became the faculty president. But with three young children to feed, clothe, and send to school, an unemployed and not too responsible husband, a smart little brother to send to college, and ailing parents to support, I was forced to ask my eldest sister to find me an employer in Hong Kong.

She did not like the idea at first. "You will stagnate here" was her curt reply. But I insisted. She told me that since I was a professional in

Manila, work as a domestic helper might make my life miserable. So she thought.

IN OUR FAMILY of eight, I was considered the most persistent, a "survivor." My mother said that whatever I wanted when I was a child, I got by hook or by crook. And except for my youngest brother, I was the only one who weathered our poverty and scraped my way through college by earning academic scholarships until I graduated, magna cum laude. I was immediately employed as a teacher in a Catholic school for boys, a young head teacher despite my youth, and a Cub Scout *Kawan* leader. After three years of teaching, I married my childhood crush. It was a decision neither my parents nor our relatives and neighbors supported.

After a few months, my sister found me a young Chinese couple who lived in very remote hospital quarters surrounded by farm land, hills, and trees. My sister was worried that I might not survive the situation since I had spent most of my teenage years in the city. "I just pray you will change your mind," she told me again and again. But the die had been cast. I had to go.

The thought of going far away and living in an unknown place made my imagination run wild, but I was undaunted. I had only one objective — to offer my children a better life. That meant sending them to school until they finished college, raising their standard of living a little bit to allow them to taste the good life and to provide them better shelter, not a shanty like we had during my childhood. I knew I wouldn't be able to achieve these simple dreams if I depended only on my husband or continued to work in our country.

I was booked for a flight four days before Christmas. The thoughtful and friendly father of one of my honor students offered to take me to the airport in his black Mercedes Benz. It was one of the many gestures of gratitude and affection that I received from my students' parents. What a great way to go to the airport, I thought — de luxe service for a soon-to-be servant de luxe! My students and their parents were aware that a couple of hours later, the "Ma'am" they used to address me as would be addressing her female employer in the very same way.

Inside the car on our way to the airport, the atmosphere was tense. With me were my husband, my eight-year-old twin daughters, my six-year-old son, and my niece Gina. From the car stereo blared a Christmas song that aggravated our sadness: *"I'll spend Christmas, all alone this year, all alone and blue. I'll be glad to walk the many miles just to be alone with you...."* No one spoke.

There were few words of good-bye at the airport. Around me I saw couples embracing. Others were teary-eyed, but not me. I deliberately hid my feelings, for I did not want to leave with a heavy heart. My final words to my husband were *"Susulat na lang ako"* (I will just write you), followed by *"Ang mga bata, huwag mong pababayaan."* (Please don't neglect the children.) It was a request that was only half-heeded. I rushed to the check-in counter where the immigration officer stamped on my passport the first day of my overseas sojourn.

I WAS QUITE fortunate to have my eldest sister in Hong Kong. Because of her, I spent only a few thousand pesos to go there. This was because we used a method called direct hiring, which means the applicant was hired directly from the Philippines through a relative or an acquaintance. Despite the clamor from applicants, this method has been abolished because of loopholes in the system. The other method is through a recruitment agency; for this, the applicant needs a huge sum of money as placement fee. Most applicants resort to borrowing money from lending institutions or even from private individuals who charge excessive interest rates. Others sell land or valuable appliances or pieces of furniture, or even their trusty carabaos, just to raise money for the placement fee. They hope to be able to get back what they sold once they find employment.

As I boarded my plane, I put on an aura of confidence. I wanted to show that it was not my first time to travel abroad. Out of ignorance, however, I discreetly said to myself, *"Ganito pala ang loob ng eroplano!"* (So, this is how the inside of a plane looks!)

Indeed, every step was a new learning experience. Even the sea of clouds below the aircraft was very exciting to see, and I was inspired to scribble these lines:

> *Oh, gentle clouds please come my way*
> *Why do you look so soft and fluffy?*
> *Will you take me to happiness*
> *Or to dreamland that will just fade away?*

These lines I have kept in my mind through the years.

MY SISTER was already eagerly waiting for me at the arrival section of Kai Tak Airport. Not having seen each other for more than a year, we tearfully kissed and embraced. She noticed that I had become thinner and was now the picture of a harried and worried person, a sign of difficult times.

She commented, though, that I looked very dignified in my trousers and matching blouse and blazer. She teased, *"Akala mo siguro, teacher ka pa, ano?"* (You probably think you're still a teacher, don't you?) Perhaps dressing well was an unconscious effort on my part to maintain my teacher image despite the job I would soon embrace. Nevertheless, my attire did nothing to erase the stigma attached to being one of the Filipino women on that flight who would soon take on menial jobs in Hong Kong. For whether a Filipino woman wears expensive clothes and decorates herself with jewelry or trinkets, or carries a *walis tambo* (soft broom), she will be identified as a DH even if she's not, as long as her destination is Hong Kong. It is not surprising that a lot of our "new rich" *kababayans* (compatriots) and those pretending to be rich, who splurge on shopping sprees in Hong Kong, abhor the sight of crowds of Filipino DHs. Because of the latter, the non-DHs are mistaken for domestics, many of whom, in an effort to be friendly, normally ask female Filipina tourists, "Day off *mo rin ba ngayon?*" (Is it also your off day today?), to the latter's irritation.

My Chinese employers were waiting for my sister and me. The first thing the lady did was to give me a sheet of bond paper filled with a long list of duties and responsibilities. I learned later that most of those who work as domestic helpers experience the same thing. I told myself there was no need for her to treat me like that because I would do the chores systematically. I did not show it then, but inside me I felt revulsion. Or maybe I felt I was going through a transition period — from being a teacher who was always in control. Later on, I came to terms with the truth that as my employer she had every right to tell me what to do. It was a bitter pill for me to swallow, but I had to act according to my role.

A biblical passage I read one night strengthened me: "You servants must obey your masters with fear and trembling; and do it with a sincere heart, as though you were serving Christ. The Lord will reward everyone, whether slave or free, for the good work he does." These words became my guiding light. The Bible also says, "No servant is above her master." Knowing this, I tried to hide the fact that I was more educated than my employers. In fact, in the résumé I submitted to them with my application, I merely indicated that I was a high school graduate. I did so deliberately because if they knew I was a professional they might expect too much from me, and since I came from a different culture, our standards were quite different.

When they gave me instructions, I obeyed them to avoid arguments even if I knew a better way. On my first week, my male employer called me and said, "Linda, do you know what this is?" He was referring to the television set. My naughtiness got the better of me. I pretended not to know and instead asked him, "Please tell me, Sir, because I do not know." He told me, with an air of superiority, that it was a television set and he showed me how to turn it on and off. I smiled secretly, for I had made him feel he was the boss.

LIVING WITH PEOPLE from a different culture is a form of direct learning, something one will never experience by just reading a book or attending school. I maximized my stay in Hong Kong by learning much about Chinese culture. I learned the Cantonese language, which was a big plus. My employers could not talk against me, nor about me, in my presence. Then I tried to learn how to use chopsticks, so that whenever they took me to a gathering, I did not go hungry even if I was looking after an excessively energetic toddler.

My being a teacher by profession also proved to be an advantage. I taught the toddler some nursery rhymes and basic information such as the names of the parts of the body, numbers, and the alphabet. My efforts paid off. The child's parents were so proud of me that they gave me a monthly bonus. They also asked me if I could recommend someone as hardworking as I was to their friends. That gave me the chance to get my two other sisters and my nieces. I was happy that they would be earning while experiencing things as I was.

My employers were so proud of me that they did not want me to have off days, preferring that I look after their toddler all the time. They paid for my off day and allowed me to go out only when I needed to send money home and attend Mass. My month-long solitary confinement made me very eager to befriend compatriots whom I met in the bus and elsewhere. I thus gained many friends from different regions of the Philippines. I collected their telephone numbers despite my employer's warning that I was not to use the telephone except in emergency situations.

As a Girl Scout, I had learned to be prepared and to do a good turn daily, and I had lived up to these lessons of my youth. I carried them with me in my work as an overseas Filipino worker (OFW). I have prepared myself for the worst that could happen, yet always prepared for the best. Knowing, too, that God helps those who help themselves, I fear nothing because I know that in whatever endeavor I undertake, easy or hard as it may seem, I always do my best.

This is why despite the status and culture shock, I was determined to put my best foot forward. I realized it was the key to staying long, happy, and sane in a foreign land and away from my loved ones.

It made a lot of sense to me to always be prepared. So as never to be taken by surprise and told to hurry up, I saw to it that I always had better- looking pants and matching shirts or blouses fit for a decent-looking maid, because I never knew when I would be going out with my employers. They were fond of doing things at the eleventh hour, or was it only a case of their planning and not letting me know until the last minute?

There were times when my habit of being prepared made me look ridiculous and funny. One winter night, as I was about to finish my kitchen chores, I was tempted to "steal" a banana for my midnight snack because I planned to stay up late to answer some letters from my former colleagues and students. I had vowed never to make myself hungry while I was abroad. I hid the banana inside the pocket of the top portion of my track suit, thinking it would be very safe there. But when I went out of the kitchen, I slid on the wet, newly mopped floor, and out came the stolen banana! My female employer saw me and the banana that had landed a few yards away. It was one of my most embarrassing moments with her.

With my male employer, I had an embarrassing moment as well. Late one afternoon, unable to resist a call of nature, I went inside the toilet but left its door open so that I could keep an eye on my naughty ward. I was in the middle of my ritual when the front door, which faced the toilet, opened wide. My Sir had arrived from work! I was so surprised that I could not decide what to do first — pull up my jogging pants or close the toilet door. In my confusion, I stood up from the loo without doing either. "It's all right, it's all right," Sir said, but for days afterward I could not look him straight in the eye. "Hope for the best, expect the worst" seems to be every OFW's motto.

Sometimes homesickness got the better of me. It was an awful feeling. At times it made me absent-minded. Once I was asked to cook steamed fish, a favorite dish among the Chinese because they regard fish as good luck. I boiled some water in the wok and waited for the right time to put the fish in. I did not realize that all the water had evaporated and I still hadn't put the fish in the wok. And Ma'am was getting impatient waiting for her lunch!

God knows I exerted my utmost efforts just to be tagged as a supermaid. I was always afraid that my working contract would be terminated, in which case I would be allowed to stay for only two weeks more in Hong Kong in order to find a new employer. This is the dreaded two-week rule, a regulation released by the Immigration Department a few months after I arrived. A few days later, President Cory Aquino chanted praises to us overseas Filipino workers, calling us the "new economic heroes" of the Philippines. The Filipino nongovernmental organizations (NGOs) in Hong Kong are still fighting for the dissolution of the two-week rule, but the Hong Kong government is adamant on keeping it in order to monitor those with illegal status, or what are sometimes called OS (for "overstayers"). In some countries, especially the United States, these hapless compatriots of ours are known as TnT (*tago nang tago*). In Taiwan they are called "*artista*" (because they keep acting). The OS are the unfortunate workers who, after having lost their previous jobs, are not able to find new employers two weeks later. They prefer to be illegal rather than go back to their families empty-handed.

HOMESICKNESS also triggered in me guilt feelings as a mother. While bathing my two-year-old ward, I would suddenly think of my own son and tell myself, "Here I am bathing someone else's child, seeing to it that he's neat and clean, but I am neglecting my own. Who could be bathing him these days?" Tears would well up in my eyes at the thought. But when I came to my senses, I would chide myself, "Why should I cry when this is my choice?"

Yes, life is a choice, and I vowed not to waste a single moment of it while I worked overseas. Having risked my children's development and given up my teaching profession in exchange for a few dollars, I told myself, "I will not go home a loser, I will not allow this job to destroy me, I will stick to the fight and emerge triumphant." Thus, despite my busy schedule, I did not let a single day pass without having spent a few hours on my personal improvement. On my rare off days, I visited public libraries, borrowed books, and jotted down interesting lessons from my readings. On not-so-busy afternoons, while my ward was asleep, I scribbled poetry and sketched the scenic surroundings with pen and crayons. I also had a passion for sending letters to the editor of one of the English dailies in the territory. These mental activities served as a panacea for my tired body and aching muscles.

Water seeks its own level. On my off days, I attended Holy Mass in an open area and observed many of my compatriots' behavior during and after the Mass. It saddened me to see that most of them sat idly along the road the whole day or in the shade of the commercial buildings in the vicinity. I joined them, but only for a while, because doing nothing the whole day and talking about people's lives are not my cup of tea. I thought of something better to fill my free time than wasteful and wishful thinking.

As if providentially, I stumbled upon a religious newsletter for overseas workers funded by the Philippine-based Divine Word Missionaries. That discovery changed my life forever. I started contributing to the newsletter and while my articles were not very good at the start, the editor was supportive and encouraged me to go on. Later, I was appointed associate editor, a job that became my apostolate for a couple of years. Although I was not paid for my work, just the sight of my articles in print and the editor's confidence in my editing were enough compensation and a boost to my ebbing self-confidence and morale. Accolades from readers restored my self-confidence, for I needed to have some evidence of my capabilities. It may be because of an unpleasant childhood experience, or because I was reared in a lowly environment, but it is very hard for me to be convinced that I, like everyone else, have a God-given talent that must be shared.

This was the reason why, despite my salary which was just enough to meet my children's basic needs and those of my sick parents, and the demands of my brother's college education, I still managed to spare some money for a correspondence course in journalism. I had to prove I deserved all the praise I was getting. My tutors' ratings became the concrete evidence that I was treading the right path.

Two years after I finished my correspondence course, Vonnie Boston, a publisher from New Zealand who had been in Hong Kong for 15 years, asked me to handle *Tinig Filipino*, a magazine for overseas Filipino workers. The job was a big challenge for me. It was a complete turnaround from stove to computers — for someone who had become an automaton for four long years to somebody who had to lead. *Newsweek* magazine picked up my story in November 1992. Here is an excerpt from the article written by Steven Strasser, its editor for Asia.

TALES OF A SELF-MADE MAID

Like many Filipina maids, Linda Layosa learned to live a double life. When she first applied for a job with a Chinese family in Hong Kong, she neglected to mention her college degree and her background as an elementary school English teacher "in order not to offend them." Once hired, she played the automaton, responding without emotion to orders. But late at night, she secretly nurtured her love of language and developed a second career, writing articles for a religious newsletter.

Now Layosa has broken out of her servile role entirely to become the editor of a magazine for Filipino migrant workers. Layosa, the third of eight children in a Filipino farming family, scraped her way through school on scholarship and stubbornness. "On the day before school, I would not eat and just sulk until my mother found money for books and uniforms," she says.

After graduating from the University of Nueva Caceres in 1973, she took a job teaching English grammar. By 1986, her salary was stuck at an equivalent of $84 a month, her husband was having trouble finding work and she worried about paying for the education of her own children. She could not resist the pull of Hong Kong, where the minimum wage for a live-in amah or maid was $244 a month. Three nights before she left home, while her children slept, "I ironed all their school uniforms, neatly piled their bleached-white socks and cleaned their shoes," she later wrote in a column. "If only I could be doubled — one to look after them and one to earn a living."

National pride: In Hong Kong, thousands of other amahs soon came to know Layosa through her newsletter columns. Then in December 1990, a local publisher offered her a chance to take over Tinig Filipino (Voice of the Filipino), a struggling monthly. Layosa seized it. Beginning with a staff of one part-time production manager, she ignored the usual formula for a Philippine magazine — plenty of horoscopes, star profiles, gossip — and instead aimed to create a "reader's magazine" built around the life of the amah.

Tinig Filipino promotes national pride and the professionalism of the DH, or domestic helper. Its columns teach manners. Its stars are the amahs who fill the pages with their stories and snapshots....

AFTER that *Newsweek* story, my life changed dramatically and I had to live up to the growing demands of my newfound career. Sometimes success can be very scary, but as the saying goes, "You cannot stop a determined person from reaching her goal. Put a stumbling block in front of her and she will make it a stepping stone." The Aquarian in me drove me more and more to explore the unknown. In my heart I knew the overseas Filipino workers needed a publication that would serve as their voice. It had to contain articles that would speak for and about them, give them guidance, information, and a pat on the shoulder. It had to be reading material with which they could identify themselves and through which they could share their struggles in their quest for the elusive dollar. It had to be nonpolitical and nonreligious. Thank God we blazed the trail and achieved our aim.

Later, with the reader's magazine came a 24-page news digest that carried news about overseas Filipino workers around the globe as well as news from the Philippines. Our initial print run of 2,500 copies soared monthly and were bought up like crazy in Hong Kong.

So great was the demand for the twin publications that we thought of expanding to other countries which had large concentrations of Filipino workers. We targeted Italy, then Greece, followed by Taiwan, Israel, Macao, and the United Arab Emirates. Thus were born two editions — the Hong Kong/Macao edition and the international edition.

We reap what we sow. With our expansion and the social outreach I was giving to the overseas workers — speeches, inspirational talks, moral support for their projects — awards recognizing my efforts came one after another. The Philippine Overseas Employment Administration (POEA) gave me the *Bagong Bayani* (New Hero) award in May 1993 for "raising herself from being a domestic helper and working her way to become an editor and giving inspiration to the overseas Filipino workers." My alma mater, the University of Nueva Caceres in Naga City, honored me with the most outstanding alumna award in March 1996. The following December, I received the *Pamana ng Lahi* presidential award of the Commission on Filipinos Overseas at Malacañang Palace from President Fidel V. Ramos himself. In June 1999, as part of the centennial celebration, I was among the women in a shortlist of awardees from all sectors who have revolutionized women's role in the Philippines.

I was interviewed for television, radio, foreign newspapers, and documentaries. I shared with them our objectives and echoed the message that we Filipino women are always ready to embrace any kind of job despite our educational attainment, if only to save our country from sinking economically and our loved ones from starving.

There was the other side of the coin. "People throw stones at a tree that bears fruit." I had to fight off the crab mentality that still plagues many of our *kababayans*. It is a disease that is delaying our progress as a people. Everywhere we go, most of us still carry it as a weapon or security blanket to cover up inadequacies and envy. It is a dirty old Filipino trick in journalism — *siraan, tagaan*, etc. — which I abhor.

I don't mind being the target of the crab mentality as long as it is done in reverse. Instead of the crabs pulling down one another, why don't the crabs who are lucky enough to reach the brim of the basket ahead help the others so that all of them can reach the top?

I have learned to be impervious to criticism and to treat my detractors' words as mosquito bites. Still, depression often strikes me. When it does, I open my old notes and read and re-read one of Dr. Jose Rizal's best poems, "Song of a Traveler," and I feel relieved. This poem, I suppose, expresses every overseas worker's sentiments:

> *Like a leaf that is fallen and withered,*
> *Tossed by the tempest from pole unto pole,*
> *Thus roams the pilgrim abroad without purpose,*
> *Roams without love, country or soul!*

Following anxiously treacherous fortune
A fortune which e'en as he grasp as it flees,
Vain though the hopes that his yearning is seeking
Yet does the pilgrim embark on the seas!

Ever impelled by invisible power,
Destined to roam from the East to the West,
Oft he remembers the faces of loved ones
Dreams of the day when he, too, is at rest.

Chance may assign him a tomb in the desert,
Grant him a final asylum of peace,
Soon by the world and his country forgotten
God rest his soul when his wanderings cease!

Often the sorrowful pilgrim is envied
Circling the globe like a sea-gull above
Little, ah little they know what a void
Saddens his soul by the absence of love.

Home may the pilgrim return in the future
Back to his loved ones his footsteps he bends
Naught will he find but the snow and the ruins
Ashes of love and the tombs of his friends.

Pilgrim, begone! Nor return more hereafter
A stranger thou art in the land of thy birth
Others may sing of their love while rejoicing
Thou once again must roam o'er the earth.

Pilgrim, begone! Nor return more hereafter
Dry are the tears that awhile for thee ran,
Pilgrim, begone! And forget thy affliction
Loud laughs the world at the sorrow of man.

MY STORY is not that special. It tells of one "ugly duckling" that has found a suitable pond to swim in. Yet the message is loud and clear: we Filipino women have a lot of things to offer to the world. What we need is to explore where we really fit in without fear of failure, without losing self-esteem, but without allowing success to go to our head and bloat our ego. As I always remind women OFWs, "Work as a domestic, but don't think like a domestic." I always tell them to imagine that they are playing a role in a movie. If they survive and are triumphant, they are good actresses.

My story is the saga of every Filipino overseas worker who has found a niche for herself by recognizing her God-given potentials and making a go of life. It is a story of enormous courage, determination, dedication, and deep love for family that are inherent in every Filipino woman's heart. In pursuit of our niche, some of us have lost our families, our sanity, and even our lives. Others, by force of circumstance, have given up their previous families in exchange for another family abroad. Others of weaker stuff have fallen prey to negative elements in other countries. As if to wake up our government and to teach the nation a lesson, several among us have suffered tragic deaths, such as Flor Contemplacion and Delia Maga in Singapore, Maricris Sioson in Japan, Maritess de Cardo in Hong Kong, and countless others in the Middle East, Taiwan, and other countries. Yet stories of courage, perseverance, faith, and determination abound, too. Ask most of those who are working in Italy and you will be startled by their individual stories of incredible courage, of how they entered that romantic country through the so-called "backdoor method" and the "baklas" system. Their adventures prove that indeed truth is stranger than fiction.

In the "backdoor method" one enters Italy by passing through another country, like Switzerland, crossing its borders on foot or through an illegal courier or a van, while the "baklas" system makes use of someone's passport with a valid visa stamped on it. The holder assumes the owner's identity, but the photograph on the passport is that of the holder. The practice is called "baklas" because the propagators of this modus operandi open the plastic shield protecting the owner's picture and replace it with the holder's. The holder has to memorize the personal details of the passport owner in preparation for his or her interview with the immigration officer.

For as long as my circumstances allow, it is my ardent desire to be every OFW's voice in my humble way. I want to bring to everyone the good tidings about Filipino women overseas workers. Just as their struggles, pains, failures, joys, and victories are mine, so is their metamorphosis.

I MAY HAVE circled the globe because of my job. I may have been branded by some quarters as a jet-setter. I may have come to love the romanticism of Sicily, Venice, Verona, Athens, Vienna, or rural England, or I may be on a par with the corporate people in highly industrialized Hong Kong and New York. I may have assimilated the traits of the hardworking, time-conscious Taiwanese, or I may have been influenced by London and Paris fashions. I may speak *"Ti voglio bene"* or *"ngo oi lei,"* or I may have adopted the stiff upper lip of the British. I may have worn jewelry made of Saudi gold or Egyptian silver, but homing is the last leg of any skyline pigeon.

When homing finally occurs, it is heartwarming to know that home, our country the Philippines, the cradle of noble and new economic heroes, is always there to cuddle us in its arms. It is always good to touch the green, green grass of home, so they say.

The young OFW's heart may belt out, *"Hinahanap-hanap kita, Manila ... Ang ingay mong kaysarap sa tenga ... Mga dyipning nagliliparan, mga babaeng naggagandahan ...* (I'm searching for you, Manila ... your noise that is sweet to the ears ... the seemingly flying jeepneys and the beautiful ladies...) Take me back in your arms, Manila.... I'm coming home to stay!"

It is also a source of joy and pride to us overseas Filipino workers to know that we are our country's biggest dollar earners and thus have contributed much to our country's economic growth despite the unsalutary effect of overseas work on our social development. With women now composing 60 percent of all our overseas workers, the typical family structure, in which the mother looks after the children, has become almost a thing of the past. Many of our children have been left to their own devices, making juvenile delinquency one of our nation's problems.

Despite the national situation, it is good to be home where our bleeding hearts, our battered souls, and our tired bodies can finally rest after an exhausting, sometimes unfulfilling, journey.

> *Sweet are the hours*
> *In one's native land*
> *Where all is dear, the sunbeams blest.*
>
> *Life-giving breezes that sweep thy strands*
> *And death is softened by love's caress.*

This is according to "Maria Clara's Lullaby," written by Jose Rizal who was an overseas worker in his own way.

To many of us who are planning to nestle, or to those who have found a new home in other countries, the many bittersweet memories of life in the Philippines will now be just a treasure pressed between the pages of the mind. To us, home is any adoptive country anywhere in the world, as long as our heart is there.

After all, the Filipino woman overseas worker will always be at home, wherever she is.

Loida Nicolas Lewis

View from the Top of Corporate America

MY FATHER, Francisco J. Nicolas, had always wanted to have a lawyer in the family, and so when I was born, his third child and first daughter, he "designated" me as the lawyer-to-be. After I graduated from the University of the Philippines College of Law and passed the bar, he gave me a round-the-world plane ticket, and a chaperone, my mother, Magdalena Mañalac Nicolas. Our first stop was the United States.

My sister Mely, who was then already in the US, was going out with someone from Harvard Law School and he set me up on a blind date. That's how I met Reginald Lewis.

We talked nonstop on that first date because we found out that we had so many things to talk about. It was fascinating, very interesting, just talking with him. I wouldn't say it was love at first sight, though, just immediate attraction. We were interested in the same things — music, politics — and we were both lawyers. As we got to know each other more, however, I began to fall in love with him. I had been with the best in the UP College of Law and dealt with them, as they say in Spanish, *mano a mano*, feeling somehow that I could dominate them. Then suddenly I met this man who was masterful. Slowly, I fell in love.

We made plans to marry and we even chose a venue, the New York University chapel. Then I developed cold feet. After the excitement of his proposal and my saying yes, I began to understand that marriage to him would mean leaving my family and my country, giving up all the ambitions my father had for me which I had accepted — running for politics, becoming congresswoman of Sorsogon, probably all the way to senator. And so I said, "I don't think I can go through with it."

We broke up. But on my way back to Manila, I was heartsick, knowing that I would never see him again. I was totally discombobulated at the thought that I would never again see this special man the likes of whom I had not met before. By the time I got to California for a reunion with friends from UP who were now studying in Stanford, I could not see colors. I was, I guess, depressed. To me there was no green or red or purple. Everything was gray. Finally, my friend Gerry Gil, who will always be very dear to me, said, "Why don't you just call him?" And I said, "That's a great idea!"

I did call him. "Darling," I said, "I'm coming back." He said, "Well, that would be great. But your father, your mother, and your family are expecting you in the Philippines. Why don't you just go back, tell them you're getting married, and then fly back here and we'll get married here."

As soon as I heard that, colors came back into my life. Instead of going home directly, since I knew that things were fine, Mely and I went around Asia for two weeks before I told our parents. Everything went well.

Initially, the plan was for me to fly back to New York, but my family said, "Loida, you are going to live in the United States for the rest of your life, but Reggie does not really know who you are unless he sees you in your milieu. Why don't you get married here?" It took some time because Reggie had already made arrangements for us to marry in two weeks, but eventually I won him over to my family's suggestion. I think he understood that the best way for him to understand his future wife and mother of his children was to see her in my surroundings in the Philippines.

There was no question about where we would live. I think that was why it was so hard for me to make the decision. I would have to follow the man I would marry. We were going to live in New York because that was where he decided he wanted to make his mark. He was a lawyer working in a big law firm in New York.

WE WERE MARRIED in 1969. At that time you could not take the bar examinations in the US unless you were an American citizen, and I was not yet a citizen. Then, in 1974, the US Supreme Court decided that this law was unconstitutional, it was a case of "unequal protection of the law," and declared that one did not have to be an American citizen to take the bar.

As soon as that decision was made public I decided to take the bar in New York. New York State allows law graduates from two schools in the Philippines, UP and Ateneo de Manila University, to take the bar without having to go back to law school in the US. So I took the bar without much ado, passed it the first time, and became a lawyer. As far as I know, I was the first Asian woman to pass the New York bar. There were no other Asian names on the list and there was no Asian woman practicing law in 1974. I told myself that if my claim to being the first Asian woman to pass the New York bar was wrong, somebody would definitely stand up to contest me. No one did.

After passing the bar, and knowing that my qualifications were good — I was in the top 10 percent of the graduating class at UP and a member of the International Honor Society, and I spoke Spanish, English, and of course, Filipino — I applied for the position of general attorney at the Immigration and Naturalization Service or INS. I was very confident I would get it. When I did not, I asked why. The only way I could find out was to sue for discrimination, which I did. After three years, the administrative judge decided that I had better qualifications than the others. I think it was a decision by default because the INS was asked to submit the resumés of the 11 lawyers who were accepted as general attorney and for six months, it failed to do so. There was no way the judge could make a comparison. There is a presumption in the law that if evidence requested is not submitted, one can assume *that* evidence is derogatory or negative and not good for the person/entity that did not submit. The judge decided, therefore, that my qualifications were better than, or at least equal to, those who were accepted, and he concluded that the only reason I was not hired was my national origin, my race, or my being a woman.

When I came to the US as a bride, the first question was what line of work would I go into. Naturally, I wanted to work as a lawyer. I started at the Manhattan Legal Services whose clientele was the East Harlem Community in El Barrio in Upper Manhattan. Reggie was a little hesitant about the job at first, but I convinced him. "Darling, you are working for a big law firm. You are working for the rich; let me work for the poor." He agreed, and offered no opposition. That was a good experience for me as a lawyer because I was working on the problems of the poor — discrimination in and lack of housing, unemployment insurance, social security. It rooted me in the type of hardships that a minority or an ethnic community has in New York City, the richest city in the United States.

The unfortunate reality is that in the US there is still racism, and it is very much alive after two hundred years of independence. Hate crimes are being committed. In a very insidious way, job discrimination still exists. If you look different from the majority, if you graduated from

168

another country, people think you are less able than someone who has graduated here, who looks Caucasian, who speaks without an accent.

The first time I arrived here I would say, "I am from the Philippines." Immediately there was an interest because people knew nothing about the country. Even my husband, when I first met him, knew very little about the Philippines and he asked me questions about it, and became interested enough in it to start reading and studying about it. So John Doe/Jane Doe knows nothing about the Philippines except maybe about Imelda Marcos and her three thousand pairs of shoes, meaning, the "notorious" kind of Filipino. On the good side, they know about Cory Aquino and the people power revolution. They have heard, too, about Marcos and the martial law he imposed. Otherwise, they know next to nothing about Philippine history: about our having been under the Spaniards for 300 years, under the Americans for 50 years, our struggle for independence during the time of McKinley at the turn of the century. For that matter, even Filipino-Americans, especially the young, know very little about the Philippines.

My husband was a corporate lawyer for 15 years but he knew that in the US real wealth would not come from practicing law. There are only 24 hours a day in which you can bill your client, after all. So he said, "I have to go to the other side, not representing investors, but being an investor myself." He tried to buy a company thrice but failed, but on the fourth attempt he was successful. He bought McCall's Pattern Co. on a leverage buyout, which means buying a company on credit. He borrowed all of the money, $22 million, to buy McCall's, and then he worked the company so that he paid off the debt and then sold the company again. So successful was he that in three years he had a 90:1 return on his investment.

Then he went to Mike Milken who at that time headed Drexel Burnham Lambert, and together they did all the leverage buyouts in the Eighties. In 1987 Reggie told Mike that he had a new deal. This was Beatrice Food. Reggie bid for the international portion of Beatrice when it was placed on auction, and Drexel Burnham Lambert backed him. He made the highest bid, almost $1 billion, and so he became the owner of Beatrice International which had 64 companies in 31 countries.

Reggie worked on Beatrice for five years until tragedy struck in 1993. He was diagnosed to have brain cancer, and in six weeks he was gone. It was the most devastating thing that has ever happened to me. I was catatonic, living on automatic pilot. But, thank God, I kept the faith and in that darkest of nights I just reached out my hand and said, "Lord, you've got to help me." Sure enough, I felt His hand in mine and slowly I took my first step. I have been walking ever since.

WHEN I REGAINED control of my life I asked two questions: What do I have here? What did my husband leave behind?

First, we had our two daughters. They needed my total attention. They would be the first priority in my life. Whatever they needed, I would be there for them. Second, he left TLC Beatrice, the company that he founded. It had to succeed. As far as I was concerned, he gave his life for the company. Failure was not an option. It had to win. I had to finish his work. And so I decided it would be better if I ran the company than have somebody else do it, because if that person failed, then my husband's work would be gone, and if I were to fail, then I had nobody to blame but myself. In order to succeed, however, I had to identify people who would help me make it succeed.

In 1994, one year after Reggie died, I took over. It was a matter of putting one foot in front of the other. For example, earnings in 1992-1993 were down. If expenses are high, your earnings are down, you have to cut costs. That's what I did. I moved the office down from the 48th floor to the 39th — a third of its former size. I also had to do the most difficult job of reducing personnel. We had to let go of 50 percent of our people at corporate headquarters. I sold the company jet; it had become too expensive. I had to sell the two limousines too. There were companies that were losing money — they were a drain on earnings. I sold them as well. Slowly, in the first year, we made $1 million in net earnings; in the second year, $10 million; the third, $15 million; the fourth, $19 million. We were on a roll.

In 1997 the biggest part of the business was the supermarket business in France. Reggie had a deal that in five years TLC would have a chance to sell the company 100 percent, or our partners would demand that we buy them out. It was like a financial time bomb. We hired investment bankers to advise us on the best thing to do in 1997 in order to capture its value. We decided that the best decision would be to sell it. Buying them out would not work out 100 percent because we were primarily financial guys, not operators. So we sold the French business for almost half a billion dollars, an excellent price, although it meant selling two-thirds of the company. It took me some time to decide, but after that I had to make the hard decision, which was to sell the entire company.

I AM ALWAYS asked whether I have felt any discrimination as a woman in a high-powered position. I have to answer that I have not. My parents raised my siblings and me not to identify people according to their looks or economic status or mental ability but instead to treat everyone according to his or her inner self. By the content of their character, as Martin Luther King put it. So I never presented myself as "a woman, treat me special or differently."

My family in the Philippines never treated me differently because I was a girl. The schools I went to — a Catholic high school for girls and a Catholic women's college — gave us a sense that we Filipino women were no different from men or were not inferior to them. We were educated in the same manner and on the same curriculum as the men. We had the same opportunities for education. We were empowered.

I think the comic strip character Blondie is the caricature of the other kind of woman, totally irresponsible, spending all her husband's salary on shopping. I believe that in the Philippines it is the other way around. It is the man who is often fiscally irresponsible. It is the woman who holds the purse and doles out an allowance to her husband. We Filipino women, I think, are especially blessed because we have a society that accepts us as equals rather than as second-class citizens.

My husband was African-American and we were well aware of the reality of racism in the United States. We had to wrestle with a decision on whether to raise our children as Asian, African, or American. So as not to confuse them about their own identity, we consciously raised them as African-Americans. They know that their mother is Asian, but they are African-Americans and are proud to be such. They are Americans, first of all, and in terms of ethnic identity, they are African-Americans.

When he married me, Reggie promised my parents that we would visit the Philippines every year. He kept his word. That is why my children know the other half of their heritage — Asian, Filipino — very well. Until they reached their teenage years, they came to the Philippines with me every year, usually after Christmas, and we would stay for a month. But like typical American teenagers, they stopped going with me around the age of 13 because their friends were not there. Theirs is a different culture. But when my older daughter, Leslie, got married last year, she and her husband came for a visit. So, you see, something said is something heard. My children have seen enough and heard enough and have been with me all their lives, so I am sure being Filipino is very much part of their personalities.

When Leslie was born, my only point of reference was growing up as a Filipino child in Sorsogon; she was just totally different from me when I was growing up. My mother wasn't here to guide me, and my mother-in-law, while she was great, didn't know how children are reared in the Philippines. It was very hard raising an American child with a Filipino frame of mind. As a result, I was always at odds with Leslie. We both had a difficult time.

For example, Filipino children never answer back, but American children do; they have minds of their own. A Filipino child listens to her parents and does what her parents say. Finally, my husband told me, "Loida, she is American; she is living in America." That fact sank in, slowly, that Leslie was an American child, she was growing up in the United States, she was not a Filipino child. When I finally and totally understood that, I was able to develop different expectations and I adjusted accordingly. It also took Leslie some time, but she's very well-adjusted now.

I, on the other hand, will always be a Filipino. In fact, I would attribute my success to my being a Filipino because I have not changed, my accent has not become Americanized, and I really am what I am because I am a Filipino woman. You can take me out of the Philippines, but you cannot take the Philippines out of me.

A FEW YEARS AGO, I helped found the National Federation of Filipino-American Associations (NaFFAA). We have just had our third empowerment convention in New York City, the first time we convened under the constitution that we approved last year. I volunteered New York because I wanted to have a convention that would be the benchmark, the standard by which all future conventions would be measured. We were fortunate to have the US First Lady, Hillary Rodham Clinton, as our keynote speaker, and the audience of Filipino-Americans just loved her. They were euphoric because it was the first time ever that a White House occupant recognized the Filipino-American community as a people. That was very significant.

Part of my function as chair of the NaFFAA's Eastern Region is to encourage Filipino-Americans, the young in particular, to learn more about their history, because if one doesn't know where one came from, one can't really move forward with confidence. That's the social consciousness and the cultural, political, and economic empowerment we are working on in NaFFAA.

We Filipinos have a proud history. I would tell that to a young Filipino-American who has lost his identity. He must realize that all of his Filipino

172

parents' and grandparents' history is in his blood. Since the United States is almost like a mother country to us Filipinos, his parents or his grandparents must have decided that there may be a better life in the US, that there would be better economic opportunities here, to give their children a better future. And so he must look at his parents with admiration because they have sacrificed for him that he can grow up independent and proud of his history, his ancestors. There is nothing for him to be ashamed of. Yes, he is a person of color, his eyes may be different, but at the same time he speaks with an American accent. He has the ability to combine the best of both worlds: the best in the Filipino — a sense of family, faith in God, a sense of community, with the best in American society — entrepreneurship, a sense of independence, all the opportunities open to him, and the determination to succeed. All that the young Filipino-American has to do is to seize the moment and move on with pride, with intelligence, and with confidence. If he keeps his goal in front of him, he will succeed.

One of the serious issues we discussed at the NaFFAA convention was that of the Filipino veterans of World War II. World War II was won by the Allies, by the United States, and by the Filipino people. That was in 1946. It is now 1999 and the veterans still have not received the benefits that should be theirs by reason of their military service. We at NaFFAA are fighting with them because they have been dealt a grave injustice. Here in this great United States of America preaching liberty and justice for all, there is no justice yet for the Filipino veterans of World War II.

Let us not forget the great contributions made to the United States by the Filipinos at the turn of the century. When the US annexed the Philippines as a territory, it needed cheap labor to work on the pineapple fields in Hawaii and to take care of the agricultural harvests in California. The Americans exported Filipino men to those places to feed the United States. Those Filipinos worked long and hard; unfortunately, migrant workers until today are still working under very, very adverse conditions.

Filipinos came to the US long before many other immigrant people. During the 1700s, a group of Filipino sailors who were in the galleon trade, ships that plied the Gulf of Mexico from the Philippines to the Americas, jumped ship and settled in New Orleans.

Those Filipinos who came over as laborers had to endure blatant discrimination. At that time no Asians were allowed to marry — they were here to work, not to propagate themselves. Again, the racist history of the United States manifested itself in the law. But in 1965 President Lyndon

B. Johnson decided to remedy this inequality. He worked for the passage of a major amendment to the immigration laws that would allow people not only from Europe but also from the other hemisphere, to come to the United States. That started the "brain drain" in the Philippines. Anyone who had a profession, or at least a college degree, was able to come to the United States and get a green card. The next wave of Filipino migrations to the United States was made up mostly of professionals: doctors, nurses, lawyers, accountants, engineers, teachers, and physical therapists.

In the Seventies and Eighties, the bulk of migration was composed of relatives. Those who had arrived in the Sixties were now American citizens and so could petition for their spouses, children, parents, siblings. According to statistics, Filipino-Americans will be the largest Asian-American community in the United States in the year 2020.

In the late Eighties, while living in Paris and with time on my hands, I thought I would volunteer my services to the American Embassy since I had put in nearly 10 years at the INS. The Embassy told me, "We need you to volunteer and be available to be assigned anywhere in the world if you want to join the Department of State." I said, "What? If that's the case, you can keep your job!!"

The next best thing was to write a book, which I did.

While I was writing *101 Legal Ways to Enter the United States*, the US Congress passed in 1990 a law allowing Filipino veterans to become US citizens. So I stopped writing the first book and worked on a second instead — *How the Filipino Veteran of World War II Can Become a US Citizen*. That became a bestseller in the Philippines. In fact, I have just met a veteran who told me that the book was the reason he was in the United States. By following the book very closely and without hiring a lawyer, he was able to become an American citizen. Later on, I went back to my first book. When the immigration laws were amended, I sold the rights to that book to Nolo Press, a California-based publishing company that specializes in legal how-to books, and they published it under the title *How to Get a Green Card*.

Where do I see Filipinos in the US 50 years from now? The future will depend on the present, and that is why I am earnestly calling on all Filipino-Americans to get their act together. What does this mean? To recognize that we are here as a community, that the enemy is not among ourselves. We must come together as a people and understand that in unity there is strength.

I like to tell the story of a father who summoned his five sons because they were always quarreling with one another. He gave them each a stick and said, "Break it." Of course, each one broke it easily. Then he took a bunch of sticks and gave it first to Juan. "Break it," the father said again. Juan couldn't, and neither could Pedro, Santiago, Pepe and Pedring. They couldn't break it because the sticks were tied together.

So if we, the Filipino-American community, can recognize that if we have unity, we would be a great force for political power, we can help ourselves economically. We will be recognized as a force if we understand our culture and if we keep the best traits we can bring to American society — our sense of family and our spirituality. Of course, the third one is hard work. Filipinos take on one job, two jobs, even three, to ensure that their families, even those left in the Philippines, are well provided for.

REGGIE AND I always said that in our old age we would retire in a city we both loved. That was Paris, which we visited before Leslie was born. Little did I know that we would have the chance to live there when he bought TLC Beatrice and turned it into a European company.

In Paris we lived what some people would probably call the lifestyle of the rich and famous. Reggie once asked me to go to a concert with him, and so we flew in his private plane from Paris to Vienna to listen to the Vienna Philharmonic Orchestra. We stayed in the Imperial Palace Hotel and then flew to London for lunch and then returned to Paris. But that was only one side of it.

The other side was that I knew if I did not hold on to something solid, something eternal, I would lose my perspective and begin to believe that the world revolved around us. Because of the kind of life we were living — we were meeting the prime minister and the president of France, for example — I told myself I had to go back to my faith. I thus sought the only English-speaking church in Paris, St. Joseph Church, and with some other women started a faith-sharing group. We would meet every week, read a passage from the Bible, give our thoughts on it, share our experiences during that week in the light of what we had just read. My doing that, I think, strengthened me for the tragedy that would happen five years later.

I took over TLC Beatrice out of a sense of duty and responsibility. I have to admit, however, that in the course of running the business, I have enjoyed the process. I am having fun. To paraphrase the title of the book on my husband, "Why should guys have all the fun?" Reggie's biography, published after his death, is entitled *Why Should White Guys Have All the Fun?*. The title was derived from a comment he made to his mother when he was only five.

I knew I would buy my own business without my husband's previous partners. Together with my sister Mely and the managing director, Dan Oñate, I bought TLC Beatrice China. I remain chair of this fast-growing chain of food retail stores in China. I feel very gung-ho about that country, especially because we got there ahead of the other multinational companies that are now trying to get on the bandwagon with the recent signing of the trade agreement between the US and China, which also paves the way for China's entry into the World Trade Organization.

By the summer of 2000, I expect to buy another food business, this time in the US. I prefer to explore another seemingly "undeveloped and overlooked" territory right here in America — the inner cities.

On the nonbusiness side, the Nicolas family is setting up The Lewis College (TLC) in Sorsogon, where I was born and where my brothers Danny, Jay, and Francis and Mely and I had our idyllic childhood. This is our way of repaying the community that has nurtured us, Sorsogon and the Bicol region, by providing its youth quality education with a strong spiritual foundation. We think this would make our parents very happy.

In the United States, the Reginald F. Lewis Foundation is funding the National Association for the Advancement of Colored People (NAACP) to teach young people in the inner cities how to run their own businesses and make them fiscally savvy. The project has been called the Reginald F. Lewis Youth Entrepreneurial Institute. Again, this is our way of sharing with the African-American communities all the blessings we have received and to bring home to them the lesson to be learned from Reggie's life, which disproved the lie that people of color cannot go to the very top of corporate America.

All of these plans will keep me very busy for the next few years.

The Lord has always been good to me. I believe that if you try to live according to His will, He will shower you with His blessings and graces. So I thank the Lord every day. I will not question His will that my love, my husband Reginald, left me early. I know that He is a loving God and whatever is His will is the best for me.

It has been a wonderful life.

Tina Liamzon

La Dolce Vita, Filipino NGO Style

THE OFFER to my husband of a chance to work at one of the United Nations' food agencies in Rome in late 1989 was God-sent. For over a year, he and I had been hoping and praying that we could take a sabbatical from work — he with an Asian NGO network, and I with a national NGO network. We were both starting to suffer from burnout.

I had been to Rome several times, but always as a tourist staying a few days each time. When the possibility of moving to Rome came, I was excited to live abroad again, after seven years of high-stress work in Manila and, before that, five years in Bangkok. I dreamt about taking a long rest and exploring Italy's ancient monuments, basilicas, and ruins, enjoying Italian pizza and pasta, and spending time to reconnect with my husband and two children, whom I felt I had started to neglect.

After several intense months finishing work obligations and buying furnishings and packing up for Rome (I hadn't had the time to think about why I was packing so much stuff, if we were just going away for a year), I took off with the children, then 12 and seven years old, at the end of June 1990 to join my husband, who had left in March. I was looking forward to having a new home, fixing it up and settling in the children and myself, and getting adjusted to a whole new life.

I arrived in Rome extremely exhausted and took a long while to recover from weeks of feverish preparation for our departure and all the *despedidas* and good-byes we had to say to family and friends. Despite our previous experience living in Bangkok, I had forgotten that moving to an entirely new environment was in itself highly stressful, given the differences in language, culture, and just about everything else. I had to

learn about my new environment, make sense of the Italian bureau-
cracy, and not feel frustrated and desperate with it. I hadn't quite believed what friends had told me about coping and surviving in Italy, which,
despite being an industrial country, can still be quite a challenge. Even
such simple things as paying bills or going to the bank or the post office
could be quite a task, they had warned. There were almost always long
queues to contend with, and I had to be able to communicate properly
with what little Italian I had started to pick up. Also stressful was having
our house burglarized two months after our arrival, while we were away
on vacation, and losing two new tires several months later while our car
was parked near my husband's office.

When I left Manila in 1990, I didn't really think much of bidding
tearful good-byes as I extracted promises from everyone, especially my
mother, that they would all come to visit, and soon. After all, we weren't
going to be in Rome for very long. I didn't realize that it would be the last
time I would see my mother alive. Otherwise, I would have taken much
more time to thank her, among many other blessings, for having allowed us to live with her for seven years, taken care of my family, provided for our needs, and overseen the children so that my husband and I
could fulfill the demands of our work without worrying too much about
their well-being. Only four months after leaving Manila, I received a call
at early dawn telling me to go home as my mother had died after a
massive heart attack. I now dread, as I'm sure every overseas Filipino
does, to hear the telephone ring very late at night or early in the morning
for fear of hearing bad news.

I rushed back to Manila for the funeral and, feeling depressed, returned to Rome a few weeks after. I suddenly felt so alone, sorely missing
my mother who would no longer ever come for a visit, and far from my
siblings from whom I had always drawn much comfort and strength.
Barely a year after my mother's death, my family experienced grief once
again when my eldest brother died from a lingering illness. I had seen
him just two months earlier when I attended the wedding of his eldest
son and he was trying very hard to be cheerful. I never realized how
badly he was coming along. I had never entertained the thought that he,
too, would be leaving us so soon. I was grateful that I could attend my
nephew's wedding, and that I did not go home only to attend funerals.

During that first year, I also found myself with much time on my
hands. It was a far cry from the Eighties, when I would get very tense and

uptight as I rushed from one meeting to another, traveled from one city or town to another, met deadlines for reports, basically tried to be a superwoman while feeling very stressed out. Life definitely turned 180 degrees in Rome. I started to get very bored and at times even felt hopeless, not even knowing where or how to start to get a life in my "new home." To fill up the time, I did a lot of window shopping and wasted seemingly endless hours complaining about the place, the wild Italian drivers, the traffic (which isn't as bad as the traffic jams of Manila), the high prices of goods and services, or just about anything else that drew my attention, which I could criticize. My boredom was compounded by the fact that my children were mostly in school, doing well and no longer really needing me with their studies and homework, and that my husband was busy coping with his job.

At least we had the benefit of many guests who came to the house to share a meal or to spend the night, but even these visits were intermittent. Among our guests were Filipinos also working with the UN, and their spouses. Through them I sought out new friends from among the new arrivals and "old-timers" in Rome. Many were UN spouses like myself, or Filipino women married to Italians, who were seeking interesting and meaningful things to do. These women willingly gave their time to teach me the ins and outs of Roman life such as the bargains to be found in the flea markets, the nuances of Roman traditions, how expensive Italian taxes were (19 percent value-added tax on most things). Life became more fun and certainly more filled, with my newfound friends. Together, we studied Italian cooking, tried to play tennis, explored some off-the-usual-tourist-track historical sites, took up Italian language courses, even tried out French class, where I quickly discovered I was the only beginner, and dropped out. Through the years, however, I also found myself mourning the loss of several of these friends, whom I had just started to get to know, when they left after their spouses' contracts ended. Thanks to e-mail, though, many of us do manage to keep in touch.

DESPITE ALL these activities, I still felt mentally bored and greatly missed the stimulation of a regular work environment. From time to time, I would get news on how things were coming along in the NGO sector in the Philippines and with my friends there. I desperately longed to be where the action was. It was hard for me to realize in the first few years that no one, especially myself, was indispensable even in the NGO world, where I thought I had made some difference. My old insecurities often resurfaced, as they would through the years, as I questioned where my life and career in Rome were headed. I was locked into a tremendous vacuum as I compared my life in Manila with my new one in Rome. Many times I felt I was losing my direction in life, as well as my self-esteem and sense of identity as a professional woman with something to contribute to society.

It must have been after getting a few opportunities to take on short-term work, whether in a paid or voluntary capacity, having the time to reflect on what was happening to me then, and the blessing of having someone from Manila to help with the housework and the cooking, among others, that I decided to end my "sabbatical." I am not sure exactly when I decided to move beyond the self-pitying stage and to try to systemati-cally explore opportunities that Rome could offer foreign spouses like myself. It was not a once-and-for-all decision, though, as many times I fought hard to think positively about what I wanted to do while in Rome.

Before I left Manila, the NGO networks I was connected with had re-quested me to take on a new role as liaison person to link them with Euro-pean NGOs and donors as well as the Rome-based UN food agencies. That request gave me an opportunity to remain in the same general area of devel-opment work, and I started to attend some UN meetings in Rome as the representative of an Asian NGO network. I discovered soon after that these meetings, with their endless government statements, bored me. Attempting to listen and make sense of all the bureaucratese was alien to my NGO expe-rience. But I have to learn along the way to adjust to the UN's bureaucratic ways, although I've refrained from attending too many typical UN meetings.

In the beginning, I also received a few offers of short contracts with-out my searching for them. One was to explore funding possibilities in Europe, which meant traveling to donors around the region; the second was an evaluation of a UN project in Nepal. I found these a new chal-lenge which opened new horizons and work opportunities for me, as I had always thought of myself more as an organization person, concep-tualizing, managing projects and activities, organizing workshops, dia-loguing with government and other sectors, and running a secretariat. I knew a lot about running networks and coalitions, having worked for seven years to build up a Philippine network at a time when networking was still in its infancy, and before that, being involved in three Asian NGO networks.

To boost my income from short-term work and regain my financial independence, I accepted a long-term consultancy that involved part-time work with a Rome-based international development NGO established in the Fifties. From 1992 to 1995, I worked as a program officer responsible for developing a grass-roots program on participatory development. I conceptualized a program on sustainable livelihoods that would bring together NGOs and people's organizations in the three main developing regions of Africa, Asia, and Latin America. The research-cum-action program we would undertake would lead to a better understanding of the factors that facilitate and/or undermine people's livelihoods. The focus was on the broader framework of livelihoods, not just the narrow context of incomes or employment. I negotiated for three regional networks to collaborate on the program with ourselves as lead organization, and we involved NGOs in over 15 countries in the three regions.

I was happy that I was able to utilize my networking skills to bring together an interregional network of people from the field and from academe through several regional round table meetings, again on the theme of sustainable livelihoods. I found much satisfaction interacting with people, not just from the Asian region with which I was generally familiar, but from others with very diverse cultures.

While I was working with this international NGO, I continued to do consulting work on the side when opportunities presented themselves. Most of these involved evaluating UN and NGO projects, or conceptualizing programs. Work took me to many different countries, including several times to the Philippines, which I particularly welcomed. After one speaking engagement in South Africa in 1991, I was asked by a colleague from the South African NGO that invited me to develop a proposal for a visitation program for a group of South African NGO leaders to learn about the Philippine NGO experiences in agrarian reform advocacy and action programs, which could be useful to their newly democratizing society. In 1994 I facilitated, with the help of a new UK-based economics organization specializing in "social auditing," the introduction of the group and its techniques to Philippine NGOs and people's organizations. Social auditing is a whole different way of addressing accountability for both profits and nonprofits, beyond financial audit.

I found myself being invited to give talks in Japan, Ghana, the US, around Italy and other parts of Europe, on such diverse subjects as an assessment of the World Bank/IMF structural adjustment programs, the effects of the WTO/Uruguay Round on food security in the South, development education, spirituality and sustainability, the people's economy, networking and coalition building. However, I never felt comfortable speaking to audiences; in fact, I was mostly terrified when I had to give these talks around the world. I had to develop techniques by which I could survive my perceived terrors. I put tremendous effort and energy into writing the talks and preparing myself psychologically to deliver them. Nowadays, I feel less stressed and tense when I do speak publicly, but I still spend a lot of time preparing for them physically, mentally, and emotionally.

Being a consultant and having to travel as part of the work have been one big adventure. Sometimes I have been the only woman in a team, and I have had to stay alone in hotels and deal with a whole range of personalities from government, the UN, NGOs, or grass-roots groups. I have become keenly aware and sensitive to cultural norms that I needed to understand and respect, especially in certain parts of Africa or South Asia where women are meant to be seen, definitely not heard.

One experience I had in South Asia was refraining from shaking hands with villagers, all men, with whom I had to meet and hold discussions. A Filipino woman I met in that country informed me that this was just not done, even if I was responsible for basically conducting the interviews, although through an interpreter. I had to be careful about the clothes I would wear, always making sure my arms and legs were covered, and even then I still attracted intimidating stares from men when I would walk by myself. In certain cities I was advised, as a woman staying alone, not to leave my hotel and walk around even in broad daylight. Although I am basically an adventurous person, I have often decided to play safe rather than court danger. I delight in strolling around, acting as a tourist whenever I can find the opportunity, which unfortunately is not as often as I wish. It is not unusual for me to go to a place, attend my meetings and then leave, with no time to explore the place or to enjoy it.

In the nine years I have lived in Rome, I have also been involved in an assortment of activities on a voluntary basis. Aside from being an NGO representative and liaison person in Europe, I was asked in 1992 to be a fellow of a loose international alliance of individuals and organizations working toward sustainability. These multiple roles have brought me to numerous meetings on a variety of issues in Europe, the US, and elsewhere. I cover several areas of interest: food security issues, agrarian reform (an area of concern since I began my career in the NGO sector in the late Seventies), and gender.

Despite my general dislike of the bureaucratic processes of UN conferences, I was active in some of the NGO processes related to the World Summit on Social Development in 1995 in Copenhagen and the International Conference on Nutrition in 1992, and the World Food Summit in 1996 (the latter two were held in Rome). In 1996, in preparation for the World Food Summit, three of us women advocates based in Rome, together with several organizations, organized an International Workshop on Rural Women and Food Security. We brought together over 30 participants from countries as diverse as Zimbabwe, Belize, and Russia.

Overall, I have had a tremendous learning experience in traveling to different parts of the world and working in multicultural settings. I have learned to be more tolerant of other people's cultures, beliefs, traditions, and religions, although I may not agree with some of the customs and practices, particularly when they involve women. The feminist in me always gets aroused and agitated when I see the terribly lopsided burden that women have to carry in caring for their families with little expectation for themselves. At the same time, I've seen many promising and positive examples of women (and men) taking the active role of organizers, at the grass-roots or intermediate NGO or network level, in promoting the empowerment of women or of people in general, of making a difference in their household, their villages, and their part in society. This I find most helpful to glimpse and I am encouraged that despite numerous problems there are many hopeful signs as well. My own limited role is to record some of these for others to learn from, and to provide particular suggestions that could improve some of the work being done.

Writing, like speaking, has never been one of my strong points. Over the last five years I have likewise had to write more or to compile and edit materials into reports. I've had to do a lot more research, think through more systematically what I've had to say, whether in a speech or in an article. I've been happy to see pieces I've written in several NGO books or newsletters, in an Italian journal (as translated), or published as reports, after literally agonizing over the writing, editing, and attempting to perfect them. More recently, I have widened my interests to include such issues as the relationship of liberalized agricultural trade and food security in the South, capacity building of civil society in such concerns as global trade agreements like the World Trade Organization, spirituality and sustainable development, empowerment and participation, and the building of an alternative economics, including the people's economy.

During that period of increasing intensity in both my paid and unpaid work, I got involved in the board of my children's school through the insistence of an office colleague who was on the board. I was the only person from the South in the board, and for the first time I had to learn how a school should be run or not run. The school was suffering from declining enrolment and from a serious financial crisis, as a result of poor enrolment. Furthermore, there was such a negative atmosphere in the school; the faculty and staff, and increasingly the students, were demoralized. My colleague suggested that I assist in smoothing out relations between the board and the staff, especially since the tricky issue of possible staff layoffs was causing much tension and stress in everyone concerned. I facilitated several dialogues among the faculty with the board on several areas of concern.

That experience left me wishing I had much more community building and conflict management skills. My NGO background did teach me how to listen more, to trust my intuition, and to have a positive attitude toward the different parties, no matter how negatively the situation was turning. A drastic change was needed in people's attitudes toward one another and toward the financial situation. They had to be willing to forge ahead as one community whose members cared for one another. The school has since turned for the better, partly from the inputs that the board and succeeding boards brought in, the new energies from a new headmaster, and an overall change in the school atmosphere. While I felt inadequate for the job, I did learn much from working mostly in an Italo-American environment.

In 1992, in one of my restless moments, a priest-friend who was enrolled for a doctorate in one of Rome's pontifical universities convinced me to take doctoral studies while I was conveniently still residing in Rome. It didn't take me long to decide to continue my studies, as I had done the same thing when we were living in Bangkok in 1980. I had resolved at that time to do something new with my life, and so I took my graduate degree in human settlements planning, majoring in rural development in an Asian institution.

I thus became a student again. When I got accepted to do my doctorate in development economics, I hadn't realized that classes would basically be conducted in Italian, which I still hadn't quite mastered, but as most of the faculty were adept in four or five languages, I had no problem submitting papers in English. That was a big relief, but having to cope in Italian with lectures and reading materials proved to be a real strain. I staggered my classes to just two per semester. Even then, I barely survived. I had been out of the academic world for too long, and it took me a while to get back to the discipline of academic reading, thinking, and report writing, which I now deeply appreciate. I had forgotten many of the economic theories I had studied at university, nor did I agree with many of them. The challenge, however, was very exciting, as I always felt that in the past I had had very little time to catch up on the readings in the social sciences. I did realize, a bit belatedly, the importance of being steeped in both theory and practice.

I found myself juggling classes between my part-time jobs and squeezing in some consulting work. The bigger challenge was starting on my dissertation. In 1996 I quit my part-time job to concentrate on it, as I realized that it was difficult to combine regular work with dissertation writing. I've had to change my topic a few times and I continue to struggle with it to obtain the final go-ahead from my adviser. Many times I have been tempted to quit, and to go on with my life prior to my dissertation. Part of me, however, doesn't want to give up yet. The goal of finishing what I have started is still there, although that may still change.

NOW THAT I'm in my mid-forties, and increasingly confronted with the prospect of several more decades to live, at most, I have been forced to sharpen my own introspection. I have found that being in Rome has also increased my living in contradictions. I have been trying to be coherent with my values and ideals, with my own lifestyle in a developed country, with its consumption and materialist values, and my own search for a "simpler" lifestyle. Like any industrialized country, Italy is highly consumerist and has influenced Filipinos, including myself, to develop expensive tastes. For several years now, I've been attending a series of workshops on ethics, spirituality, and sustainability in Assisi and these have helped me to focus on this issue even further; so, too, has my exposure to the international sustainability alliance to which I belong, where a number of partners are part of simple lifestyle movements.

In the Assisi workshops, participants, though coming mostly from the Christian faith, are also Buddhists, Hindus, Bahai, etc. Living together for several days in serene Assisi, and to some extent experiencing the spirit of St. Francis and St. Clare, have helped me to center on spirituality and sustainability, essential elements for the survival of the world, and my own role in promoting these values. Some participants have strongly pointed out the discrepancy and unsustainability of our increasingly consumerist world, particularly for those who live in the industrial world, including myself. The promotion of the Earth Charter, a declaration similar to the Universal Declaration of Human Rights but dedicated to calling the world's attention to respect the whole of God's creation, is part of the project of these workshops, which I try to disseminate. My religious friends in Rome have also taught me, through their example, what simplicity in lifestyle is, satisfying and fulfilling as their lives manifest.

One of the wonderful things about residing in Rome is having thousands of other Filipinos living and working in the city, which always makes me feel I'm not missing some aspects of Philippine life. After all, I can regularly buy an assortment of cooked Filipino food, even fresh *ampalaya, talbos ng sili,* at the makeshift *turo-turos* at the Filipino church centers, or at the park near Eur Fermi, close to where I live, or other parks in the city. My family can attend Sunday Masses in Filipino or English in any of the over 30 Filipino church centers in the city. I can ask for directions in the center from an Asian I see near a bus stop, and almost always it is a Filipino woman. Very often I am asked if I work full-time or part-time, and I invariably say I work part-time, to indicate my many part-time responsibilities as wife, mother, NGO worker, volunteer, student, etc. As an advocate of migrants' concerns, together with several religious and a few lay friends, I helped produce a monthly newsletter for the Filipinos in Rome. It lasted almost two years. For the Philippine Centennial in 1998, six of us Filipino women, mostly UN spouses, produced a handy resource guidebook for the Filipino in Rome, as our contribution to the celebration.

I have sorely missed my extended family, my source of constant support, as well as my friends back in the Philippines, although having e-mail these past few years has certainly brought me closer to home. At the same time, I have been blessed with my "sisters" in Rome, some of whom have come and gone. The others who are still here have not just helped me cope with the physical and material necessities of surviving in the eternal city, but have also led me to deepen my spiritual quest through our regular Wednesday ecumenical bible study and prayer group. Through the years, being a member of this group has become a fundamental part of my life in Rome, where I've learned more about God's word as well as shared prayer requests, praises, and thanksgiving for His never-ending flow of favors and blessings. These are things I had taken so much for granted, or at least never fully acknowledged or appreciated in the past. Our sessions have helped me to absorb the bible's teachings, even as I try to reconcile other interreligious teachings I have read and discovered, while working with a variety of groups and individuals of different religious backgrounds and beliefs.

More recently, I've had the support of a smaller group of women friends. We try to encourage individual members' aspirations, as we collectively and singly move into new directions, including learning new skills in our midlife, and plan ahead to furthering our goals and fulfillment of life.

Throughout our stay in Rome, my husband has been my constant pillar of support. He is always ready with encouraging words during my moments of insecurity, and he gives me the freedom to pursue my myriad interests and passions, and to discover my inner stirrings. He was very understanding of my unceasing complaints in our first years in Rome, and my consistent harping to go back to the Philippines, even *sans* family. From a relationship sometimes described by some of our friends as rather competitive, given our similar concerns, background, and general skills, we have developed what I believe to be a relationship that is much more complementary and facilitating of each other's growth and development. Being together in Rome with only our small family to provide the emotional and moral support to one another has helped bind us more tightly as a family. For this I am ever grateful. I've learned to appreciate that my husband is the mainstay of our financial resources that allows me to do the things I've been doing. He has told me that maybe we could exchange roles in the near future and that he can in turn become the consultant pursuing his interests, while I become the primary income earner. It is an idea to which I'm very open.

My children, too, have become a real source of joy, despite often trying times as they passed through their own adolescent difficulties. I've had to learn new skills and adopt new attitudes as a mother, particularly in being more accepting. Just as some of my skills in working and dealing with NGOs and others helped me in my role as school board member, or working with various other organizations, they have helped me cope and understand my children a little better. My recurrent guilt feelings at my seeming neglect of their needs in their earlier years have not helped, and I avoid replaying them in my mind. I am glad, though, that we never at any time completely gave up on one another, and that our relationships are now much more relaxed and basically supportive and congenial. We are finding new avenues for interaction and enjoying each other's company, hopefully more and more.

While my children study in an American school, raising Filipino kids in an Italian environment put a tremendous strain on both my husband and me and on our children. Many times pressures from several cultures have created an identity crisis for my kids, as I'm sure other Filipino children living abroad have generally experienced. We continually remind our children they are *Pinoys* and must therefore behave or act as such, whatever that may mean sometimes. Yet, having lived outside the Philippines for the major part of their lives, they have also become as much American, or even Italian, in many ways, a reality that my husband and I have found hard to accept. Peer pressure to conform to different norms would contradict whatever we as parents would say.

Over the years, and through our tears and frustrations with one another, between my husband and myself, between the children and ourselves, my husband and I have come to realize, even if a bit reluctantly, that while we hope our children will imbibe what we believe are strong Filipino traits and values, such as family closeness, we also understand that they have equally imbibed Western traits such as early independence and speaking out their minds. Many of our clashes have sprung from this, and it has helped us as parents, and our children, to understand where we are all coming from and to appreciate the need to try to integrate the best values from the cultures to which we are exposed. I know it is a dilemma shared by many Filipino parents who raise their children abroad for a prolonged period.

LIFE IN ROME has certainly evolved for me — from the initial excitement, then restlessness and boredom, even frustration and despair, to seeking new challenges and opportunities where they present themselves. While I still have moments of discontent and impatience, gone are the days when waking up in the morning would leave me wondering what I would do next with my life, and before I knew it, the day would have passed by without my having done anything worthwhile, resulting in strong feelings of frustration with myself and the erosion of my self-esteem.

I have accepted that home is where my family is. And it is where I should be, and that, for the moment, is Rome. Much as I pine to be back in Manila or some other part of the Philippines, as I will eventually be over the next few years (even if my family and friends no longer quite believe it), I have learned that I make my own life and I should make it wherever I may be. It is therefore on the day-to-day that I must focus, while not losing sight of the longer-term vision.

My regret earlier on was that my career has not gone on a straight path, or at least not as straight and clear-cut as I would have wanted it to be, with a stable and regular income. The terrible vacuum that I often felt no longer bothers me as much. I am less discontented, even as I follow the same "career path" of a so-called international or global "NGI" (nongovernmental individual). A friend recently pointed out that in fact my career has taken a clear direction but not in the traditional mode with which I had been looking at it. What I perceived to be the lack of semblance of a career which covered so many diverse, often seemingly unrelated, types of work and activities, completely lacking a sense of being whole, is in fact a career that is often grounded in a multicultural setting that involves among others, linking groups and individuals with shared concerns and interests, learning and sharing new ideas, new skills, and new approaches to problems and work.

All these, I have realized, are part of a continuum, beginning as far back as my student activist days in high school and in university in the early Seventies, to my decision to work on social justice and development concerns with NGOs whose work my extended family could never quite understand, and now includes migrant issues — to living in Bangkok, then Manila, and now Rome.

I am hopeful that I can still finish my doctoral studies by the year 2001, while I continue to pursue many interests, causes, and activities. I am particularly excited and challenged in this promising yet worrying turn of the century where we can help to shape what the next millennium will be like, with a much greater concern for the earth's sustainability through a rediscovery of, and a return to, spiritual values.

I also want to continue with the things I relish doing. These include going places, taking relatives, friends, and friends of friends around to discover the beautiful churches and ancient sites in the city, exploring the museums alone or with others, doing *tai chi*, going to concerts, sharing a meal while discussing the latest news and *tsismis* from home, maybe even taking up ballroom dancing, which I enjoy, while we are still in Rome. Our home has been open to relatives, friends, and acquaintances when they visit, and we continue to enjoy hosting all those who pass through our *pensione*.

I tell myself that I should never live in mediocrity and resignation to my situation, unlike the way I started out living here. God has made life simply too full and exciting for that.

Elizabeth Medina

Discovering
My Filipinas
in Chile

I AM A FILIPINO woman, born in 1954 in a Philippines then living the apex of its Americanization, to parents just recently recovered from the shocks and hardships of the war, whose ultimate dream became immigration to the United States. My education created in me a total identification with American culture and a desire to leave my country, which I saw as a strangely silent, empty place, though I was deeply bonded to her at the somatic level — in my love for the rich smell of her moist, fertile earth; for the calm warmth of her seas; for the soothing murmur of her bamboo forests and country streams.

My family immigrated to San Francisco in 1973 when I was 19 years old, but three months later I left the poor basement apartment that my mother had installed us in (perhaps provisionally, perhaps forever — she did not say), to forge my own way of life. I did this because I did not identify with my parents' materialistic values nor with their fear of a hostile world. I was an idealist and this was not well considered by my mother, the head of our household. My father, Juan Medina, who had stayed behind in Manila until his retirement from San Miguel Corporation became formalized, died of a heart attack in Honolulu, when he was traveling to join my mother and siblings six months later. Unlike my mother, he supported my idealistic aims, but he was never a forceful presence in my life. My father was a charming and cultured man who was, however, withdrawn and reserved within the family, preferring to leave the important decisions in the hands of his astute, take-charge wife.

I had just become a member of Siloism, a movement for simultaneous personal and social change founded in Argentina in 1969. Five young Chileans arrived in Manila in 1973 and one of them became my teacher at the Alliance Française. They had escaped the Chilean coup by a hair, part of a large group that spread out to several countries to make known the ideas of Mario Rodríguez Cobos, whose pseudonym was Silo. Though I was afraid of my family's censure and of being brainwashed, I took a gamble because their expressed ideals were mine — to work for self-knowledge and a new, nonviolent, planetary human consciousness. I went to live with a Chilean couple in Berkeley, then later found an apartment which I shared with another young woman. In my mind, I then became an American and began a new life.

For almost 10 years I lived in the US, but I was really within a microculture that existed in parallel to the mainstream. I had no contact with other Filipinos, only with Americans, Chileans, and Argentines. In this sense, my story is not a typical one. I did not finish my college education because I had to support myself working as a secretary. My free time was devoted to the movement activities: group meetings for self-knowledge and study, seminars and retreats, and, in 1973-74, campaigns to call public attention to the Chilean and Argentine Siloists who were imprisoned and tortured by the military regimes. Later we studied stress reduction techniques which I and my friends later taught in free courses at the University of San Francisco, the YMCA, to public school teachers, and in our groups of personal work. After living in the Bay Area for five years, I moved to Washington, D.C., and started groups there. It was in 1981, when I attended a public event organized by movement members to "Humanize the Earth" in Mexico City, that I met my future Chilean husband.

Because of love, I returned to the Third World and painfully severed my ties with the US. I had never become a US citizen because some part of me didn't want to give up my nationality. By the time I wanted US citizenship, it was too late. I had learned Spanish in the movement, but when I arrived in Chile I could not understand the cultural codes and I might as well not have known the language, considering how little it served me. I was also now a part of a German-Jewish family — an odd situation, as Germans, according to my American education, were supposedly barbarians whose culture was to be disparaged, if not shunned. On the other hand, Jewishness, according to my Filipino Catholic culture, was synonymous to "bad person" because the Jews had killed Christ. As for the language, though my father had spoken Spanish, I believed it had nothing to do with me and so resisted speaking it. I grieved within myself for the loss of American music, American books, American food, and my American friendships. I was now a housewife, financially dependent on my partner and responsible for running his home. We were also immersed in a movement culture in Chile, but a much more numerous one that was extremely hierarchical and vertically oriented, like Chilean society. For six years I was to struggle with attitudes I could not understand: chasms between the social classes, between the sexes, and with my own marginality as a foreigner and as a woman who firmly believed she was a free agent, but who now found herself bound by strict social rules and narrow roles.

There was, however, an upside. I was in an interesting place where I could make a meaningful contribution. The military regime was in crisis and the movement became an important democratic political force. We were nonviolent organizers and the first ones who dared to openly enlist people to the cause of calling for Augusto Pinochet's resignation and free elections. A party was formed — the Humanist Party, with a colorful and positive discourse. When the 1986 revolution took place in the Philippines and ousted Marcos, I became its spokesperson when we showed a video of it at meetings in the poorer municipalities of Santiago. I risked deportation with my activities, but I simply tried to be discreet and intelligent. At any rate, the Marxists and Communists — and the defenseless poor — were the main targets of military and right-wing violence.

I began to understand my new milieu and found myself bonding with Chileans, who were, after all, quite similar to Filipinos in their warmth and hospitality toward foreigners. Anywhere I went, I was automatically accepted and even fussed over. A typical reaction was, "Ah! Marcos made a fool out of Pinochet!" In the early Eighties, Ferdinand Marcos's refusal to allow Pinochet to land in Manila, forcing the dictator to fly directly back to Chile, was a diplomatic embarrassment that gave the entire country something to laugh about. It probably was the only moment when Marcos became the most well-liked politician in the world. Another stock response was, "Julio Iglesias' gorgeous ex-wife is a Filipina!" For the first time, I was around people to whom meeting a Filipino was practically a cultural event, because to them we were exotic and special. Besides which, in terms of sensibility, of "skin feeling," I always felt at home even if I didn't understand everything that was going on. It was so unlike in the States, where one could understand everything that was happening and yet not quite feel emotionally at ease.

After I became a mother to my wonderful daughter and son, my assimilation became complete. I came to value and respect the Jewish traditions and love for culture that Lisa, my Berlin-born mother-in-law, communicated to me. When I went back to school, I began to understand the Chileans' past and their cultural mindset. In their history I saw the reflection of my own country's past and suddenly realized that the profound meanings of our own colonization by Spain had been forgotten; only their shadowy outlines remained in our history books.

DISCOVERY of Chilean culture brought with it many gifts. In Chillán, an old city south of Santiago, I met poets for the first time. I realized that Chile had great traditions of theater, poetry, literature — and democracy. As I began to understand how Latin America perceived North America, I also saw the parallels between my own country's experience of economic and political co-optation by the US, and what had happened in Chile when US business and geopolitical interests banded with the local aristocracy and the military to overthrow the Allende government.

Chile is like the United States because her strength also arose from the symbiosis between her colonial society and successive waves of European immigrants, beginning with the educators and artists who were attracted to Latin America after the establishment of the new republics in the early 1800s. There was a German wave in the mid-1800s which transformed the thickly forested south into a stunning replica of Bavaria, and the English built Valparaíso and its burgeoning shipping industry when the city was the most important port in the Pacific, before the construction of the Panama Canal. Today, Yugoslavs, Palestinians, Spanish, Italians, French and German Jewish immigrants manifest their cultural presence through their sports and social clubs. A large wave of Jewish immigrants arrived in the late Thirties, when Chile was one of the few countries that accepted them.

My marriage became my direct education on the Holocaust and its tragic human consequences. It is simply different when your mother-in-law tells you about how, at the age of 16, she was told at school one day that she and her brother could no longer continue coming. My husband's father, whom I never met because he died the same year my father did, lost his parents in Auschwitz and himself succeeded in getting out of prison camp only because the camp commander, his former classmate, looked the other way as he escaped. After my daughter was born, my mother-in-law gifted me with a pair of diamond studs that her mother had saved from confiscation by the Nazis. She wore them, Lisa said, only on special days. I treasure them as well.

One day I met a young Jewish Chilean, a translator like me, who had studied in the US. When I told him I was Filipino, he said that in the 16th century there was Inquisition activity in Manila and the people were asked to inform the authorities if they learned of people who prayed over lit candles on Friday nights. The Inquisition is not even mentioned in history classes in the Philippines. My children, who have been raised together with their cousins almost half of the time in their grandmother's home, today sometimes light the Sabbath candles with her on Fridays, and each year they sing and pray with the entire family at Passover before enjoying a scrumptious dinner. I was glad to support my 11-year-old daughter's decision to convert to the Jewish faith and have her bat mitzvah, because I knew it meant that she loved her family and felt grounded in a tradition of faith and survival.

It was another subtle paradox that in Chile, for the first time, I became part of a close-knit Filipino community — the one that revolved around the Philippine Embassy. There were only about 35 Filipinos then in Chile. Most of them were either missionary nuns and priests who labored in poor urban areas in Santiago and isolated rural communities in the south, or Filipino women married to foreign businessmen and diplomats. At a celebration of Philippine independence, I met a Filipino scholar who was pursuing advanced studies in Santiago. He confessed to me that he had been active in the university movement in the Seventies to abolish the teaching of Spanish in the Philippines, and that he now regretted having done so.

But the most significant revelation took place at the Embassy's Christmas dinner in 1990, when I met a Spanish-Filipino who had lived in Santiago for 40 years. He told me that when he was 13 years old and living in Laoag, Ilocos Norte, he had known my grandfather. I was electrified. My grandfather, Emilio Medina, had been executed in 1945 by Filipino guerrillas for collaborating with the Japanese. My father had never spoken of him to us (just as my husband's father never spoke of his own loss). There had only been family legends. This man, Angel García, was the first person I had ever met who had spoken to me about my *Lolo*

Emilio. García gave me the names of people I could interview in Laoag to find out more about my grandfather's death. It so happened that in one month I was set to go to the Philippines with my husband and children. It would be nine years since I had last visited my homeland.

My husband accompanied me on my first trip to the north, and we interviewed several people. We went to the church in Narvacan, Ilocos Sur, behind which my grandfather was executed along with some 18 others. I learned that in the northern provinces the Filipino guerrillas had killed more people than the Japanese had. Later, through correspondence with my aunt who was 16 in 1945 and the last of the family to see my grandfather alive, I learned that his killing had had political undertones. He had been the rival of Ferdinand Marcos's father for a congressional seat and was one of the most important prewar politicians in the influential north. Modesto Farolan, the man appointed to succeed him as governor of Ilocos Norte and who held the position for over two years until war's end, was not, however, death-listed by the guerrillas. My aunt informed me that he was a Marcos cousin.

Most incredible of all, as we drove northward, we saw them: the 400-year-old churches from the Spanish era. I was wonderstruck because I recognized the landscape before me as not Asian, but Latin American.

ON MY RETURN to Santiago, everything suddenly fell into place in my mind and I realized that, though I was indeed North American in mentality and in my educational formation, I was nonetheless Filipino in my soul. And what was "Filipino"? It was, first of all, being a descendant of Indians who, like the Indians of the Caribbean, Mexico, Central and Latin America, had become vassals of the Spanish crown when Columbus discovered the New World. Second, it was being the inheritor of the historical and cultural tragedy of our serial colonization: first by the Spanish for 377 years, and then by the US for 45. This meant that the indigenous inhabitants of the Philippine archipelago had suffered the destruction of their cosmology after the conquistadors arrived in 1521. But in 1898, when the Hispanic Filipinos put an end to Spanish rule with the revolution they had begun in 1896, the Americans immediately annexed the Philippines. In the ensuing 45 years, US rule erased our Hispanic Filipino memory and identity. By totally revamping our educational system, America then gave us the double legacy that became our cultural karmic burden: of wanting to be something we could never be — white Americans with brown skin — and of renouncing the Philippines because we could do nothing for her; she already belonged to the privileged others. We would be better off leaving her for the real Land of Promise — the United States — and choosing assured material comfort above the perils of laboriously carving an uncertain destiny in our damaged, despoiled country.

I also realized that I was the continuation of my grandfather's spirit. He was a nationalist, a gentleman, an idealist — a complex and courageous man. The war had placed him in a position of checkmate. As a prominent citizen of Laoag and a former congressman, his decisions became heavy with implication. When, instead of fleeing to the mountains like the elected governor, he dealt with the Japanese in the interest of protecting lives and property, he walked into no man's land and became marked for death. He was indeed, in technical terms, a collaborator. But to me, the violence of the Filipino "bad" guerrillas effectively mooted the issue. Emilio was executed by order of an American, a self-designated major named John O'Day, a miner before the war who, as a guerrilla leader, made himself notorious as a killer and rapist.

My grandfather was captured as he tried to reach the Americans who had landed in Darigayo in preparation for the advance on the north, and who had already issued strict orders to the guerrillas to stop all killings.

All of these revelations had to be written down and passed on to my countrymen and women, and this is what I have done. Had I never left the Philippines, had I never lived my American dream and later followed a new dream of love to an unknown continent, I could never have realized that my Filipino heritage was so vast and rich; nor could I have heard its compelling voice, asking to be rescued from oblivion, and finally understood.

CALIFORNIANS were pretty much the Americans that I expected to find and become one of. I already knew that the warm, easygoing, humanitarian G.I. was a mostly mythical creature that arose from the liberation of the Philippines in 1945. However, in San Francisco I did find, to my joy, the American culture that I sought: tolerance — I would even say an automatic acceptance — of all cultures, a strong Asian presence, and an utterly relaxed bonhomie that I have come to consider the very best trait of the ordinary, unassuming but tremendously creative, resourceful, and fun-loving American.

That, however, was San Francisco in the Seventies. In Washington, D.C., in the Eighties, I received a totally different impression of who and what America was. There I became aware for the first time of how deeply etched into the American psyche the color line was, and of the continuing corrosive effects of racial violence on Americans' collective life. I also acquired the beginnings of a new consciousness that official America — the White House, the Pentagon, the State Department, and the International Monetary Fund — was an entirely separate dimension of the American reality. They constituted the spheres of power, influence, and might. They were the economic, political, and military juggernaut that policed the world in the name of the American people.

In California I had felt accepted and esteemed by my bosses. I felt I was considered their equal, albeit fulfilling a different function. In Washington, D.C., I had another feeling. There was a subtly imperial air among the senior lawyers and partners in the environmental law firm I first worked for. I detected for the first time the aura of privilege and wealth from which Anglo-Saxon American culture derived its most subtle glamour and power. Then, when I worked for the World Bank, I was crushed by the realization that I was no longer a professional (in California one was a professional if one earned one's living doing what one did), but merely "nonprofessional staff," which meant that I had no degrees from the most important universities in the world, nor was I being groomed for political and economic protagonism in my home country. It was in the World Bank where I determined never to be a secretary again, when I realized that there was a glass wall between those who were important and those who were not, and that I was being sent unequivocal signals of what my place was. Ultimately, not even a tax-free salary and an excellent benefits package could adequately compensate for the feeling of being a party to my self-devaluation. Though I was glad to learn what I did from that world, I left with a deep sense of release.

As a volunteer worker for the illumination of the greater world, I also realized that in the United States people talked about information but did not like to discuss ideas and — even less — feelings and inner experiences. There was a great fear of the emotions, near panic at any prospect of opening oneself up to almost certain manipulation and emotional damage. In the end, I became just as frightened by the alienating reactions I received from those I ingenuously approached to suggest the need to humanize our interactions and relationships. In Chile, however, though people were much more comfortable simply being together, they didn't have much interest in ideas or in what was happening in the larger world. They were also curiously unable to verbalize their feelings, in contrast to Americans of the "New Age" self-help culture, who seemed to verbalize too much without saying enough, tending to use language about the emotions mainly for complaining and demanding attention.

Whereas in the States, to be an individual with a clear personality was a guarantee of positive feedback, in Chile it was the exact opposite: it guaranteed that people would soon leave you alone because they preferred the company of people who looked, acted, and talked like them. They were not comfortable with individuality. It was a society that worshipped tradition, where it was de rigueur to toe the line and not stand out, and that often punished talent unless it was backed by a prestigious family name, a prestigious national or foreign university, a prestigious anything.

Chileans, however, clearly had a deep identification with their country. Any Chilean who lived abroad never let go of the dream of someday going home. They were in this sense very different from Americans and Filipinos. Whereas Americans seemed to like living in the States because it was, above all, logistically the most comfortable place for them to be, even Chileans who had attained great professional success abroad always missed the land, longed for their *empanadas* (meat pies), and pined for their future reunion with the beloved family. They rhapsodized about their country spontaneously and feelingly, even humorously.

Filipinos, on the other hand, were silent. They avoided discussing anything. Though unfailingly cordial, they were hermetic and inscrutable. Filipinos mostly dreamed of retiring in the Philippines, but only those who had been raised there, and only if they could take back a well-lined wallet. Otherwise, they simply resigned themselves to exile. Chileans who returned to Chile for visits took with them their beautiful, happy children, well-dressed and carrying gifts and toys for their cousins, aunts, and uncles. Filipinos took enormous bales of foodstuff, as if the jumbo jet they would travel on were carrying out a mission of disaster relief.

Americans, of course, either carried a briefcase or a knapsack, and a novel. They wandered all over the world to see, to take photographs, to record data, to establish alliances, and then they returned to their country with anecdotes, new impressions, new conclusions to air in their well-informed conversations. But always in a tone of scientific observation, somewhat removed from it all, objective observers, distant, unidentified.

Always much too busy, too jaded, too "been there, done that." Only war or mass death and destruction could produce deep emotion in them. They seemed to need to go out to the Third World to make contact with simple humanity, but in controlled doses. They had nothing new to learn about anything. Theirs was a well-informed kind of ignorance.

When I was leaving for a new life in the US, I was ecstatic and expectant. When I was flying to Santiago de Chile for the first time, I was full of optimism and conviction that I would feel instantly at home. Both times I experienced deep disillusionment, although in the United States it was a gradual and subtle process, whereas in Chile, though it was almost instantaneous, I unconsciously denied it for many years.

And yet, thanks to the United States, I developed autonomy and affirmed my right and my capacity to create my own way of life. Though she was impermeable to my attempts to change her, she allowed me space for experimentation and learning.

Chile was my chance to express my rejection of authoritarianism. It was there where I learned about democracy, how important it was to think about politics and participate in social mobilization. She was also my difficult testing ground, where crude experience taught me that such basic concepts as women's rights and fraternity, equality and justice, were still just words outside the US. And yet, paradoxically, she made me remember what I had forgotten for many years — that the Third World was as good a place to live in as the First, and that in many ways it was better, precisely because there was so much to be done, so much new ground to be broken, and thus one could still make a difference. Finally, she allowed me to develop important and unsuspected aspects of myself that would enable me to return to my country with a glad heart and a project of cultural renewal.

AS FOR THE Philippines, though I abandoned her, she never left me and finally reclaimed me as her daughter.

She could never have achieved it, though, without the collusion of her cousin, Chile, who conspired with her to lead me home. For Chile was not only where I learned about my grandfather, but also where I discovered the first and most important biography of Rizal, published by the Spaniard W.E. Retana in 1907 in Madrid. During my studies in Santiago in 1990, I learned of the biography upon reading a book on the unpublished letters of Miguel de Unamuno. When I obtained a copy of the biography in Madrid, I realized it had to be translated into English so that the Filipino youth could learn about Rizal from one who could tell them about those times, because he had lived through them as a conscious witness.

Difficult years followed after my marriage ended in 1993. My mother, Felisa Seno, now became my pillar of strength, sustaining me through economic uncertainty and emotional hardship, giving the support only she could provide in a dark time of abandonment and isolation. It would be thanks to her that I would later succeed in publishing my translation of the Rizal biography in Chile, in time for the Centennial.

In 1998 my mother's ancestral legacy to me became clear. Once again through serendipity, I discovered that her birth mother was a young girl named Petra Cañete, from the legendary family of *eskrimadores* of Cebu, who trace their lineage back to the arrival of the conquistadors. I finally understood the origins of my mother's tough warrior-woman nature, my deep identification with the poor, my anger at injustice and oppression.

Thus, a girl who believed she had no country and no birthright discovered that she possessed one of the richest histories of all. Fate had interwoven the destinies of the Philippines, Spain, and the United States in hidden strands that created the invisible pattern of my life; and Chile, on the continent where realism was married to magic, revealed to me the unity to which my heart had been blind before — revealed the burden, the magic and the promise of being Filipino.

I am who I am because of three countries, three worlds. My children have three families on three continents and they are richer and happier for it, just as I am. In the end, I can say that I discovered that the world does in fact belong to us, and we belong to the world. The First, Third and Fourth Worlds are within us. The Philippines, the United States, and Chile have all given me and taught me to accept the best and the worst of each of them, and to love them all, as I have come to love all of myself. The most meaningful task is to continue to grow and build on the basis of learning, experience, acceptance, and to realize that you are the continuation of the world. You are a force that can destroy, and that can create.

What is most important, then, is clarity with respect to one's goals, built over a basic awareness and acceptance of who and what one is. In the end, yes — the First, the Third and the Fourth Worlds are within us, and we are empowered to join them in our own lives and create a new New World.

Lucia "Ciay" Misa

The Way to the Heart Is from Inside Out

EVER SINCE I can remember, my biggest blessing (and oftentimes my downfall) has been my impulsive nature. I have always trusted my instincts and they have led me to uncharted territories. Yet I have always felt protected and fearless. I recognize in me my mother's Batangueña pride, strong will, and passionate temper. From my father, I inherited sensuousness, a love of nature, and romantic idealism. Although I lost my father when I was 20, I have felt connected to him all these years.

My rebellion against conformity and tradition has always been innate. It is no wonder that 20 years ago, at the age of 28 (pretty late by today's standards), I broke away from my mother's protection and from the rules and rigidity of claustrophobic Manila. Being the fifth child with seven siblings must have made me independent and resourceful. After a month's visit to my sister in Paris, I found myself in America, specifically in Boston, with $300.00 to my name, actually a loan from a friend. With sheer determination, my fiancé and I were able to secure visas at a time when travel outside the Philippines was banned.

Once in Boston, I was in my element. I was free to do whatever I wanted to do and to be whoever I wanted to become. But living conditions were very limited: I was trapped in the suburbs and living with my fiancé's cousin. The promised job fell through. I did house chores to pay for my keep and accepted menial contracts here and there. In those nine months I saved every cent to pay back a wealthy uncle who had lent me the money for my ticket. That Christmas was my loneliest. I resisted calling home because I had left without my mother's blessings. She had become widowed by then and started an export business. My family presumed that I was doing well.

My fiancé's cousin and her husband decided to open a retail store on Boston's Newbury Street that would sell Philippine wicker furniture and accessories. They asked my mother to be the supplier. The store, which I named Sari-Sari, was a big success. But my engagement to my fiancé fell apart, and so did my commitment to the store. Fortunately, our next-door neighbor, the biggest florist in Boston, was looking for a direct source of baskets for his many stores and offered to set me up as a partner in the basket business. From one frying pan, I jumped into another. Yet, as always, my Papa assured me it was a good decision. I remember that after I accepted the partnership, I called Mom and exclaimed, "Ma, *hindi na tayo pobre!*" (Ma, we're no longer poor!)

I knew nothing about operating an import company. My background was communication and television production, but there I was, across the Boston Flower Exchange, with a basket import company we called Luzon Imports. I hired a helper every now and then, but for the first few months I was alone, unloading containers, mopping floors, accounting for money that poured in. Beautiful baskets from the Philippines were a prime commodity then.

I worked hard and played hard. I even had my wild days but stayed away from Filipinos and gossip. Eventually, my mother and I bought out my partner and I continued to operate the small but profitable company.

I never envisioned myself getting married. I had been living with Michael for three years when my mother and my grandmother came to visit. I had to justify my living with this man. So the prospect of marriage came up, and it was effortless and timely. Here was a man who never complained about anything. I was convinced he was the only man who could bear living with me.

When I gave birth to our daughter Cristina, Michael had to take over the New York Gift Show for me. From then on he became involved in Luzon Imports, and he gave up his own cash-strapped business. We worked very well together, and every Christmas traveled to the Philippines for vacation and business. In 1986 I was blessed with my son Eric, whom I have always recognized as my father's reincarnation.

The year after Eric was born, we refinanced the brownstone building in the city that my mother had helped us buy. Its value had increased tremendously. We were able to purchase a beautiful home by a lake in New Hampshire two hours away from the noisy city. I fell in love with this enchanted paradise. Here my children spent the most wonderful weekends and summers carousing in the woods, swimming to different islands, communing with the animals, and living the essence of yoga in the wild. To reinforce this, I taught "balance and movement" at their Montessori school for several years.

I became attached to the pristine waters. To this day, whenever I go to New Hampshire, I make it a morning ritual to dive into the lake whatever the season, except when the lake is frozen. Many a night I have swum under a full moon, singing with the loons. It is here that I learned how to windsurf, and to watch for deer and moose.

In 1987 my brother Lito, who was my first meditation teacher, encouraged me to start conducting workshops during my annual home visits. That same year, I experienced my "spiritual awakening" while studying with a delightful couple, Angela and Victor, in Greece. They taught a controversial free-form yoga that broke all traditional rules of this ancient practice. Just by watching Angela in ecstatic meditation, I recognized the source as sexual energy. I decided to try it in evening meditation. Sure enough, as I relaxed and let my breath fall all the way to my sexual regions, a dynamic energy penetrated my skin, physically exploding every cell in my body. I was very conscious of hot steam from my groins spiraling as cool energy along my spine. The energy engulfed me entirely. It then melted away the hard armor of muscular strength I had developed through all those years of fanatical practice, the result of my obsession with perfecting the poses and always being too hard on myself. I realized that I was stuck in my front body, always pushing forward.

It was exhilarating to discover the back body. I learned to fall, let go, inward and out to energies bigger than myself. I finally understood how energy flowed through my body. The next morning I was doing extreme forward bends, the only pose I could not do in all those 10 years of rigid yoga training. Angela and Victor used powerful visualizations that my new inner body was obeying literally, word for word.

From that day on, my whole body chemistry changed. I was no longer loose and flexible. Now I was doing yoga from inside out and it made me more sensitive to pain and suffering. My hands could now massage and heal. I found myself dancing endlessly without any effort, led simply by the natural fluid motions of my body. Life slowed down, my morning exercises turned to prayer and praise to my Maker. What started in 1972 as an obsession to beautify my body was transformed into an exploration of inner beauty. The body's well-being came as an after-effect! The new openings in my body literally flowed through my heart, and I became a better wife and mother.

I was so empowered by Angela that unconsciously I became attached to her tutelage. I organized a workshop in Boracay for her and Victor that catered mostly to their European students. An attempted military coup d'etat, however, abruptly put an end to it. Instead, I attended their workshops all over America. I wanted to learn more and more. One day, at an all-women workshop in Harbin Springs, California, the umbilical cord was severed. For seven whole days Angela ignored me completely. She tore me to pieces when I asked her a question in class. I was so hurt, even if she anointed me goddess of water at the end of the seminar. Afterwards, she wrote me a beautiful card explaining how she could not understand it either but she knew that she had to put an end to the childish hero-worship. She acknowledged me as her equal. It was then that I was initiated as a teacher. That was the year before I held my own first workshop in Boracay.

THE YOGA I practice is the path of inner body exploration. This is the fruit of my many years of studies with various yoga masters. *"Talikwas"* was a reminder for both them and me that what we came to explore was a life process, a discipline that required a complete reversal of our thought patterns. It was "soft belly yoga" then, and after the first workshop we baptized it *"Talikwas,"* meaning inside out.

In 1989, in response to my students' queries — What lessons can we take home? How do we practice without you? When will you be back? — after a five-day yoga workshop at Mount Banahaw, these words and images came to me dreamlike, flowing through my pen:

Talikwas	*Inside out*
Yakapin ang dilim	*Embrace the darkness*
Talikuran ang pangarap	*Abandon your dream*
Ibuhos ang laman	*Empty what is within*
Bumalik sa sinapupunan	*Return to innocence*
Ang puso ng tao	*The heart*
Ay bubukas lamang	*Opens to receive*
Ng patalikwas	*Only from inside out.*

As in many acquired skills, *Talikwas* involves defying gravity. By falling into our center "pit" and waiting for the deep belly exhalation to bounce back up, we release the spine's energy that allows us to stretch in all directions. As the energy spirals up to the chest cavity, it literally "opens" the heart and the eyes. The effect can induce drastic life changes.

There is a lot of resistance to this intimate physical exercise. It is safer and more appealing to be encased in beautiful external poses or *asanas*, as they are called in India. But what the body truly feels inside is the essence —

the sophisticated art of effortless fluid movement from a dynamic and balanced center is more enduring in the end. Mount Banahaw was the ideal setting for this process of emptying, waiting, and listening. We imbibed the sweet breath of the mountain wind. We melted in the healing waters of the waterfalls. We absorbed the earth's energy through the soles of our feet. Powerful imagery from nature translated into electrical currents that touched our skins, opening each pore, until we could once again feel specific body parts that had hardened, numbed out, or collapsed from trauma and pain. Armors of hard, tight muscles gave in as fears and tensions were washed away by the rhythmic breath.

In the mornings we spent four hours of uninterrupted relaxed breathing, visualization, stretching, and soundings. I used my hands, and at times my whole body, like a hammock to support the students in places where they needed to fall. Once they found a deep, delicious breath in their back bellies, I would guide them with simple visualizations: "As you release your imaginary tail, glide forward slowly with the belly breath, spreading your wings from behind. Keep falling back to gather spaces with your breath, while the outer body just goes along for the ride. Feel new life at the back of your knees. Now connect to the floating energy from the back of your ears to the spaces over your head." It was fun, but in reality it was intense work that required very precise concentration.

After a sumptuous lunch, we embarked on spontaneous adventures. We meditated and merged with the mountain's sacred elements. At night, while the world slept, we floated in the cool rivers. In the echoes of the pitch-black caves, we discovered our voices after blowing out the candles. We cried under the Sacred Falls. We slept on top of Mount Kalbaryo under the moonlight. At sunset we meditated amidst dancing winds and sky. We did backbends on rock altars, balanced on top of enormous boulders. We snaked our way into narrow twisting tunnels. We climbed, walked, and swam in complete harmony with the mountain's breath and our newly awakened breathing.

These wild activities were a first experience for many. Howling like a pack of wolves and chanting in little "chapels" inside the sacred caves seemed so natural at the moment.

In the morning sessions we discovered that those who had never had any yoga training had an easier time tapping the deep energy source, unlike those who were trained to hold poses by muscle and flexibility.

In preparation for these five-day workshops, I usually arrived the day before to unload my ego and surrender to the mountain. I had to be alone. At

208

that time, 10 years ago, Mount Banahaw was completely safe and unspoiled. It was an indescribable experience to be one with nature. Most unforgettable was the night of the full moon. Fascinated by the life of St. Francis and his love for the caves of Assisi, I requested our caretaker's sons to escort me to the mountain's "belly." This was the sacred cave used by the locals as a confessional where they would crawl in one at a time and weep their sorrows. My remarkable encounter with the full moon is recorded in my journal:

Communion with the Full Moon

The earth stood still
As I traveled into timeless space
To my past, present and future.
Ah, precious longest six hours of pure existence
Until every pore lay open to receive her Beam.
As she emerged atop the mountain,
I followed obediently with silent guides.
Up, up to the Secret Cave they delivered me.
Every leaf, every stone, every insect
Pulsated with life, basking in her light.
I melted into the rocks and the soft earth.
Whole body breathed with the crickets' song
Until my eyes finally merged with hers-
Eye to eye, soul to soul.
As the seconds stretched to hours,
My feet led me into my womb/tomb cave
Where solitude and companionship,
Life and death, joy and pain are one.
Conversing with my shadow cast upon the wall,
I met old friends and new friends.
Then came my deepest slumber into eternity.
It must have been twilight
When she roused me in all her glory
Pouring her radiance into my being.
Dreamless sleep engulfed me again
Until she bid me farewell at dawn.
As I gazed up, she slowly dipped into the daylight.

WHILE MICHAEL was obsessed with business and the material world, I had become involved in healing, teaching, and meditating which opened doors to a whole series of creative impulses. We started spending a lot of time apart. He was often out of town participating in all the major trade shows, flying to the Philippines twice a year, going to sports events with his friends. With fellow free spirits I traveled to exotic nature retreats, usually mountains and oceans.

To open my throat chakra, I started taking singing lessons from a talented soprano who used exactly the same images as my breathing techniques. Singing arias was fun and challenging. I apprenticed with an extraordinary rolfer and exchanged sessions with a pranic master who recognized my "movement by feeling." I worked with a world-famous Filipino filmmaker who edited a video of my workshop so that his son could learn the principles of *Talikwas*. Finally, I recorded my *Talikwas* song with a popular songwriter and singer whom I idolized. It seemed that every wish I made came true, only because I was merely following instincts and impulses. I traveled to Bali with a dear friend, climbed the vortexes of Sedona with my family, visited a Hopi reservation and made friends with a Hopi elder, and had so many other exciting adventures. The climax of it all was my life's dream to climb Mount Apo, the tallest mountain in the Philippines.

For many years the magnificent mountain where rare species of plants, birds, and insects thrive had been "held hostage" by leftist terrorist groups. Fortunately, it was protected from tourists and thrill-seekers. When the leftists abandoned the mountain I made plans to climb it, but each time I tried, something would prevent me, such as inclement weather and my two pregnancies. But in May of 1996, I knew it would happen. Annafer, one of the participants in *Talikwas*, invited me to visit her forest home at the foothills of the mountain's base and promised to procure the best guide for me. My family started discouraging me. "Don't be foolish, it's too risky... there are all kinds of kidnappings lately... the weather is too dangerous..." I appreciated my family's concern, but I knew that I was going to be safe. I trusted Anna and so I pursued my plan. It reminded me of my first escape to America, that one can pursue one's dreams without the help of an overprotective family.

The whole journey was magical. At Anna's artist's studio, I met Susing, my guide. He decided that Jun, the cook's 14-year-old son, would join us. We took the only trail used by the villagers, and it started from Anna's backyard! As we hiked through each village, I enjoyed the warmth and friendliness of the mountain people, who greeted us with beautiful smiles. There were breath-

taking views of waterfalls, rivers, and foliage laden with all kinds of wildflow-
ers. Atop the mountain the following night, I was in heaven. What a grand
sensation of being 10,000 feet high under the glorious night sky! This was
my special union with God. Life was rich and full. I thought of my children,
and my husband Michael who was so understanding.

In 1991 Michael and my mother developed a new line of products called
Twigs. Michael designed a whole line of topiaries, wreaths, trellises, balls,
and fairy furniture, and my mother breathed life into them using a black
vine from the jungles. These were used by florists as bases and armatures for
dried and silk flowers. Twigs became a sensation overnight, creating a niche
in the floral and craft industry, and Michael made a name for himself since
all the major distributors wanted to sell the line. Chinese suppliers immediately copied it, but their vines were brownish and lacquered and did not
exude the same charm and warmth as Twigs. I was thrilled for Michael, and
stayed in the background. I was glad that unlike me, he enjoyed working
with the salesmen. Everyone thought he was the owner.

My mother became increasingly uncomfortable that Michael had taken
full control of the business and that I was relegated to purchasing and managing the employees (no easy job). I did not worry about it. I trusted him. I
became more and more involved in my *Talikwas*. He was happy. I was happy.
Finally, a confrontation regarding money and control erupted between my
mother and Michael, and I was caught in the middle. It was a no-win situation. It affected me deeply and caused the first big dent in my marriage.
Somehow the problem was temporarily resolved by a message conveyed to
me in a dream — that I was not to meddle and that Michael and Mom each
had to deal with their own issues. They settled the issue eventually, but it left
a permanent strain in their relationship.

PAIN, IT IS SAID, is a masterful teacher. I remember when I first encountered Thelma, the bone-setter shaman in 1994. My students had been raving
about her healing powers and suggested that we meet. They told her I was an
excellent teacher of breath-work. She looked at me and started her diagno-
sis: "Your eyes are sagging (somehow I had started running a fever), your
cheekbones are caving in, making your face even smaller, your shoulder is
out of alignment, and since you were carried the wrong way in your mother's
womb, you have a block in your energy flow. I think you need help."

With that, she started clawing at me like some wild animal, almost
breaking every bone in my body. Somehow I trusted her. I melted under her

power and started crying. I admitted that my marriage was suffering. I remembered and felt all the pains I had blocked in my late teens. After she was done with me, my body was aflame, throbbing. I felt vulnerable and wounded, yet relieved and somehow empowered.

The next day I proceeded to Mount Banahaw for my fourth workshop. I was still weak from the slight fever, and felt very subdued and low-key. Yet my students later told me that I had improved tremendously from the previous year and that I had become more human and approachable. The energy of the workshop was overwhelming. Many participants were grappling with intense pain: either cancer, the recent death of a loved one, or major life crises.

I myself was dealing with the cancer of my sister Reza who, like me, had migrated to America. A few months earlier, she had dreamt that she had breast cancer. Her doctor later confirmed it when she went for a checkup. Uncannily, it was on the same day that Mariel Francisco, my soul mate and dearest friend who organized my workshops in the Philippines, came to Boston to take her sister Bette to an alternative healing center for cancer. I ended up teaching *Talikwas* to the terminal patients there in exchange for attending classes on natural healing from raw foods and wheat grass juices. Diet became a major part of Reza's healing. Bette eventually passed away in the Philippines, while Reza had a mastectomy and fought her disease like a gladiator. When she attended *Talikwas* that year, she gave strength and inspiration to everyone.

At the end of the workshop, I shared this poem which Benilda Santos translated into Filipino. Benilda is a poet who inspired me to write in verses and taught me that words can also allow me to fly and spread my wings.

The Path of Pain	*Ang Landas ng Sakit*
Within the Sacred Receptacle	*Sa loob ng banal na*
	Sisidlang-Katawan
Life ebbs and flows	*Umaagos ang ilog ng buhay.*
Absorbing every vibration of emotion.	*Sa bawat pintig ng damdamin*
Rhythmic movements	*Walang tigil ang indayog:*
fly and fall	*ang paglipad at pagbagsak*
sway and bounce	*ang paghapay at pagtalbog*
open and close	*ang pagbukas at pagsara*
suck in and spill out.	*ang pagsipsip at pagbuga.*

Blood curdles; pus, tears,	Nakukurta ang dugo; nana, luha
semen alchemize.	at tamod naghahalo.
Heart, nerve, vessels throb and burst;	Puso, ugat, daluyan ay kumikibot
	at sumasabog
As violent forces defeat the weaker,	Kapag ang Sisidlang-Bukas
	ay dinahas
Boulders collapse:	Guguho ang mga tipak na bato
Bruising	Manunugat
Piercing	Manunuot
Shattering	Mangwawasak.
In the dark stench,	Sa masangsang na kadiliman
Worms feed on decaying bowels	Gumagapang sa binti
	ang mga uod
	Na naginginain sa nabubulok
	na dumi
Until all is still and numb.	Hanggang ang lahat maging pipi
	at manhid
Then from the deep Source	Mula sa malalim na Bukal
The great avalanche pours out	Bumubulwak ang daluyong
Exhaling in opposite directions	Inihihinga nang patalikwas
Melting petrified bones	Ang naaagnas na buto at
and prehistoric debris.	sinaunang latak.
As the swirling currents caress	Samantalang hinahaplos at
and cradle	kinakandong
	Ng bumabalisungsong na tubig
The primal howl is released	Pinawalan ang mabangis na
	ungol
To celebrate the silent pulsating	Upang ipagdiwang ang payapang
of new life.	tibok
	Ng bagong buhay.

THERE WAS A TIME when the world of the shaman was beckoning me. The call was triggered by a skiing accident. I lost my balance and landed on my right wrist. It was strange to hear the thumb snapping out of its joint. Overnight my right hand swelled to at least double its size, ugly and deep black and purple. The next day I went to work feeling helplessly handicapped. All my employees advised me to put my wrist in a cast. I knew I had to work on the thumb that night, and so when the whole house was asleep I retreated to my yoga room and started focusing on softening the throbbing pain.

With eyes closed, I directed every breath to melt the hold of the skin on the bones. After two hours I felt I was ready. I knew I could now touch it with my left hand, step on it with my right heel, and put my whole weight on it. I kneaded it with all my strength. I felt no pain at all. After about an hour or so, I opened my eyes. Voila! the black and blue was gone and the swelling had subsided. The next day, my employees were astounded. They started regarding me with some kind of strange respect and coming to me for minor injuries.

It was at this time that I devoted myself to two dearest friends who had contracted AIDS. They called me their witch doctor! I massaged one of them until his last days at a hospice. Eventually, I delivered his ashes to his family in Oaxaca, Mexico. It was a truly profound experience. My other friend is doing well today, living normally with minimal symptoms. He even does my personal bookkeeping for a fee. He has taught and inspired me deeply about life and death.

I always felt that my friend Jane was some kind of sorceress. I knew she had something to teach me, and I was drawn to her mysterious energy. I was always intrigued by her story of falling victim to the dark forces of the *babaylan* or shamans in the Philippine province of Antique where she had spent her summers as a child. At age 14, she was suddenly struck by a life-threatening ailment which no doctor could diagnose. She felt as though her whole body were on fire. A team of five shamans worked on her, but it was a man called Levi who ultimately healed her. We talked about the experience again during a *Talikwas* workshop which she asked me to conduct for a faculty group at Cornell University in Ithaca where she lives. Upon her prodding, I set off to meet Levi on my next trip to Antique.

The lure of Antique was equally strong. I wanted to feel it, smell it, swim in its clean waters. This was where Jane and her sister Lani grew up. Here Lani learned from her *yaya* (nanny) to connect to the earth elements and the spirit world. Eventually, Lani became a famous artist in Montreal, inspired by her mother who taught her how to design her abstract landscapes.

My friends thought I was so lucky that my husband allowed me to go on these trips. Little did I know that he was already in his own world away from me. Anyway, Mabel, a fellow free spirit who had spent a good part of her childhood in Antique, volunteered to escort me and my son Eric around Antique. I loved to travel with Eric and to watch the world through his sensitive old man's eyes. He found joy in petting dogs, climbing trees, and taking tricycle rides. Mabel also arranged for us to meet an anthropologist who had just written a book about the *babaylan* healing tradition. We met some of the local shamans, although those she interviewed lived up in the remote mountains. We slept in the convent where Mabel had studied and met this incredible mother superior in her eighties who, inspired by a vision, had built the school from nothing.

It was relatively easy to find Levi. Everyone in the barrio knew him. A tricycle delivered us to the neatest nipa hut surrounded by all kinds of flowering plants. As Levi's wife greeted us, all the children and grandchildren appeared from the adjoining huts to see what was going on. She went to fetch her husband who was fishing in the back of the fields.

Levi turned out to be a most charming and gentle patriarch. I was drawn to his lovely home, his wife, and his whole family. We talked about Jane and Lani. He had little to say about powers and healing. My curiosity in learning the techniques of his "profession" seemed rudely invasive. I felt awed. How was I to understand these people and their culture, and the healing powers that evolved from being deprived of doctors and modern medicines? I could sense that Levi's power came from his humility, simplicity, and pureness of heart. His wife stood by him. His children tended their neat home and garden. The feeling of ease and spirituality pervaded this little hut leading to the rice fields.

The time we spent with Levi was spiritually reinvigorating. After saying good-bye, we went out to swim in the great warm Pacific. I was thrilled to see Eric swim his longest stretch of freestyle, while I basked in the caressing waters. I remember feeling connected to the texture of my homeland. I knew this was where I would turn to dust one day. I was happy. The trip was a big revelation. The shaman's call had come to an end.

Now I could focus on my little family. The healing power I learned from the shamans need not be effortful or threatening to my center, my home, and my family. It was time for me to nurture my nest and be fed there. From this nurturance I could then offer my services to others. I came home brimming with good intentions and new insights.

But it was too late. My husband was already out of our nest. Four months after my triumphant climb up Mount Apo, Michael announced he wanted to leave me. I had naively regarded the big open spaces between us as ideal and healthy for a union of 17 years. We were both so devoted to the children. I never imagined he would actually abandon them.

215

Cultural differences surfaced that we never dealt with during all those years of "compatibility." He said our backgrounds were too different. While my family was close-knit, his was "respectful of each other's privacy." Mine was "invasive and needling." I argued that at least in our family we aired our grievances, even violently at times, while his small family was forever divided by cold, polite wars. He was excluded from these wars because he was the angel, the one who avoided any confrontation, never took sides, and was always pleasant and light. He also brought up the issue of control. He said he wanted to find someone who could love him without demanding changes and without verbal abuse. But those issues belonged to the earlier years of our marriage!

There was a time when I fantasized spending the rest of my life with another man who could share my dreams and interests, but when faced with the reality of divorce, I clung to my family for dear life. I knew that the worst victims would be my children, then aged 14 and 11. And they did suffer. Cristina started rebelling, getting into all kinds of trouble. She was sensing something sinister. I was always depressed and in tears. I would lash out at her at unguarded moments. Her grades plummeted to D's and F's. She hated the private school she was in, and mocked the rich brats there. Then she started hanging out with streetwise kids. It got so bad that one day, unable to stand the situation anymore, I blurted out that her father was leaving us. She was in shock, which turned to anger, but suddenly she embraced me and confessed she thought I was just angry with her all the time.

My sweet son Eric cried with me, and then just kept quiet, leaving me more worried. He and Cristina both went through the usual therapy sessions. It helped somewhat that many of their friends came from broken families. Nine tortuous months passed before Michael finally left. He was cold, distant, and uncommunicative. I was desperate for him to change his mind. After all, this was our first major crisis. We had never fought before; in fact, everyone thought we were the perfect couple. The truth was there was very little communication between us. Every time I tried to get a passionate argument going, he would laugh and ignore me. I learned to be self-sufficient. But this was all too sudden — was I not worth a second chance?

I could not accept the rejection. Michael agreed to go through some therapy, but only to convince me to release him. The more I clung, the colder he became. When I asked him what all that good sex was about, he answered it was just a physical release for him. I started hating him. This is the hardest stage of a divorce — when a person who is supposed to leave is still in the same house, and in the same place of business.

My mother came to spend almost three months with me to see if she could salvage my marriage. I remember that long night in New Hampshire. We huddled all night till morning like old friends, discussing the contrasts in our marriages. Hers was financially difficult but emotionally rewarding. Mine was the opposite. At dawn I finally came to a decision. I had to let Michael go. He had never loved me. I felt very close to my mother, even to my father whom I now appreciated as my mother's husband and mate. My mother and I shared many tears.

By the time my mother went back home, she had succeeded in restoring my long-lost faith in the Catholic religion. At my weakest point, the only solution I found was to offer my pains to the Lord, trusting in his love for me. I felt relieved and strong. It felt good to be in church with my mother and to receive communion once again. That summer I arranged for my children's first communion with a priest friend in New Hampshire.

OVER THE YEARS, I had started relishing being alone in New Hampshire. Now it became my solace, where I faced life's tragedy. I meditated and soaked up the animal spirits that dwelt there. As I swam in tears, a pair of loons would come very close to comfort me. They danced and sang to me on my morning swims when everyone was still asleep. I remember many beautiful nights communing with the stars, chanting to the Comet Halle Bopp. It was a time for healing.

I met Pat, a loon lover who connected me to a whole network of artists, healers, and evolved people of the earth who lived in a nearby town. They were all supportive of *Talikwas* and my dreams of teaching there. When Michael stopped going to New Hampshire, I purged the house of his presence, got rid of half its contents, converted its ambiance to ethnic American Indian, and named it *Talikwas* Center. But as reality seeped in, my dreams crumbled away: this would never pay for the children's private school that was nurturing them so well. This would not feed us.

Slowly I had to direct my energies to Luzon Imports whose employees and their families were my responsibility. Michael had made me believe that I was not capable of talking to the banks, to the big clients, and to the salesmen. Accustomed to running the company as a cozy little

217

business, I felt inadequate and insecure to take charge again. It took many months before I gained confidence, and when I finally asked Michael to leave the company he was so surprised. I allowed him to collect unemployment, not knowing he would vacation for over a year. The years that followed were years of challenge and empowerment.

I was left with two houses to manage. I also had to collect rent from three tenants upstairs. It was exhausting work. Fortunately, the timely visits of old friends helped me throughout this household crisis.

Problems also started to affect the business. My manager of seven years resigned. Boston's record-high employment made it very difficult for me to find new employees. Michael had made some decisions that set me back financially. One of them was to move to a larger showroom/warehouse with a much higher overhead. My mother bailed me out, but I still have to catch up with outstanding loans.

Nevertheless, it was good to be in charge again. However, when the economy is good, the crafts industry suffers. People buy appliances instead of florists' baskets. Fierce competition and new market trends upset budgets and plans. Sometimes, when nothing seemed to work out right, I was tempted to give up. But somehow light would appear at the end of the tunnel. I survived each day and tackled the next as it came along.

Things were not easier at home. In the summer of 1998, as Cristina turned 15, she vented her anger like a volcano. She defied me in every way she knew. I was fortunate that my family and friends rallied to comfort me. I hung on, entrusting my daughter into God's loving hands. With the help of her wonderful teacher, she settled down and decided to stay at her old school instead of going to the correctional boarding school to which I wanted to send her.

Michael finally found a job, and we started court proceedings. The court case kept getting delayed because his job required him to travel. As I write this, it seems the property settlement case is coming to a close. To minimize my children's traumas, I have struggled to keep them in their present school and to keep our house in order.

In the past four years, my friends have noticed that I never look like I lack sleep, that somehow, despite my ordeals, I am rested and strong. The many hours spent in my yoga room in Boston have sustained me. There I have sobbed and howled. After emptying, I would always reach a state of peace and calm. I did a ritual of pouring out, emptying, and receiving for as much time as I could steal. This meant before the crack of dawn, or late at night till the wee hours of the morning. And on Thursday nights for the last 20 years, I have never failed to treat myself to Boston's best yoga class, conducted by one of the most insightful yoga teachers I have ever met. Barbara trained with Angela at the same time I did and has been teaching "soft belly" yoga since then. She is my mentor who constantly reminds me to do less and less as I tackle the most extreme poses.

Another major factor in my healing has been the comfort I have found in bonding with my sisters and female friends. I remember my first Christmas without Michael in 1996. I had to give up my annual retreats to Mount Banahaw since I had to be back in Boston for the gift shows. I became very close to my younger sister Bobbie and my best friend Patsy, with whom I share a similar fate. Women seem to be more comfortable with pain. In Boston my friends who were artists and writers gifted me with a lot of beautiful insights. After class Thursday nights I always consulted Ali, my yoga classmate of so many years, for her motherly advice. There were many e-mails and letters of support. I particularly cherish this postcard:

"I only wish you love and softness and kindness my heart can muster. I wish I could sing your pain and it will dissolve in this thick Paris air — How can you sing your memory so it does not fall into the abyss of forgetfulness? Women are good at diving — but sometimes it is difficult for others to hear our voice, we incise into the thick air, the ocean water with sharp knives but there are no traces. And when we lie down our tears feed our ears. But it is this depth of sadness that leaves no trace — is the greatest melancholy of our belly, our exile. Perhaps then, we will remember the love that this place holds. I rub your belly like the full moon. Luckily its light can only make us naked. My dearest friend — the desert is quiet and beautiful.

Love, L."

TODAY I AM living in my own *Talikwas*. It has been 20 years since I first moved to Boston. Things seem to be falling back into place. The business is picking up, thanks to my mother's resurgent creativity in designing a new line of baskets. Cristina is getting sweeter and mellower. Eric is excelling in school.

Now it is time for the hardest hurdle: the final *Talikwas*. It is about forgiveness. And how the heart has to open from the back, in order to receive from inside out. I shared this with my sister Chita, who had e-mailed me earlier about the issue of forgiving:

"I have been bothered for the last two years by a shortened tendon in my left groin. Of course, I should know what to do with it, with all my yoga breathing. For the most part I can blow it away and retrieve the lost spaces. But the tightness keeps coming back, even while I sleep. I am just about done picking at it. I realize this hardness is a manifestation of my resentment to Michael. I tell you, sometimes it pays to get help. I organized a sweat lodge in New Hampshire last fall — did I tell you? The American Indian elder who guided us through the ritual was so powerful. As I entered the pitch-black lodge, I knew right away that I was doing this for my kids, and for myself. That I had to forgive Michael! Something 'organic' happened, and when I saw him the next day at Eric's school play, I sat beside him and chatted away, without the least pretense — it was REAL! I felt relaxed, calm, and elegant. Cristina's eyes popped open. I knew this was all she had to see. She was all smiles, pointing me out to her friends who sat beside her ... Unfortunately, it did not last long. Money issues came up again that got me angry. But soon, Chita, very soon?"

I had not written a poem for the past five years. But one day in New Hampshire, after my morning swim in the icy waters, I soaked in the hot bath, chanting my gratitude to God, and I knew I was ready to let go of the things of the past. As I rushed to get paper and pen, I knew I had come a long way.

Morning Breath

Every morning
I plunge into my darkness
Swimming in the hollow tunnels of my bones.

I sniff my spine,
Lick my tail,
Yawn into the songs in my kidneys
until I touch the ocean belly.

Here I watch each cell
Explode into stillness
Echoing silences in shadows of deaths.

Setting the
World's Women
Free

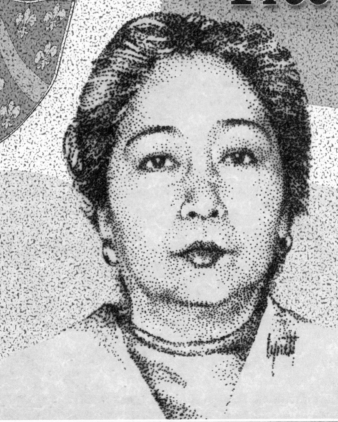

THIS ALL BEGAN when we had lunch in the wonderful room of the TLC Beatrice International office on top of midtown Manhattan. The glass wall displayed a panoramic and breathtaking view of New York's park and skyline. It evoked a wonderful and relaxing feeling. Beside me at the luncheon table was Galina, the Russian project officer who had been assisting me in my work as director of a training program on human rights advocacy for an organization in Washington, D.C. The training program on human rights involved very highly educated women from 21 countries of the former Socialist bloc.

I first met Galina at one of the cocktail parties given for fellows from Romania, Lithuania, and Mongolia by an international organization in Washington, D.C. The difference in our nationalities never bothered us. We immediately found common ground and became good friends. When my company needed someone who knew the former Soviet countries, I remembered Galina and invited her to work with my organization. Working with her, I soon realized, was like working with a systematic, efficient, intelligent, and dedicated *kababayan* or *kapatid,* proof that sisterhood is global.

On that memorable day at TLC Beatrice International, Galina and I had just come from a meeting at the Open Society Institute, more popularly known as the foundation of the billionaire George Soros in New York. His foundation has been funding our training project. Since we had a few hours to kill before our flight back to Washington, the invitation to lunch with Mely Nicolas was timely and most welcome.

I was eager to see Mely again. I had seen her years ago at the international airport in Manila. We were both queuing for the immigration passport check. She had come in from New York and I had just flown in from Thailand. Our women's rights activism had drawn us together for several projects in Malaysia and the Philippines. Now here we were in Manhattan chitchatting in English, exchanging views with Mely's corporate team in New York. Rey Glover, the bright and provocative civil rights activist turned big-time corporate lawyer/businessman, was trying to understand the women's movement and why Galina and I are so gung-ho about women's human rights. Among other things, we discussed perspectives about the impact of the women's movement on corporate management. I mentioned that not too many studies have been done on the managerial styles of women, but that I believe their contribution to corporate management is the council type, a consultative decision-making process that brings about team management. Like most men, Rey argued in favor of the efficiency and speed of a hierarchical organization. I said such a structure is undemocratic, militaristic and dominating, and tended to be insensitive to employees' needs. He said the democratic, consultative type takes time, and efficiency and speed of action are usually sacrificed. I didn't disagree.

I posited that an organizational structure and managerial style, whether hierarchical or flat, should depend on the objective, purpose, and philosophy of those who establish the organization. It was a good compromise position since I believed that in such a discussion no one had a monopoly of truth or correctness. We agreed that there were trade-offs to everything.

Going back to the women's rights issue, Rey said that if women want to have equality, they must be prepared to take on an equal share of men's responsibility and burden. I have no problem with that. I said, "I can pay for my own dinner. I don't need a man to do that. I have no problem paying for a man's dinner too. It's usually a man who has a problem with that." At the back of my mind I knew that what I said assumed that a woman has equal opportunities with men, can act on opportunities that come her way, and earns her income equally with men. Unfortunately, not too many men understand what women mean when they complain that they have no "equal opportunities." Men fail to see that women's opportunities are limited by society's perception of the nature and role of men and women, cultural and legal barriers, and women's choices under given circumstances.

Rey commented that the women's rights movement has caused confusion among men. "It used to be that it was expected of a man to open the door for a woman. Now I am never sure if I should open the door for her or not," he said. I understood his dilemma and so replied, "If you're not sure what to do, stay away from the door."

Am I glad my man has no problem with opening doors for a woman. He and I are both sure that either of us can open the door for each other. Although I'm labeled as a feminist, I don't mind if a man opens the door for me as long as that is not made a justification for society to give me fewer opportunities that life can offer or to pay me less. Between my husband and me, being a man or a woman has never been a problem with regard to who is going to do what. We believe in interchangeability of roles which gives each of us so much more freedom to be ourselves. I can cook or do house chores for him, and he can cook or do house chores for me. If he needs me to climb the ladder for electrical work he wants to do or to crawl under the sink for his plumbing at home, I can do that too. If I don't have time to wash my clothes, he'll gladly do so for me. He'll say, "No sweat, the machine does all the work anyway."

Maybe that's why we're as close as ever, even if I practically live in suitcases. My work base is Washington, D.C., and I travel to those new independent states of the former Communist bloc for two to three weeks almost every month, while he lives in Los Angeles, California, to take care of his business and his almost-90-year-old mother. We try to keep in touch about two or three times a day every day wherever I am, thanks to modern communication technology that has greatly contributed to globalization and to our relationship. Of course, we also find time to be together. I fly to Los Angeles for Christmas and he comes to Washington, D.C., when I'm in town for more than a week. We visit the children and grandchildren whenever we can. He's not difficult to please. Give him a round of golf and a good Italian meal, and he's content. I'm content too, especially if he cooks the meal. We're more friends than husband and wife. I think we have found friendship to be our basis for a comfortable, lasting relationship.

But back to the lunch with Mely and her team. We had so much fun talking, but soon it was time to go. Before we left the beautiful dining room, however, Rey told me something that stuck in my mind. "There is really something about Filipino women," he said. "From the nannies to corporate presidents, no matter what they say and do, at the end of the day they know the meaning of power." I took that as a great compliment and a very powerful statement.

ON THE FLIGHT home I told Galina, "I think that when I retire, I'll write a book about my lifetime advocacy. The book's title will be 'Stay Away from the Door.'" The title will be symbolic of so many things — the many doors of destiny and opportunity in one's life, the choices we make in shutting out or welcoming in people, the door that connects the public and private domains of men and women, or the door that leads to the interchangeability of women's and men's roles. Until one is sure of what one wants, however, it may be best to stay away from the door. Staying away is not always a bad thing. It often becomes necessary to look at things from a distance to gain a broader and clearer perspective. One could relate it to Kahlil Gibran's statement: "A mountain is always clearer from the plane."

The title couldn't wait for my retirement. When I was asked to write an essay about my life and work in the countries that have only recently emerged from the "iron curtain," I knew that I couldn't stay away from the door that long. Sooner or later I would have to write about myself, a job I am not too good at. There is always this contradiction in me. To most people I appear to be very open, yet I really do not wish to reveal too much of myself or of matters closest to my heart. I am all over the place, but I don't really want to be public property. That's why I have never run for any public office. I would rather be a political strategist than a political candidate. I like to meet people and to know more about them and about the world, but I prefer to walk the streets alone and go anywhere in anonymity. Some people know me more as a litigation attorney, while others know me as their political science or law professor. Some know me as a feminist; others see me as a human rights activist in general. Very few know me as a businesswoman, a life partner, a daughter, a mother, or a grandmother.

There has never been much time to reflect or write about myself. But there have been many times when I wondered: *There must be something providential about tyrants, pain, and suffering.* These are the experiences that test my faith and make me reflect. These are the situations that draw out the best in me. I am usually peaceful, patient, lazy, and tolerant, but my anger at unfairness and injustice brings out the fighting spirit, the boldness to move forward, to open doors even if it costs me my life. This is perhaps the reason I am doing so much work in human rights advocacy instead of simply tending my garden and being chauffeured as prim and proper little Miss Daisy.

Lately I have been very busy thinking of my work, of others, responding to e-mail from friends and colleagues all over the world, writing and reviewing projects, scrutinizing budgets and financial reports, developing advocacy training courses and analytical tools, conducting workshops, and traveling. Within 12 months, I traveled to 15 countries at least once or twice — to Ukraine, Bulgaria, Poland, Hungary, Kazakhstan, Kyrgyzstan, Uzbekistan, Russia, Mongolia, Belarus, Czech Republic, Germany, France, Netherlands, and Switzerland. In addition to managing the global human rights advocacy training program of an international nongovernmental organization (NGO), I am also providing technical assistance as needed by the women's human rights advocates in the new independent states (referred to as NIS countries in human rights reports).

Surprisingly, I have never felt like a stranger in any of the countries I've been to. I quickly developed personal ties and friendships with more than a hundred women in these countries even if I didn't speak Russian and regardless of whether they spoke English or not. I picked up a few Russian words from Galina and other friends in the region that helped me get by in times of difficulty or when I decided to get lost and go shopping by myself. The human rights fellows in Kazakhstan with whom I worked taught me how to count in Russian after I complained that I didn't understand the reply to *"Skolka?"* (meaning "how much?"). Now I know how to say the numbers 1 to 10 in Russian. I am learning from those I am training, just as they are learning from me.

One way of finding out what the market is like and who a country's trading partners are would be just to walk into the stores, see what products are on the shelves, and read the labels that tell you where they are made or who the distributors are. Even if the print is in Cyrillic, there are still ways of finding out the links of the product. Women are traditionally the shoppers, so they can tell you a lot about a product, its quality and affordability. After all the traveling I have done in the last 15 years, I can now say that leather, cotton, and trinkets are good buys in India; good quality leather bags and boots (so classy and comfortable) are made in Italy; genuine fur coats are so cheap in Kazakhstan; amber and silver are commonly sold by sidewalk vendors in Ukraine; good wines and cognacs are produced in Armenia, Bulgaria, Kyrgyzstan, and Uzbekistan; the lowest priced Salvatore Ferragamo perfume I have seen is at the Duty Free shop in Sofia, Bulgaria; Russia makes beautiful *samovar*s and delicious varieties of chocolates and candies; Mongolia's best export product is cashmere; the Czech Republic has exquisite crystalware. I could go on and on.

What about the people? The people I have met and worked with in these new independent states are all warm, hospitable, and not very different from me or my friends in the Philippines or the United States. We may look different, but we share the same feelings and commitment. We give each other gifts and *pasalubong* pretty much like we do in the Philippines and in the other countries of Asia and the Pacific. Women are the same all over the world. We all like to talk, eat, shop, and laugh. We're always thinking about our family and buying things for them. Unlike Americans, though, women in the former Soviet Union like to dance and sing, whether they're lawyers, judges, professors, government officials, or heads of organizations. The women in the former socialist countries work hard and long hours on their advocacy strategies just as I worked long and hard with them, but we all know how to have fun. We sing in buses, dance on boat cruises and restaurants, and ride horses in Mongolia whenever we can take a break. That suits me well as a Filipino. Now I look at the map of the world and in each of the countries I've been to, I see the faces of friends and I think of home.

THE ONE BAD PLACE to be in other countries as a Filipino is at the borders where stupid immigration officers scrutinize my passport, take away all my papers for "registration" and make me wait indefinitely. The American and Russian members of my team of trainers breeze through and then wait for me on the other side of the border controls, never knowing if I'll make it across or not. Heck, I'm supposed to be the head of the team, and I'm the one left out! My colleagues quickly go through those immigration officers' cubicles while I am discriminated against, simply because I am a Filipino. Sometimes my United Nations picture I.D. as official representative of an accredited NGO helps me through those unreasonable and ignorant immigration officers sitting in their "passport control" booths. At other times they couldn't be bothered.

The same problem bugs me in the United States. When my assistant calls the embassies of the countries I am scheduled to visit to check on visa requirements she is asked, "Does she have an American passport?" and told, "Oh, if she's Filipino she has to get a visa." A former administrative assistant who worked with me once got into an argument with a visa officer of an embassy in Washington, D.C. The officer had made a remark that he had to check my documents well because I was a Filipino. Peeved by the discriminatory attitude, my assistant bombarded the officer with questions: "Did you look at what her occupation is? Did you see that she's a lawyer? Did you see how many countries she has been to? Did you see that she is a resident of the United States? Now, what makes you think she wants to live in Uzbekistan?"

In addition to the inconvenience of getting a visa, Filipinos have to pay the fees too. What's with being a Filipino, anyway? This is really something that Filipinos and the Philippine government should seriously think about. Why do other countries make it very difficult for us to enter their territories? How do we open those doors wider? Are other countries so afraid Filipino men and women will give their citizens stiff competition? Why are American citizens welcome in almost every country in the world?

One would think the Americans are the best people in the world, if one were to judge by the immigration rules of the various countries. But the United States of America is no different — it discriminates against people who enter its territory, in spite of its proclaimed advocacy of human rights. Sad to say, it is in the United States where I have met the most racist and prejudiced people. They only try to be more subtle about their racial prejudice and refuse to admit it even to themselves. But I experience it every time I come back from my overseas trips. It's not so much with the US immigration people. They can't say anything wrong with my documents. It's the customs people who are discriminatory.

No matter where you are coming from and no matter if you are a resident of the US, if you carry a Filipino passport, customs people will likely make you go through the inconvenience of opening up your luggage for inspection. They say the rule is for the customs officers to make random checks, but it's clearly discrimination if the pattern shows that

Filipinos, whether US residents or not, are most likely picked for that "random" check. Of course, Africans and citizens of other Third World countries will complain about the same thing. Yet, no customs officer will ever admit that s/he is discriminating on the basis of nationality. Who do these people think they're fooling? Why do Filipinos and selected other nationalities have to prove that they are not carrying contraband? It's because they assume we're the kind of people who carry contraband! Now isn't that discrimination? Of course, some American passport holders may be checked too, but such instances are very rare. The American and Philippine governments need to check that out.

IN ONE of the visioning exercises I conducted during an advocacy training for women from the socialist countries, the participants said, "We dream of a world without borders." A Croatian woman said, "We used to be of one nation. Now I have to say that I am Croatian. It hurts that people we used to be identified with have to classify me as being of another nationality." Another participant from Bosnia-Herzegovina said, "I agree with her completely. I feel the same way. Why do I have to show that I am from Bosnia when I travel?" These are women talking. In those countries the women can work together, but the men have been fighting for years. Until now a peace-keeping force has to be there to prevent another war. Women are talking about peace; they want peace. Why are the men fighting? What's wrong with men?

In one of the training workshops, a participant from Belgrade said, "We used to be called Yugoslavians, but now we don't know what we are." The original kingdom of the Serbs, Croats, and Slovenes was united under Marshal Josip Tito's Communist regime. After Tito's death, Communism waned and nationalism rose. From what I heard from the stories of the women in the training, the wars made no sense. They were all about the competition between male egos using nationalistic sentiments to promote their political ambitions and mobilize the people against each other. With all the male-dominated political in-fighting, Yugoslavia split into several countries. Croatia declared its independence in 1991, Bosnia-Herzegovina became independent in 1992. Macedonia and Slovenia also declared their independence. Today, only Serbia and Montenegro, including the two autonomous regions of Kosovo and Vojvodina, remain of the former Yugoslavia. Here's what I learned from all the wars: *Beware of leaders who use nationalism*

or religion to fan their egos and promote their political ambitions.
It is they who have caused world catastrophes and great human suffering. Their fanaticism and excesses kill people. History has too many
of them.

In 1998 a team of women's human rights activists from Belgrade,
Subotica, and Kosovo was formed as a result of a workshop conducted
by my organization. I had been working with them to design and refine their advocacy strategy on the issue of violence against women,
using the human rights instruments and the State's accountability of
its obligation. Although Yugoslavia had already been expelled from
the United Nations, the human rights norms nevertheless proved to be
useful tools for organizing and developing strategies to improve the
lives of people. Two days before the North Atlantic Treaty Organization
(NATO) intervened in the conflict between Serbians and the Kosovars,
I was in communication with the Yugoslavian team, helping them raise
funds and facilitate the transfer of seed grants for their initiatives.

Dictatorships and tyrants have been thrown out by small beginnings. There are ways of doing so and I have had first-hand experience with it in study groups, teach-ins, and human rights activism –
from the grass roots to the highest court in the Philippines. When I
heard that NATO dropped the first bomb in Kosovo, I slumped in my
chair. I felt as though all my efforts and energy had gone to waste. I
thought of the wonderful, energetic, intelligent, and hopeful women I
had been working with. I worried about their safety and welfare.

The Serbian and Kosovar women were working together, trying
to find effective ways to change the situation in their country for the
better. Why couldn't those stupid men stop fighting and find peaceful
solutions? Then here comes the super bully called NATO, bombing all
other possible strategic solutions away. Didn't the military strategists
know that Slobodan Milosevic's power was beginning to be questioned
by the population that supported him? Didn't they know that his cred-
ibility was being eroded by his neglect of the economy and his mis-
placed emphasis on the power of the police? I didn't know if by writing
to the wonderful and amazing women in former Yugoslavia I would
be putting them in danger. Having lived through martial law myself, I
understood the risks. Then I got a touching letter from a woman named
Mirjana that captured the frustration of women who were putting their
lives on the line for something better. She wrote:

Dear Emelina,

Just a few days ago our group finished a project we want to submit to WIDTECH. We made a plan of education and development of women's social and economic rights with great enthusiasm. Now it seems to me that it was a hundred years ago... Just now I hear bombarders flying above my head going to Belgrade, where Jasna, Maja, and thousands of people wait in shelters in fear and despair...I'm in touch with them by Internet and phone, they are still working. They are terribly afraid, me too. I suppose that Rrita and Anda are also in danger, their town is in flames, and bombed.

This is, Emelina, why I said in Poland that Universal Declaration of Human Rights are very nice but only a piece of paper (although I never thought that things could be so bad). We need new morals, international ethic and international justice, and moral and responsible people who can defend them, including universal human rights. One can't stop human catastrophe making greater human catastrophe. One can't protect human rights violating human rights. The greatness of one person or state can be measured by the manner of their relation to weaker persons (minorities). My state made many mistakes, but now, western countries are making A TERRIBLE, HUGE MISTAKE, whatever their aims are. It was expected that such an intervention could only start a fire, and atrocity, the consequences could be terrible not only for people in the Balkans, but wider. Emelina, I don't want to disturb you, I even don't know why am I writing this to you. Perhaps because I've just got Maja's e-mail, and on TV, I heard announcement of new air strikes, and jets over my head, and here is our finished project. Emelina, they are going to hit people who were three months on the streets, demonstrating and asking for peace and tolerance and change of this politics, as Maja and Jasna did. Now all these people are wondering what is the international community doing, and they are more and more angered naturally. YOU CAN'T IMPORT DEMOCRACY AND HUMAN RIGHTS BY BOMBS, JUST OPPOSITE. We were fighting here for h.r., women's rights, freedom of media... NOW ALL OUR RIGHTS AND FREEDOMS ARE SUSPENDED, because this is wartime. And what now? And what after now?

Sincerely,
Mirjana

I was angry at NATO for being politically naïve. As both Serbs and Kosovars I met with after the bombing admitted, the NATO intervention and military strategy succeeded only in strengthening a bad leader. It drew attention away from Milosevic's incompetence and weaknesses in governance. The air strikes were reported to be necessary to flush out, drive out, or weaken the military force of Milosevic before NATO ground troops would be deployed. So, aside from so much destruction, what did the bombers accomplish? Is Milosevic out of power? As of this writing, he is still there. When the bombing stopped, the media in Yugoslavia reported that the country and Milosevic "had won."

The future of Kosovo remains uncertain, even after the NATO bombing. Anda, the young, very pretty, and intelligent fellow from Kosovo, told me of her experience as a refugee in Albania during the NATO bombing. She and her family returned to Kosovo to find only the structure of what used to be their home. She said to me, "There is nothing in my house now." She had traveled from Kosovo to Albania by bus for 14 hours to get her plane so she could arrive in time for our workshop in Budapest. She had to go the roundabout way because she couldn't go through Belgrade, which was the usual route out of the country. She did not want to miss the women's human rights training.

She asked about the other members of her team. She said the difficulty of communicating and the dangers of traveling to Belgrade, and even being seen meeting with Serbs, now make it difficult for her to work on the same project as her Serbian colleagues. She told me she would still try to contact her colleagues in Belgrade and to develop a separate strategy that could help rebuild Kosovo. I asked her if after the bombing the KLA's position of obtaining independence instead of autonomy had gained more support among the Kosovars. Shaking her head, she replied, "We can't survive as an independent state now. Not in many, many years. We don't even know how we can survive as an autonomous region. There is one thing I know. After all the violence seen and experienced by the Kosovars committed by the Serbs, it will be very difficult for us to live with them again."

IN RECENT YEARS, the world trend has been toward political fragmentation and economic globalization. This is the context that all men and women have to live with; this is the situation in which human rights have to be viewed and applied. The women in the former socialist countries that I work with today have the same problems as other women all over the world that I have worked with before. Those who have not been to as many countries as I have think their problems are unique. They are not.

In Russia the team of women undergoing human rights training is dealing with the issue of discrimination against women with regard to their pension. In general, women get less pension in their old age because the maternity leave benefits are deducted in the computation of their retirement benefits. They asked, "Why do women get penalized for giving birth to the next generation?" They have a point. Men suffer no deductions in their pensions for fathering a child! In Russia both men and women work and support their families. Working women are doubly burdened by housework and child care when they get home. The women complain that the men don't work when they get home; they just get drunk on vodka.

The Albanian team is also working to refine strategies to reform the maternity benefit law and for the government to provide adequate support for child care. It used to be that the State supported maternity leave for one year. After socialism, the State support has been greatly reduced. I suggested that if the Albanians want to survive the switch from socialism to capitalism, they should begin by reframing their minds. As in most of the countries of the former Soviet Union, Albania's economy is in transition. The reduction of social benefits requires the development of alternative support systems. The women welcomed the examples I gave about how women in other countries are coping and how governments are trying to address the problem of maternity and child care.

The team from Macedonia, Belarus, and the Czech Republic is working on the issue of sexual harassment and violence against women. The Ukrainians, Bulgarians, and Uzbeks are addressing the problems of ignorance of women's human rights and lack of access to justice. The Mongolians and Lithuanians are talking about labor problems in the context of globalization. The team in Kyrgyzstan is working on women's political rights; that in Kazakhstan, Azerbaijan, and Armenia, on various economic and social rights of women. The team in Bosnia-Herzegovina is focusing on the issue of women's lack of participation in economic decision-making. The Croatian team is working on women's health rights.

One day in late 1998 in Uzbekistan, I was traveling by car from Samarkand to Tashkent with Mavluda, one of our fellows there. As we passed by cottonfields, Mavluda pointed to the women who were working there. She told me about the cases of women getting skin disease due to the fertilizers. She told me how the reduction of government-subsidized medical benefits after the end of "socialism" worked to the disadvantage of women. Immediately my mind raced to the same problems of women workers in the rubber plantations in Malaysia and the agricultural plantations in the Philippines. What is worse in the Asia Pacific situation is that there is no government program in place for free medical services for these poor women workers. In the United States, health care is also a big issue because not everyone can afford health insurance. Yes, the problems are the same. Some cases are just more serious than others.

I am impressed with the dedication, discipline, warmth, and optimism of the women in the former socialist countries. They are all concerned and interested, especially in the economic development issues affecting their countries. "Politics affects your economics," I remind them. They want to know more about how globalization is affecting them. They are eager to learn and work for the improvement of their situation. They are the hope of their countries. Even after the NATO destruction, women in the Balkans kept their sense of humor and of hope. When I met with the Yugoslavians, I said I was glad they could still laugh and that they had not given up hope. One of them responded, "We cannot let hope die. It's the only thing we have right now."

In the United States and the Philippines, traditional human rights lawyers and activists understand and mostly work on civil and political rights. Very few understand or even know how to handle economic, social, and cultural rights. Economic, social, and cultural rights are the collective rights that the former socialist bloc tried to address. The realization of all human rights, however, requires more than just knowing them. Realizing human rights requires organizing and advocacy skills from the grass-roots to the government level.

My grass-roots work and women's activism starting in the Philippines and in the Asia Pacific region gave me the insight and the experience of working on issues that cut across political, civil, economic, and cultural rights. I am grateful to the women in the poor communities of Davao City, Philippines, for having given me first-hand experience in developing strategies to solve their immediate political, social, economic, and cultural problems. Their problems required me to put to good use my political science and legal training as well as analytical and strategic thinking. Both the documented and undocumented successes confirmed that my "unconventional" and nontraditional type of lawyering was needed for structural and cultural changes in society.

I thank the women and men in those poor communities for having dared to open the door of my then small law office and for having involved me in finding solutions to their problems. The cases did not mean more money for me, but they gave me more knowledge and greater confidence than money or college degrees could have given, knowing each time that I fought the good fight and won. My friends thought I was crazy for handling such cases. One colleague told me, "Emelina, you're a very good lawyer. Why do you want to be a social worker?" It wasn't just social work. There were too many families of human rights victims knocking at my door, they scared my mother. She said that the only time she could sleep in peace was when I was overseas. She feared that I'd be picked up by either the military or the rebels and I'd just disappear. The untold struggles of women and men to better the lives of their families and communities gave me invaluable experiences and insights that refined my understanding of women's human rights. These forced me to learn how to use these rights effectively.

As more and more women articulate their problems and issues, it becomes more obvious that political and economic rights could not, and should not, be separated. These rights complement and contribute directly to the achievement of the other. To address pressing social problems effectively, human rights advocates must not only agree in principle that political and economic rights are "indivisible, interrelated and integrated," they must also urgently develop strategies and take action. This is where my energies have been focused in the past few years — on helping others develop effective strategies to move an inert mass, to empower the powerless in the economies in transition. To help open doors wider.

The women in Central Asia and Eastern Europe themselves will have to test their mettle by engaging the political, legal, economic, and social systems nationally and internationally. They will need a clear vision, fire in their belly, and the support of others who believe in the concept of countries and nations without borders. The seeds of women's activism in the region have been there all along, perhaps only waiting for fertilization from cross-cultural encounters. I have entered the newly opened doors of countries that used to be behind the mystical "iron curtain." Only time will tell if my presence and interaction in the region made a difference.

The time may have come for women to stop talking about their human rights. They should just act on them to the limits of their humanity. My job, however, requires me to talk about women's human rights. Many times I have thought of shutting up and going out the door — only to open another one. When I told my daughter that I was thinking of getting out of human rights employment and starting my own business honing economic rights, I thought she would become concerned about the loss of my stable income and benefits. Instead she said: "Oh, you've already done that in the Philippines and Malaysia, haven't you? You're already a pro in that. So it should be no big deal for you." What a booster from a daughter who thinks Mama can't fail!

I see as many doors that are waiting to be opened as there are opportunities in the world. I'm in no rush. For now, I'll just finish this story. Until I decide where I want to go and what I want to do next, I'll stay away from the door. No one is expected to open doors for me.

Coco Quisumbing

On the Air
from Singapore

IF YOU'RE a Filipino woman abroad, there's one thing I can say about you with some certainty. You are never alone.

Thanks to the Filipino Diaspora, there's a ready-made *Pinoy* community for you to either join or avoid just about everywhere in the world. Not only that. It seems everyone on earth has encountered, or at least heard of, a Filipino woman, and on that basis has formed certain notions about you.

So a Filipino woman travels not only with her parents, relatives, and alma mater as her "ticket," for compatriots to scrutinize as they try to figure out where she belongs in their community. In the eyes of non-Filipinos, she travels with all Filipino-kind.

She is expected to know every other Filipino ("My uncle worked with a Filipino in the Navy"). And whatever she does contributes to the collective image of the Filipino. Corollary to this, the collective image is shone on her, and she is expected to be like every Filipino anyone has ever met.

So it is that in Singapore many taxi drivers react with incredulity when I tell them I'm from the Philippines.

"You not Filipino!" they assert.

"Yes, I am," I reply.

"You don't talk like Filipino."

"Many Filipinos talk like me." (Wrong grammar, I know, but sometimes you have to give up your standards to get your point across.)

"No, they don't."

What can I say? These men, who probably have never been farther from their island state than nearby Malaysia, know better about the Philippines than I do.

To be frank, I don't speak like most Filipinos. That's because I speak for a living. As a television news anchor, I'm paid for my better-than-average voice, diction, and articulation with only a slight hint of a Filipino-American accent.

Still, it is galling to meet people who strongly believe that all Filipinos speak with heavy accents, or perhaps in broken English, that it's easier for them to believe I would lie about my nationality than to give up that notion. This, in a country where locals speak with such varied accents as *Sing-lish* (the local pidgin), Teochew (a Chinese dialect), Malay, Indian, and slightly Oxford English.

Why so many people find it easy to lump all Filipinos into one, I don't know. It's sad to note that many Singaporeans, like that infamous erroneous Oxford dictionary entry, equate "Filipino" with "domestic worker." Sadder still, these workers occupy such a low rung in the social ladder that other Filipinos rush to differentiate themselves in order to get better treatment for themselves. In 1994, when word spread that I was moving to Singapore to join the regional business news channel Asia Business News, advice began to pour in before I even left Manila. "Don't go to Orchard Road on Sundays. That's when all the *Pinay* domestics go and the shopgirls will treat you badly. Or, if you must go, dress up and wear all your jewelry."

I learned early on that when it comes to determining social stature terminology is the key. I used to tell people that I was in Singapore on a "work permit as a TV news presenter." What I meant to convey was that I had the official blessing of Singapore's Immigration Department, rather than being *TNT* (*tago nang tago*, meaning an illegal worker). Mistake. In Singapore "work permit" connotes a low-level job paid a pittance. Real estate agents don't want to show you apartments; banks don't want to help you open accounts. It turns out there is a huge difference between "work permit" and "employment pass," which is extended to those with "skills" and salaries above a certain level. I had an E.P., but it took me more than a year to train myself not to use the two terms interchangeably.

While I didn't exactly follow the Orchard Road rule, I did use external signals to preempt any possible prejudiced behavior. Whenever I looked at apartments, went to the bank, or did any business transactions,

I wore a business suit. And I immediately presented my name card — proof of professional employment — to everyone with whom I had to deal. I didn't realize it then, but a former colleague had noticed my attire on such occasions. She even mentioned it as we reminisced about our Singapore days in New York recently. An American of Chinese descent, she said she first thought it was kind of silly ("Why couldn't you just dress casually when looking at an apartment?"), until she realized that it made a difference in the way I was treated.

You would think I would have a slightly easier time than most and not encounter too much prejudice simply because of my job. I was on television, after all. But because of the nature of the media in Singapore, I wasn't necessarily famous.

A typical conversation in cabs and other places, before 1997, would go like this:

"Where do you work?"

"I work for Asia Business News."

"Sorry, I haven't seen that magazine. Or is it a newspaper?"

"It's television."

"TCS?" they'd ask, referring to the Television Corporation of Singapore, the national and, until a few years ago, the only broadcaster in the country.

"No."

"But how can you work for TV but not TCS?"

I would then have to explain that Asia Business News was a regional news organization based in Singapore that could be seen all over the region via satellite and cable but was not widely available locally because cable was relatively rare.

In the past two years, much to the delight of expatriates, cable has been installed in many more homes in Singapore. As a viewer myself, I must say I missed Manila TV, where even before the days of cable we had five terrestrial channels with a wide variety of local and American entertainment, news and public affairs programs. In contrast, the TV fare in Singapore until 1997 was very thin. And even with less money and often antiquated technology, Manila productions seemed more creative and better produced.

A landmark for me in local recognition was when a man I passed on the street said, "Hi, Coco." Since I wasn't used to being recognized on the street in Singapore, I assumed we had met before, so I stopped to reply. It turned out he didn't know me at all, but had seen me on TV.

EARLY 1995 was an interesting time to be a Filipino in Singapore. Not dangerous, though a lot of people back home asked me if it was. It was interesting because the danger was for Singaporeans in the Philippines. A few months after I moved to Singapore, a Filipino domestic worker named Flor Contemplacion was hanged for killing another Filipino maid and the latter's young ward. Even though Flor had been convicted, sentenced, and imprisoned for two years, news of her fate was not publicized in the Philippines until a few days before her execution. Perhaps Filipinos thought she was given a quickie and unfair trial, or perhaps the issue was stirred up by political groups trying to win support for the impending congressional elections. Whatever the reason, the reaction to Flor's hanging was violent. Protest groups burned the Singapore flag. Bombs exploded outside the Singapore Airlines office in Makati. Singaporean diplomatic officials and businessmen received threats.

Such expressions of outrage did nothing to improve the image Singaporeans held of Filipinos. In fact, it led some of them to believe that Filipinos were a violent, unreasonable people. Add that to the common misconception that all Filipinos were qualified only to be domestic workers. (And, because of the Contemplacion case, potential killers.)

During this period, many of my colleagues and other people I met plied me with questions: Are they always that violent? Is it legal to burn flags in the Philippines? Isn't the government strong enough to keep this unrest in check?

To me, their questions showed that very few people knew much about the Philippines. Even though I had never labeled myself "Filipino" because I thought of myself more as a "human being," I realized that I was at this time a spokesperson for my country, and in the bigger picture an ambassador, an example to the uninformed of what Filipinos can be.

My usual answer was that they couldn't judge the whole country by the actions of a few; that law and order was generally good but had its weakness; that our democracy guaranteed freedom of expression even though some people took it a step too far; and that, in my view, many Filipinos who didn't have all the facts of the case, might have thought Flor was a victim of a flawed, prejudiced Singaporean legal system.

At that point, when the Philippine government had chartered a plane for domestic workers who wanted to go home, I did a story on how the sheer number of Filipino domestics in Singapore helped spawn a whole economic sub-segment. A mall on Orchard Road called Lucky Plaza is filled with cramped stalls that sell Filipino snacks, soy sauce, *adobo,* and *sinigang* mix. Other stalls rent out Filipino videos. Some travel agencies specialize in trips home. The savvy Singaporeans have built booming businesses for money remittances and door-to-door delivery service to the Philippines.

While working on that story, I found out that at that time, 1995, there were about 70 thousand Filipinos in Singapore, a nation of roughly 3.5 million. And while 60 thousand of them were domestics, that meant 10 thousand were not. More than a thousand, in fact, were architects. So many skilled workers and professionals (the head of consumer products multinational Unilever was a Filipino), yet Filipinos were generally seen as menial workers! Or worse, as sex objects.

While I mourn the negative traits ascribed to Filipinos abroad, it must be pointed out that some of these are borne out by facts. On the other hand, I think it naive of non-Filipinos to lump all *Pinoys* into one and I resent having to bear the burden of the actions of others simply because we have the same nationality.

I was shocked to learn that there are places in Singapore where men can go and buy the sexual favors of Filipino women, nationality specified. Business hours are usually Sunday afternoons, when most do-mestic workers take off from work, because most of the women-for-hire, if not all of them, are domestic workers.

I've also learned that many Filipino women are quite willing to be mistresses of married men and that these men are not ashamed to talk about their Filipino girlfriends. At an ABN cocktail party, one financial analyst who was a frequent guest on my show told me that he had a Filipino girlfriend for two years when he first moved to Hong Kong. A few minutes later, while we were on another topic, he mentioned that his wife and children joined him in Asia a couple of years after he moved. It doesn't take an idiot to figure out the timing; he was already married when he left England. Yet he thought nothing of telling me about his Filipino girlfriend. Did he think it was a point on which we could "bond"? He obviously didn't think I would be offended by such a revelation, or that I would think less of him.

A colleague, another British (at the risk of generalizing, is this a Brit thing?), also confided that he was seeing a young Filipino woman. This confused me because I had thought he was married. He was. When I ran into him at the bakery downstairs from our studio, he proudly introduced me to his gal. Should I take consolation from the fact that these men were not ashamed to be going out with Filipino women?

There's a phenomenon in Singapore known as the SPG, or "Sarong Party Girl." She's typically a young Southeast Asian woman who hangs around bars and clubs picking up white men. The economic exchange is not cash-based, nor as straightforward as for a prostitute, but her aim is generally seen to be personal enrichment. Thankfully, descriptions of SPGs usually mention nationalities such as Malay, Thai, or Indonesian, not Filipinos, but most white men can't tell one from the other and try to pick up any small brown girl they see. Even in respectable clubs and hotels, I've had to deflect some very aggressive introductions on some of my nights out. Those are the times I wish I were more famous, so drunken men wouldn't mistake me for an easy pickup.

ALL THESE STORIES about the issues a Filipino woman faces in Singapore come from outside my workplace. I was very glad that the people at ABN were very open-minded about Filipinos; they just didn't know very much. In the early days there were only four Filipinos in the company — all women, and in different departments. Besides me, there were Mai Tatoy in our marketing and public relations department; Alexa Kirk, who had grown up in Canada and worked in distribution; and Nancy Kwee, a graphics artist who had married a Singaporean and lived in Singapore for so long that she spoke with a *Sing-lish* accent. I didn't know she was *Pinay* until she told me.

I was the first anchor ABN hired from outside the United States or First-World Asia. The rest were American-Asians or Singaporeans or Japanese. Once again I felt I'd been called to represent my country. On my first week at work, many told me I was "very professional." I didn't quite know how to take that compliment. Did they expect less of me because I came from the Philippines?

Even though I had had 10 years of broadcast journalism before I joined ABN, in the early days I felt I had to prove myself to the editors, all of them American, all over again. If I made a point in a story, I was asked, "What makes you say that?" I thought, "I've spent more time in Asia, and in TV than some of those editors. Why do I have to support my conclusions by sending the original wire stories for them to read? Would they do this to a white woman? Would they do this to a man?" Those suspicions will never be answered, but I am happy to report that over the five years I spent at ABN (which later became CNBC Asia) I won enough respect so that I no longer had to defend my news judgment. In fact, the editors trusted me so much they saw no need for a morning editor to look over the scripts for the first show. I even mentored many of the younger staff, teaching them how to choose stories, how to arrange them in order of priority, and how to write clearly and concisely.

Another role I felt I needed to play was to ensure fair and accurate reporting about the Philippines. Every TV show has a limited amount of time, so stories get on the show depending on how important and interesting the producers and editors find them. It's easy to fall into the trap of covering only the big Asian economies — Japan, Hong Kong, South Korea. I would point out stories about the Philippines, both the positive ones and the negative, and explain why I thought they were important enough to mention. A story about a minor Japanese company, I argued, was not so important as a typhoon in the Philippines that closed down not only the stock exchange but virtually the whole country.

I've helped colleagues with the pronunciation of Filipino names and given them background to help frame stories in context. There was a time when it seemed every script that mentioned the Philippines described it as "the sick man of Asia." I campaigned against the automatic use of the term. Now, I'm not blindly patriotic and can point out the faults of my country as well as its worst critics can, but I feel it's not good journalism to use terms carelessly. When my editor pointed out that my country did, at that point, have one of the weakest economies in the region, I replied that there are times when such a term is in context but must ABN mention it every single time it mentions the Philippines? Later, during the regional economic crisis, the Philippine economy held up better than did those of its neighbors.

Every time another Filipino joined our newsroom, colleagues would be very curious to see how I would react. They either expected us to bond automatically because of shared nationality, or have a deliciously antagonistic rivalry. I noticed, however, that they didn't have such interest when another Singaporean or another American was hired. Though potential rivals, we Filipinos became friends instead, not just because we got along well but also because we shared the same sense of responsibility. Along with Maria Ressa of CNN and Veronica Pedrosa on the BBC, Twink Macaraig, Rico Hizon, and I were the few Filipinos on air internationally. We carried the image of the Philippines to the world.

What do some financial analysts and professionals have in common with some taxi drivers? They're surprised when I tell them I'm from the Philippines. And I do tell everyone I'm from the Philippines. Sure, I went to high school in Hawaii, but I've spent most of my life in the Philippines and I see myself as a product of Philippine, not American, education and values. And I've come to take an almost mischievous pride in flabbergasting those who don't think professional quality can come from a developing Asian country.

DESPITE ALL the negative things I've mentioned so far, I have to emphasize that I have enjoyed living in Singapore very much. It is a pleasant and easy country in which to live. No traffic, no winter. Very good infrastructure, consumer goods from around the world, excellent food of all price ranges, lots of movies, and a great airport with cheap fares. Thanks to my job, I have the wherewithal to enjoy what the country has to offer.

To me, one of the best things about Singapore is that it is a relatively uncrowded island and so one can enjoy the outdoor life, an unheard of luxury in Manila. I've learned how to water-ski and roller-blade in seaside parks. The zoo is great and parks are plentiful. The beaches, while a far cry from Boracay, are easily accessible. A word of warning, though: keep in mind that Singapore has one of the world's busiest harbors. On my first month there, I went to the playground island called Sentosa, a 15-minute walk across the bridge from Singapore. A friend told me it was a great place to sit on the beach, read, and just relax. But I like to swim. When I emerged from the water, though, he said, "I've never been in the water. Can it be very clean, do you think, since there are so many ships just out there?" I felt I needed a penicillin shot right then and there.

Singapore is also a place where I have made wonderful friendships — with both Filipinos and non-Filipinos. Although I didn't specifically seek out the *Pinoy* community, quite by chance some of my closest friends are Filipino and I like to think it's because of affinity rather than some forced association.

One of the most common complaints people have about Singapore is that it's boring, that it lacks culture. I think it's very difficult for a place with so many various ethnic groups to "lack culture." I've celebrated Chinese New Year, had a Hari Raya feast at the home of a Muslim friend at the end of the fasting month of Ramadan, and walked through Little India during the Deepavali Festival of Lights. If "culture" means cultural events, the government has made strong efforts to develop that side. The annual film and arts festivals have improved dramatically in only a few years. I've sat on the grass at historic Fort Canning for the local dance company's "Ballet Under the Stars." I've seen concerts from Michael Jackson to the Gypsy Kings, Tina Turner, and a major Indian *bangra* music star.

In short, I've generally liked life in Singapore because I've had access to things I could not get in Manila. I also revel in the fact that I can have "a life." My last five years in Manila were devoted to law school at the University of the Philippines, newscasting for RPN Channel 9 at night, and doing consultancy work for various United Nations agencies during the day. Since I studied and worked till 11 o'clock at night, dinners, shows, and concerts were events I could rarely attend. When I moved to Singapore, even though I had to wake up at four o'clock in the morning to anchor the "Breakfast Briefing" show on ABN, the very fact that I could get together with friends in the evening was a major improvement. Could Singapore be more exciting, more stimulating? Yes. But it could be worse.

Again, thanks to my job, I can also afford to go home quite often. Manila is, after all, only three and a half hours away. I am enjoying the best of both worlds.

I ALSO ENJOY the freedom from all the expectations Filipino society piles upon a woman.

In Singapore I live alone and no one questions that. For all the years I had my own apartment in Manila, I was constantly called upon to explain and even defend my housing. "Why don't you live at home?" "It's a good thing your father lets you live on your own." And because my mother lived in Bangkok just before I moved abroad, "Who looks after your dad? You should stay at home and take care of him."

A Filipino woman over 25 has to explain why she isn't married yet. No, it's not because I put my career first. No, I'm not "too picky." Marriage just hasn't happened yet.

Just as marital status and relationships are scrutinized by all and sundry, so are career moves, as if your entire life belongs to the greater society. "Why didn't you become a lawyer like your parents?" I am asked this question all the time, even though I was already a recognized newscaster on Channel 9 and obviously had a more-than-decent job.

When I moved to Singapore to join ABN, I did some publicity interviews with the Philippine media. One of the most common questions was, "Why did you leave Channel 9 — whom did you fight with?" Repeatedly I explained that there was no adversary at my old place of employment; the opportunity to move to an international level, cover the whole Asian region, stretch myself and earn more money was too good to pass up. Still, one reporter wrote, "When asked why she left Channel 9, Coco was coy..."

Ah, the freedom of being an expat. You aren't expected to fit the local mold because you aren't from the place. You can't help it. You have a built-in excuse.

Ironically, I see the same phenomenon among Singaporean *balikbayans* (those who returned home after several years abroad). Often they first move away to pursue undergraduate or graduate degrees and then stay on to work, usually in the UK, the US or Australia. Upon their return, culture shock. They move back into their parents' homes, partly because rents are so prohibitive in Singapore, but mostly because of family pressure. Once there, they are expected to center their lives on their parents'. Not only do they have to account for their movements, they get pressured to get married too. At parties they reminisce fondly about their days away and long for the opportunity to leave again, and I realize that one major reason I enjoy my life in Singapore very much is that I feel so free here.

I had no such excuse for not fitting the mold while living in the Philippines. I felt that as society constantly measured me against its yardstick, society was consistently disappointed. I was, and still am, independent, outspoken, and intelligent. Not exactly the demure, feminine, self-effacing Filipino woman idealized by the Maria Clara character in our national novel *Noli me Tangere*. (Does no one remember that she is a tragic figure?)

Even worse, my mother was a role model of the opposite sort — she is a scholar, a diplomat, and a globetrotter. My long-suffering father, who claimed to prefer that we grow up more "traditionally" and bewailed our "liberal" upbringing" (or so my mother claimed), may have preferred that my mother stay in the Philippines where his own career trajectory to the Supreme Court kept him. However, I suspect that he's got a liberal streak of his own. First of all, he married a woman whose brilliance and ambition matched his. Also, he never actively tried to force his children into the traditional archetype. In fact, he conspired with my mother to raise my sister and me to have minds of our own. We grew up aware of the world around us — the entire world, not just the Philippines. So we understood that there is no one correct mold. Unfortunately, the traits my parents honed in us that make us so comfortable in the big wide world (my sister Jay lives in the US) seem to do us a disservice in our own homeland.

I'm not the only one who feels this way. I know many Filipino women abroad, both single and married ones, who relish the freedom to grow unfettered and unmonitored. This is not to say that all Filipino women overseas are cut from the same cloth, nor am I asserting that no strong women remain in the Philippines. But for those who are abroad, what they miss the least about home are the *intriga* (intrigue), the *chismis* (gossip), the feeling that people are not only always watching but also always judging. Even though, as I mentioned earlier, there is a Filipino community wherever we may move, the pressure to conform is much less because the world in which we live now encompasses so much more than just the Filipino point of view.

Yet, if conformity means to be and to act like the community around you, why doesn't our Filipino society recognize that a great number of its women are independent, intelligent, outspoken, and greatly skilled — and revise its expectations of them? After so many generations of women who have displayed those traits, why are their kind still considered "abnormal"? And why do so many of us feel we can comfortably be ourselves only abroad? A house is not a home in itself — isn't "home" where you can be yourself without fear of criticism or punishment? Why, then, do very many Filipino women have to leave home to feel at home?

Juanita Salvador-Burris, Ph.D.

Changing
My Corner
of the World

IT WAS SATURDAY morning and I could not sleep in. I was scheduled to be on a panel downtown on tax increment financing sponsored by the Neighborhood Capital Budget Group. Deputy heads of various city departments had been invited and I was to sit on the panel of neighborhood representatives that would be impacted by a one-million-dollar pilot program called Neighborhood Investment Fund.

I skipped breakfast at home and took the train to the Fine Arts Building downtown. I was glad there were muffins and coffee. But the panel organizer, John Paul Jones (my dear advocate of tax fairness and public accountability), and the usual workshop materials were not there. John was stuck in an old elevator in another landmark building, and we could not start without him because he had organized the whole event.

I sat by the wide window ledge on the tenth floor of this gorgeous building and marveled at the panoramic view of Lake Michigan and Michigan Avenue while enjoying my coffee and muffins. I saw Buckingham Fountain at the center, and on either side of it, a stone monument of Native American Indians on horseback. Around the monuments and on the parkway were abundant flower gardens, and in the background, vast, beautiful Lake Michigan. I closed my eyes and took my "Kodak moment" shot with my mind's eye.

I wondered how many Chicagoans knew this particular spot and this particular view of Michigan Avenue. I felt privileged to know this unusual vantage point; I have had opportunities to be in a few buildings along this "Magnificent Mile" with its fantastic views for executives. And here I was now with a view I could enjoy — for the moment.

Chicago is indeed a beautiful city, especially in this part of town. It was Daniel Burnham, the visionary architect and urban planner, who a hundred years ago made sure the public would enjoy and have free access to the lake by prohibiting the construction of buildings on the east side of Michigan Avenue. This was the same Daniel Burnham who did the city plans of Manila (including open-space Luneta or Rizal Park) and Baguio City in the Philippines, and Havana, Cuba. Today, the 20 miles of Chicago shoreline along Lake Michigan are public parks enjoyed by every citizen, poor or rich. Occasionally, a developer proposes a different use of parkland and the battle cry is recalled: "Forever open and free!"

Presently, I heard sirens blowing but could not see any motorcade. I remembered that President Bill Clinton was to be in Chicago that day to give a graduation address at the University of Chicago, my alma mater. The ceremony was scheduled to start at 10 in the morning and I had noticed "No Parking" signs posted for blocks as I walked to the train station. I wondered what the President would choose to say to the university's Class of 1999. He apparently had not been invited by the graduates; *he had asked to be invited*, after having chosen where he wanted to give two or three commencement addresses this year. In keeping with the controversial nature of both his presidency and his personality, some graduates, parents, faculty, and alumni were pleased that the President was honoring the university. Others, however, were displeased because they felt he was not an honorable man (the Lewinsky affair); still others were prepared to protest and demonstrate against the bombing in Kosovo.

I heard Jackie Leavey, the gray-haired white liberal director of the Neighborhood Capital Budget Group, calling us together to begin since John Paul Jones and the conference materials had been extricated from the elevator. We were relieved and hugged him. He had been so stressed out; putting the conference together, moving the office the week before the workshop, and then getting stuck in the elevator this morning with the conference materials! While many Chicagoans love landmark buildings, their antiquated elevators can provoke anxiety much of the time.

I listened to what the city officials said about their new program initiatives, the new financing tools, and how these were designed to benefit the low-income communities of Chicago, areas currently designated for "redevelopment." These are neighborhood areas which suffered decades of disinvestment and neglect because of the deep institutional racism toward African-American communities on the south side of Chicago.

The city officials described how the Local Initiatives Support Corporation (LISC) had pulled together and persuaded a dozen banks to advance the $1 million capitalization of TIF/NIF. TIF/NIF is the city's innovative attempt to help current homeowners with limited incomes fix up their homes. The $1 million would be given out as grants to qualified limited-income homeowners to enable them to fix up the exterior of their homes. The grants would range from $10,000 to $17,000, depending on whether the home was single family, two units, or four units. My community of Woodlawn welcomed the program as an alternative to the redevelopment plans which were primarily for the construction of new homes expected to sell for between $150,000 and $200,000 per home.

Given that the neighborhood had been poor for so long and that the middle class had long ago left for the suburbs, those left behind wondered who would be buying into the neighborhood, next door to their old, unfixed up homes. Thus, the whole community could be "spruced up" to promote "gentrification." This is what happens to low-rent poor areas when middle-class people buy the cheap houses, fix them up and eventually raise the rents so that low-income people cannot afford to stay. To many people, this is progress, the only way they believe development happens. To others, this is to be fought since poor people have no other place to go.

When it was my turn to speak, I acknowledged my community's appreciation for the home fix-up program, but pointed out how limited the impact of $1 million was in one community. I was critical of the for-profit banks that had not fronted a $1-million fund for a low-income community. Instead, a not-for-profit financial intermediary had to scrounge around from their supportive banks to get the fund together. How could a million dollars be a big risk to any bank? I was critical of how the same banks had left the neighborhood 30 years ago and contributed to further economic decline. People in the neighborhood had to depend on currency exchanges which charged high fees for check cashing and, unlike banks, put no money back into the community. Banks also practiced "redlining," a systematic refusal to lend mortgage monies to specific low-income neighborhoods, which ensured that homeowners could not get access to credit with which to buy or fix up their homes.

But the real problem in the Woodlawn community, I said, is the lack of jobs: too many African-Americans in Chicago's low-income neighborhoods have no access to jobs, and it is this pervasive condition in the community that demands redress. I spoke of how deeply fundamental a job is to an individual's life. I spoke of knowing many in my community who, for two or three generations, have *never* had jobs, and generally have a debilitating helplessness and lack of initiative in creating their days, much less their future.

I cited the importance of land to poor rural people in the Philippines, where I was born and grew up. And how people demand land reform and the right to have land for the landless, so that every citizen has the opportunity to live and make a living. I said that in Chicago, and in fact in the United States, we should demand jobs for the jobless, given that the economy is going great and yet millions are unemployed.

There was loud applause for what I said. I was surprised at their enthusiasm. When I went back to my seat, the officials leaned over to me and asked me to go with them to the banks and corporations to get them to give funds and jobs to their programs. "Come with us, Juanita. We need you," they said. The other African-American neighborhood representatives agreed with what I had just said and dispensed with their usual long presentations. It was quite an experience for me to have them step back and give a Filipino-American the "last word" on jobs and economic empowerment. I went home feeling satisfied that I had been an effective voice for the low-income African-American community where I live and work. But I was even more pleased with the way my references to Philippine land reform resonated with the audience. Poor people around the world have much in common. We all want to get out of poverty.

ON MY WAY home from the train station, I noticed that the area around the University of Chicago looked bustling. Then I realized that at that hour, one in the afternoon, the graduation ceremonies might be ending. Sure enough, as I crossed the Midway Plaisance to Woodlawn Avenue, the street where I live, President Clinton's motor entourage was turning the corner from the campus and was headed east toward the lake. I saw the President talking inside the limousine and then waving at the few people on the street. Yes, I did see the President of the United States, at close range from the sidewalk, driving through *my neighborhood!* It isn't often, in this big United States, that you find the President in your neighborhood. He'd been to Chicago many times before, but never to our side of town.

Early that evening, my husband and I walked to the campus—after a late afternoon drenching rain—to see what the quadrangle lawn looked like, as set up for graduation. The University of Chicago had always had its graduation at Rockefeller Chapel which can sit 2,000. But the President's presence today called for a larger space and so, for the first time, the graduation was held outdoors. I was curious about the popularity of the President and the security aspects the university had to deal with. I wondered if many people from the surrounding community came to shake his hand. I could not be there to be a guest or a bystander, so this was my way of imagining, at the end of the day, what everything must have been like.

It was very interesting to see how they packed thousands of folding chairs into every available space in only one section of the quadrangle, a temporary stage in the middle just outside the Social Science Building where I had spent my graduate school years, and tents set out all over the lawn with water coolers on tables to alleviate the heat. It was quite simple, no frills, just chairs, tents, water. Reading through a copy of the convocation program, we learned that the President had spoken at the very end. The program said simply "Remarks." Following tradition, the convocation address was given by a University of Chicago professor. Well, the University of Chicago is kind of snobbish that way. It is the faculty that have power here.

While soaking in the bathtub that night, I played *"Magandang Bituin"* (Beautiful Star) by Richard Tann on my CD boombox and reveled in my memories of the day. Then I realized it was June 12, *Araw ng Kalayaan,* Philippine Independence Day! There must have been a parade downtown on State Street by the Filipino-American community, and I was not there. This is the story of my life. I happen to be a Filipino living in America, working as a community development person in an African American community. I have little connection with Filipinos in Chicago. *"Kung ang hanap mo ay ligaya sa buhay . . . tagabukid man may gintong kalooban, kayamanan . . ."* I began to weep, recognizing the seeming inconsistencies in my life, yet my heart was full that day. At the end of the day, I was very pleased at where I was and what I had been about.

So let me tell you my story, where I am in life now, where I came from in the Philippines, and how I got to be who I am now, at home in the world.

I AM a community development "professional." I have been one for five years now, as executive director of a small community development not-for-profit corporation which I also helped found, together with some members of my church and residents on my block who had been active in the block club. I have told our organizational story many times in terms of how our board of directors grew out of a block club — neighbors and community residents who chose to organize at a different level of organization — to shape and develop their community in the ways they wanted. Margaret Mead once said, "Never underestimate the power of a small group of people to change the world." I saw, at least, that our corner of the world could change.

We are developing a co-housing project based on a development approach from Denmark, which clusters a maximum of 25 to 30 homes to have common grounds with a common house for dining and recreation. The philosophy of co-housing is to develop a strong sense of community and neighborhood as the housing project is being developed. We have also started a small elementary school, where class size is limited to 20, compared to Chicago's average class size of 35. It is a movement that started in New York City to address issues of providing quality public education with increased participation from parents and community in support of the work of teachers in a smaller classroom.

Our efforts at creating job training and employment, as part of a comprehensive economic development strategy for the neighborhood, have met major obstacles and challenges. Political power was used over us. A vacant Art Deco public library we wanted preserved and transformed into a Business Enterprise and Community Arts Center was demolished. Yet our neighborhood was designated as a federal Empowerment Zone precisely to promote economic and cultural revitalization. Though we targeted a particular industry with significant growth trends for job training and employment, we never got adequate funding for it. With a 4.2 percent unemployment rate nationally, it is hard to convince anyone that our small community of 27,000 has 55 percent unemployment among those of working-age people, even though it is just next door to the biggest employer on the south side of Chicago, the University of Chicago, and its University of Chicago Hospitals.

We also address environmental concerns at the neighborhood level by working to transform vacant lots into community vegetable and flower gardens. Residents come to know one another, look out for each other's vegetable plots (mustard greens and cabbages get stolen occasionally, and tomatoes are stolen all the time) and share the satisfaction of growing food for themselves and others while improving the neighborhood. Sometimes the community garden can transform lives, as when several drinking buddies drink for only four hours instead of eight because they have to tend their vegetables every day.

This work at the community grass-roots level has been, and is, fulfilling for me even though I have been underpaid the whole time. Part of me believes I should be paid what I am worth in the market, especially with a Ph.D. from one of the world's great universities and a diverse and responsible work experience. Another part of me simply acknowledges the reality of my job being of low social status in the hierarchy of professions. This is a fact because it is dominated by women; the same is true of nurses, social workers, teachers, and child care providers.

I live my life the way I do because I am a true believer in social change. I believe that individuals can change their communities, their society, or their country and, of course, the world — to better the world for themselves and for those who will follow them. Where I grew up, in Sta. Mesa, Manila, I observed the community as it was, transformed every day from a rural-like community of wooden and nipa houses, rice fields, big old mango trees, and two rivers (Pasig and San Juan) we could swim in, into an urban neighborhood filled with middle-class homes and apartments of concrete hollow blocks, fences, and gates, and neighbors whom we did not know and who did not want to associate with us "poor folks."

We had two churches and two town fiestas: one for the Aglipayans (Philippine Independent Church), the other for the Roman Catholics. The long standing, poorer residents of Bacood tended to be Aglipayans; the newer middle-class residents tended to be Catholics. My parents were Catholic and middle class (by virtue of my father's being a white-collar employee at Shell Oil Company) but we were renting two rooms from Lelang Eyang, who was Aglipayan, matriarch of a large extended family and one of the original residents of the town who lived on a widow's pension. I was constantly fascinated by the two different worlds in which I was living. I enjoyed having two town fiestas in May, as well as the socio-economic and political competition of who had the most bands, who had the biggest name movie stars for the stage show, and the ultimate neighborhood debate on the question *"Alin ang mas masaya?"* (Which one is more fun?).

The dichotomies I saw in my community (rural/urban, poor/middle class, traditional/modern, uneducated/educated) were also present in my family. My mother and my father met at the YMCA on Arroceros Street where my mother was a cafeteria cashier and my father a tennis-playing YMCA member who worked for a multinational company. She was from rural Camiling, Tarlac, where she had finished grade five. He was born and raised in Arlegui, Quiapo, and educated at San Beda College. When I was growing up, I always felt *Inay* was traditional (uneducated) and *Itay* was modern (educated) in values, beliefs, and basic outlook on life. *Inay* listened to Rafael Yabut for news every day while *Itay* read the daily newspapers and encouraged me to be well informed on current events. And even though they were both Catholics, *Inay* was religious and a daily churchgoer in our small parish church; *Itay* went only on Sundays, stayed at the back of the church, and often preferred to go to San Beda chapel or San Sebastian Church "downtown." Occasionally, my mother would be defensive about the YMCA being a Protestant institution, especially since *Itay* was a dues-paying member, but *Itay* would always affirm he was there primarily for recreation and physical fitness. In the Fifties, the YMCA must have been a great health club for him. I also saw it as a lower middle-class social club to those who were familiar with the lifestyle at Wack-Wack, Club Filipino, or Army and Navy Club.

THIS THEME in my life — of social change from traditional to modern — is probably my equivalent of a myth, in Joseph Campbell's terms. It shaped the way I interpreted my experience in a systematic, mostly unconscious, way during my formative years in the Philippines. When I was a student at Holy Ghost College, I was very conscious of social class differences among my fellow students. Many were brought to school and fetched in cars while I took the veritable jeepney, strategizing morning and afternoon on how to get a seat without having to walk all the way to school or all the way home. When I was given a ride home from some birthday party, I would contrast the celebrator's neighborhood with mine. My classmates' streets in Quezon City were asphalted; mine was still a dirt road — *baku-bako ang Bacood,* I would say.

I also wondered about the fair-skinned *mestizas* in school who spoke Spanish most of the time and had their own social circle. Some carried last names of the rich and famous, but since I was not invited to their birthday parties, I did not really know where or how they lived. I was particularly intrigued by the *internas*, those who stayed in the college dorm because their parents lived in the provinces. They seemed to be monied, were often landowners, but they seemed traditional, if not conservative, in thinking and behavior. I always envied them when the school year opened because they would have wonderful stories of how they spent their vacation months in all kinds of wonderful nature settings. I had lost those places to urbanization and did not have an ancestral province to go home to.

In graduate school years later, I chose to do my Ph.D. dissertation on the question of social class differences in parental childrearing — in values, beliefs, and practices that determined variations in IQ and cognitive development scores among preschool-age children — in my own community of Bacood. I interviewed people who had watched me grow up and those who did not know me, Aglipayans and Catholics, lower class and middle class, parents who lived in the slums along the abandoned railroad tracks and parents who lived in big houses, with cars, television sets, refrigerators, and air-conditioners. I wanted to know if the middle-class children could be projected to have better futures — that they would most likely succeed in their schooling — because their parents "had in their heads" modern ideas and beliefs like human potential, developmental processes and stages, and the human capacity to create environments which promoted and nurtured the intellectual development of children.

My anthropologist/adviser loved my thesis. He had big plans for me. I was going to be a "lily pad" in the Philippines in his cross-cultural network of bicultural social scientists who would do major research together. I still don't know why I didn't go along with his plans. I often remember what I said then: "I wasn't born Filipino to teach American graduate students in Harvard." I made a choice to not accept a postdoctoral fellowship with him at Harvard; instead I decided to join a new and emerging national minority mental health center for Asian Americans that was being established in Chicago by the National Institute of Mental Health. That, I believe, was the single most important fork in my road of life. "I took the one less traveled by, and that has made all the difference." The year was 1977.

That was also the year Jim, my American husband of five years, got excited about purchasing a "rehab special," an old Victorian house we could fix up ourselves in an interesting neighborhood of Chicago. We talked it over with some good friends (another Filipino-American couple), looked in several interesting neighborhoods, including "Hot Halsted," and wound up in the same neighborhood of Hyde Park we were already living in.

The nice Victorian red sandstone house we found was perfect for our small extended family. We were going to bring up our children together in a bicultural setting. As fate would have it, however, the following year, Jim met a retired professor of social ethics at the University of Chicago Divinity School who inspired him, and later me, to join in the formation of an intentional community. How Jim and I made the decision to be part of this community is worth telling.

I was in Stockton, California, doing field research on the needs of elderly Filipino farmworkers for the Asian American Research Center. I was having a great time connecting with the Filipino pioneers who had come to America between 1910 and the 1920s. I found out that they had arrived when they were young 18-year-olds, recruited from rural areas in northern Philippines to work in California's burgeoning agricultural industry. They were fired up with the dream of making money, and a future, in America. But they did not make money; they were overworked and underpaid in those "factories in the field." They also experienced severe discrimination. "No Filipinos and dogs allowed" signs were posted in business establishments. The one factor that had the most impact on their life was the absence of women. Filipino women were not recruited to work in the farms; our culture then probably prohibited women from traveling, period, much less to strange foreign lands. There were strong anti-miscegenation laws in the United States. Filipino men and American women did not socialize, except on those dance floors where it was 10 cents a dance. I was learning about Filipino and American socio-cultural and political history. More importantly, I was there to document their needs as elderly rural farmworkers so that they would be eligible for social services that other senior citizens were already receiving.

Meanwhile, my white husband from Minnesota was learning so much about African-Americans and the civil rights movement from the retired professor who had brought Rev. Martin Luther King, Jr. to Chicago in 1966 to march for open housing. (That was the year I started graduate school

in Chicago and was clueless about city politics, paying as I did more attention to the Vietnam War and US imperialist actions in the world.)

Our contrasting experiences — one in Stockton, the other in Chicago —
had different effects on our consciousness. I was being moved to dig deeper
into my collective unconscious by connecting with the past and present experiences of Filipinos in America. I was developing my awareness of racial
prejudice and discrimination in America, toward Filipinos in particular. Jim,
on the other hand, was being moved to broaden our definition of extended
family. (It should be noted that he had already gone out of his traditional
definition of family by marrying me, someone who was not his own kind.)
We had gotten beyond family blood ties to creating a small extended family
of good friends whom we had known for decades. Now we were being asked
to consider being part of an extended family of people who were entire strangers
to one another! What did we have in common? Yet this community was seeking to be interracial, interclass, and intergenerational, precisely to transcend
the taken-for-granted divisions we make in American society.

The time to make a choice was drawing close. Jim and Reverend Pitcher
had found a semi-abandoned 21-unit courtyard apartment building in
Woodlawn that was within the group's affordable price range. The individuals and families who had been meeting for a year every Sunday for potluck
suppers, singing, and fellowship were making decisions to move into the
building and finally become a community there. I realized that what we
were faced with was the loss of our own dream —— the dream of rehabbing
our own Victorian house and becoming our own extended family with a dear
Filipino American couple. Was I (were we) ready to give up that dream? For
the sake of what — someone else's dream? Or do we embrace this larger
dream and make it our own? We said we would. That was 20 years ago, and
we are still in Woodlawn. (Incidentally, Jim and I celebrated our twenty-fifth
wedding anniversary and our renewal of marriage vows in the lovely Victorian house and garden of our dear Filipino-American couple friend. It is a
beautiful home and we love being in its space, and are we glad we didn't
have to rehab it ourselves!)

AFTER 20 YEARS of living in an intentional community in the largely
African-American community of Woodlawn on the south side of Chicago,
who can I say I am?

Four years ago in a Landmark seminar, I learned how to define who I
am, not in terms of my Philippine identity, nor of my past, but in terms of a

future to be created in the realm of possibilities. The idea of *being as possibility* was a paradigm shift for me. I knew about paradigm shifts as in global consciousness change due to the Copernican, Newtonian, French, Industrial, or Atomic Age Revolutions. I was not aware that I could revolutionize my own consciousness. From that day on, I declared to myself: *"Who I am is the possibility of boundless energy for the building of community and for the preservation of the earth."* This is my everyday mantra.

For many years prior to Landmark, I had often said to myself: *Ang hindi tumingin sa pinanggalingan ay hindi makakarating sa paroroonan.* (She who does not look back at where she came from cannot get to where she wants to go.) It gave me an anchor in the Philippines. I kept looking back to where I came from. But did I know where I was going? So I didn't go to Harvard because I said I wasn't born Filipino to teach American graduate students. I must have had this deep sense of obligation to teach Filipino students. The fact of the matter, however, was I was living in America. I recall Fr. Ed de la Torre's anecdote of a similar predicament. The large billboard on Taft Avenue read: JESUS IS THE ANSWER. Father Ed would say: "But what is the question?" Now I understand that "framing" the right question is critical.

Being of Filipino identity continuously shapes my thinking and action but it doesn't define my whole being. There is a time when being Asian American is simply an enlargement of my Filipino identity. Like garments that one layers in the wintertime, I put on the long sleeves of Asian American or the thick sweater of person of color when I feel the need to be included myself or to include others in the warmth of my identity. I remember how I resisted being identified as American at the Earth Summit in Rio de Janeiro in 1992. I was quick to take that off because the United States government under President George Bush refused to sign the air quality treaty. What I did then was join a large group of American environmentalists and other nationalities who protested outside the official Earth Summit meeting place. I was also happy to be working every day in the secretariat with the Filipino delegation, even as I was an American representative for the Hyde Park Community Environmental Action Council and the Chicago Asian American Women's Network

Two other important periods in my life may serve to illustrate this enlarging sense of identity which is Filipino at the core. After staying home for two years to raise our son, I decided I needed to have a work life. I found an interesting job with the City of Chicago Commission on Human Relations to be in charge of their New Residents Program, i.e., Southeast Asian refugees moving into Chicago from the camps. I am sure they hired me because I was Asian but perhaps also because my Jewish friends had recommended me. The Commission addresses racial relations in the city. It keeps tabs of racial hot spots to prevent racial strife or racial incidents from occurring. Now that Southeast Asian refugees from Vietnam, Cambodia, and Laos, among other places, were moving into Chicago's neighborhoods, it was necessary to insure that they would be accepted, if not welcomed, as the new ingredients in America's melting pot.

I worked with a dozen resettlement organizations within a Refugee Consortium structure of collaboration. Chicago's history is replete with stories of how different ethnic groups replace one another in a geographic area in an ever changing configuration of neighborhoods which is always rife with socio-cultural tension as they accommodate one another. While refugees were concretely learning to distinguish a refrigerator from a chest of drawers, they somehow had already learned that blacks, and not whites, were to be feared. Perhaps they had learned this from white Americans, or from earlier Asian immigrants to Chicago, few of whom settled in the Southside, perhaps because it was predominantly black. Filipinos, Indians, Koreans, Pakistanis, and now the Southeast Asian refugees, all wanted to live on the Northside. During this time of my work with the city government, the election of the first black mayor of Chicago was becoming a distinct possibility.

I put on my thick sweater of person of color and worked on the Harold Washington campaign, quietly, after office hours. I did not want to lose my job, which could have happened if my boss had found out I was working for the opposition candidate. It was a very nasty race. Racism was so blatant in the campaign to keep a black man from the office. Grass-roots support was high as we organized coffee fundraisers in people's kitchens, church halls and basements and elsewhere all over the city. Lo and behold, on April 8, 1983, Harold Washington got elected as the first black mayor of Chicago! It was a narrow margin that put him at the top, thanks to a coalition of minorities: blacks, Hispanics, Asians, Jews, white lakefront liberals. Then, lo and behold, when the Transition Committee members came to interview the section heads of the Commission (which included me for the New Residents Program), my work caught somebody's attention and in a few weeks I was being offered a job in the mayor's office. I was sure it was because I was Asian-American and they wanted the mayor's staff to represent the ethnic diversity of the people who had voted for him. From my personal perspective, I was just ecstatic to have been chosen to be part of a significant movement for social change that was just beginning in Chicago.

I had a Hispanic boss, one of four senior management aides to the mayor. The others were Polish-, Jewish-, and African-American. The chief of staff and the deputy were also African American. The four years I worked in the mayor's office were the best time of my work life. Every day I experienced being valued for my ethnicity and the different perspective it brought to an issue. I was also affirmed by many colleagues for my personal competence. For 18 months, I was assigned to the infrastructure sub-cabinet cluster.

I learned a lot about the operations of the Departments of Streets and Sanitation, Water, Sewers, and Public Works. I also learned much about how entrenched the patronage system was and the sticky politics of hiring, firing, and promoting minorities through affirmative action. My highest personal work satisfaction grew out of my being coordinator of the Mayor's Task Force on Solid Waste Management. It had members who represented diverse, often conflicting, interests. After more than a year of substantial discussion and give and take on the goals and implementation plans, we created a consensus on what to do with Chicago's garbage for the next 25 years. I also pride myself on the "discovery" of a group of poor black families on the far south side of Chicago (called Maryland Manor) who did not have potable drinking water. They had been written off (they didn't count) but I made sure the problem would not go away until they had safe drinking water.

For the other 18 months, I worked in the development sub-cabinet cluster which included the Departments of Planning, Economic Development, Housing, Cultural Affairs, and the Mayor's Office of Employment and Training. During this time I had to learn to do complex but quick public policy analysis. If some new federal legislation was being contemplated which could affect a city like Chicago, I could be asked to pull in the relevant department and prepare the necessary background data for a possible mayoral position in a few days. I always had my thinking cap on and kept myself informed on a wide range of issues. I never knew what would show up on the mayor's office radar screen.

These are the highlights I remember: staffing the first-ever Hispanic Business Development Task Force, insuring that a neighborhood recycling center in Osaka was visited by the mayor as part of the sister city program, planning a sesquicentennial celebration with a strong Native American component *(Chicagou* was the settlement on Lake Michigan that the Potowatamee Indians built before the white settlers came from the Eastern United States), and securing grass-roots support for the city's first neighborhood infrastructure improvement program to be financed by a $10-million general obligation bonds issue. I learned a lot about the necessary cooperative interplay between the cluster departments before effective results could happen that would truly benefit the people of Chicago.

ALTHOUGH MY Philippine identity was known to almost everyone, it was not really relevant in my day-to-day work. I myself was to benefit from my position at the mayor's office when President Cory Aquino was invited to address a joint session of the United States Congress and I wanted to see and hear her. Gallery seats were hard to come by and I was to have used a Congressional Black Caucus member's seat. The morning I was to fly to Washington, however, my five-year-old son James reminded me that we had not had dinner together as a family for four nights in a row. So I gave up being part of the historic event of hearing a Philippine woman president address the US Congress and stayed home to enjoy dinner with my family. Since Rene Saguisag was her press spokesman and Rene was a friend from college days in Mendiola, I had to "settle" for him in Chicago months later to get a feel of what Cory is like and what it meant to work for her.

After EDSA, I burned with the desire to return to the Philippines. We had not been back since 1979. Jim was ready for a sabbatical from his community development work; I could get a year's leave of absence from city government after helping Mayor Washington get reelected. James was six years old and I had high hopes that a year's experience in my home country would imprint many happy memories for his whole life. Jim and I thought we would spend our time with my family and friends, travel around the country, enjoy a period of reading and writing, and generally have a good time.

Mayor Washington got reelected to a second four-year term in April 1987. *Buklurang Pilipino for Washington* got out the votes and contributions from the Filipino-American community. We arrived in Manila in early September after visiting Jim's relatives in San Francisco and Seattle. The first week I was back, I got word from then senator Rene Saguisag to consider working in his Senate office as chief of staff. Surely, I could contribute something while I was in the country. *Ang hindi tumingin sa pinanggalingan ay hindi makakarating sa paroroonan.* How could I possibly not work? You gave four years to Mayor Washington; why not one year to Rene Saguisag? Jim was incredulous when I agreed to work for Rene.

I started work in September at the Senate offices located at the Philippine Veterans Bank building in Port Area. It was wonderful to see Manila Bay and Luneta every day. They brought back happy memories of my two years working with the cultural attaché of the American Embassy in Manila, the man who had made it possible for me to fly my wings on my 24th birthday and apply to the University of Chicago. But the daily traffic from our rented house in Quezon City, via Makati for James's elementary school, to Malate for Jim's Tagalog class, to the Port Area for the Senate office was horrendous. We survived it for a year, but we could not see ourselves being able to live with it year after year after year. To be sure, air pollution was a serious health hazard. More important for me, however, was the symbolism. Traffic congestion was symptomatic of our inability as a people to discipline ourselves personally and our unwillingness collectively to be governed by impersonal rules that applied to everyone.

We had returned to the Philippines to ask ourselves also whether we wanted to live there — to give ourselves sufficient time and space to consider the question seriously. I thought working in the Senate would be a good vantage point from which to discern whether public service was a good place to be. Rene was also attracting people who wanted to work on the Bataan Nuclear Power Plant issue, which was connected to the whole IMF/World Bank/Marcos crony deals that interested me. Although my experience was city governance and management at the local level, I thought government and democratic processes should have much in common, across the board, if common good was the bottom line. At the end of the year, we decided we could not make a decent salary in public service or in nongovernmental organizations that were attractive to us. Everyone in the Philippines already knows that, but I guess we had to know it experientially, deep in our guts, at least for a year.

I do believe now that I have found my true calling in local community development. I have to reconcile myself to the fact that in this occupational setting, my hard-earned Ph.D. does not necessarily count for either higher social status or higher compensation. In some sense I am overqualified, but in another sense I have learned to utilize my training precisely to understand the complexities of society and to raise the right questions. Certainly not for research but for action and social change. I also have to reconcile myself to the meaning of the adage "You bloom where you are planted." Though I grew up in the Philippines and was nurtured in its formative soil until the age of 24, I really grew up and matured in America as a person. I had political interests but I did not get politicized experientially in the Philippines. I was not at the University of the Philippines where I could have become a *Makibaka* member. Instead, I was shaped by reformist Irish priests who encouraged us to be in leadership roles and to work for change from within. The Jesuits were no different. *Some are born to die for the revolution; others have to build after the revolution.*

I created my own revolution within me. I enlarged and expanded my identity to be inclusive of other races and cultures. But every once in a while, often on such dates as June 12, my being Filipino surfaces to the top of my consciousness and I try to observe, even for a few moments, the meaning of being Filipino. Philippine music has a way of getting straight to the heart. *Kung ang hanap mo ay ligaya sa buhay . . .tagabukid man may gintong kalooban ....* As do Filipino friends who still want to share our common histories and culture. We gather for food, friendship, and an occasional project like promoting *Simbang Gabi*, helping Bishop Nepomuceno build facilities for solar-powered electricity, or helping Sen. Raul Roco to become president of the Philippines. Someday these dreams could materialize. But it will require millions of revolutions from within.

SHARIFA ZEANNAT ALI-SALIH is the regional director of nursing at the Ministry of Health in Makkah, Kingdom of Saudi Arabia. Born in 1948 in Turtle Island, Sulu, she received her early education at the Jolo Central Elementary Pilot School, went to high school at Notre Dame of Jolo, and completed the nursing course at Philippine Women's University. She has been an overseas Filipino worker in Saudi Arabia for 22 years. During that time she earned several distinctions: the first nursing director of the Hera General Hospital in Makkah; the first nurse and only foreigner to become a member of the Scientific Committee of the Ministry of Health for the Hajj Health Program; the first Filipino expatriate to become a member of the Faculty of the Nursing Institute; the only expatriate to hold a key position in the Ministry of Health.

She has initiated and organized several incentive and educational programs in her region. During the Gulf War crisis, she was an active participant in the contingency plan organized by the Philippine Consulate General's Office in Jeddah and chaired the medical committee for the plan. She helped as well in the peace process between the Philippine government and the Moro National Liberation Front. In 1984 she was instrumental in the restoration of the recruitment of medical personnel from the Philippines, which had earlier been discontinued.

She has received numerous awards and certificates of merit and recognition from the Ministry of Health in the Kingdom, among them the "most outstanding nurse of the year" and a certificate of appreciation from the Directorate of Makkah Health Affairs for her "exemplary achievements and contributions in promoting the health service of the region." The Philippine government has given her the San Lorenzo Award for Outstanding Overseas Contract Workers (1994) and the Presidential Pamana ng Filipino Award (1998). Philippine Women's University recognized her in 1995 as an outstanding alumna.

She has written a book, *Intensive English Course for Nurses,* which has become part of the region's educational and training program for nurses.

She is chairperson of the Committee of the Nursing Service in Makkah and a member of the Philippine Nurses Association.

TITA ANGANGCO has been the director of the Information Technology Services branch of theManagement Board Secretariat in the government of Ontario, Canada, since 1994. Under her leadership, the office, which was a fragmented and ineffective branch when she took over and overhauled it, has become a model of service capability, recognized for its leading service quality, low costs, and business effectiveness. Her previous assignments were at the Ministry of

Housing as manager of nonprofit programs in the Housing Operations Division for three years; corporate planning manager of the Social Housing Wing for five years; manager of the Satellite Information Centre for seven years. She also worked as a research and policy development analyst at the Ontario Housing Corporation and as research officer at the Ministry of Correctional Services.

Before immigrating to Canada, she worked in the Philippines' Commission on Population as research and evaluation manager.

She majored in psychology at St. Theresa's College in Manila and in 1979 earned a master's degree from Harvard University where she specialized in applied reseach methodology and applications.

DR. EUMELIA "NINI" BAUTISTA DE GARCIA was a nuclear safeguards inspector at the International Atomic Energy Agency (IAEA) of the United Nations for 10 years until her retirement in May 1999. Although she was based in Vienna, Austria, her work took her to Japan, Korea, and China, among other countries, where she inspected nuclear facilities such as nuclear power plants, plutonium reprocessing plants, enrichment plants, and fuel fabrication plants.

Born in Cavite City, she has a chemical engineering degree from the University of the Philippines, an M.S. in chemistry from Adamson University, an MBA from the Ateneo de Manila, and a Ph.D. in nuclear chemistry, *sobresaliente cum laude,* from the Universidad de Madrid in Spain. She was the first Filipino woman to earn the doctorate with highest honors. She has received two IAEA fellowships: one for postdoctoral work at Centro Nuclear Ezeiza in Buenos Aires, Argentina, on environmental monitoring of plutonium, and the other, in nuclear chemistry at Junta de Energia Nuclear in Madrid.

Before joining the IAEA, she worked for years at the Philippine Atomic Energy Commission, starting as a scientific writer and working her way up to become chief of the chemistry research division. She had also been a consultant to various corporations, a project leader and research scientist at the National Science Development Board, and a professorial lecturer in chemistry at the Philippine Women's University Graduate School. She has edited various national technical and scientific journals on atomic energy; presented papers at international and national congresses, symposia, and seminars; and authored the first preschool science book in the Philippines, *Me and My World,* which is now used as a textbook. In 1999 she was editor in chief of *Celebration*, a coffee-table book on the Filipino migrant community in Austria.

The Civic Assembly of Women gave her a science and technology award in 1978 for outstanding work in research and development in nuclear chemistry. She is a member of the American Nuclear Society (Vienna chapter), the International Nuclear Materials Management, Radioisotope Society of the Philippines, and the Philippine Association for the Advancement of Science, among other professional organizations.

She is married to Manuel Garcia Peso, a businessman from Spain, and has two stepchildren.

CECILIA MANGUERRA BRAINARD is a writer, editor, and teacher in the United States. Born and raised in Cebu, she immigrated to the United States in 1969. She has authored eight books and received several awards, among them a California Arts Council Fellowship in Fiction, a Special Recognition Award from the Los Angeles City Board of Education, and an Outstanding Individual Award from Cebu. She teaches creative writing at the University of California in Los Angeles Extension, and has lectured and performed in universities and art centers in the US such as UCLA, UC Berkeley, University of Connecticut. She has lectured as well in various universities in the Philippines.

She is married to Lauren R. Brainard, a lawyer who was a Peace Corps volunteer in the Philippines (Maasin, Leyte). They have three sons. Home is Santa Monica, California, but Mrs. Brainard makes regular visits to her home country.

VIOLETA CENTENO-BELTRAN is a medical doctor based in Chicago, Illinois, USA. Born in Manila in 1930, she earned her medical degree at the University of Santo Tomas and started her private practice in Malasiqui, Pangasinan.

Upon arriving in the US in 1966, she underwent internship at the South Chicago Community Hospital in Chicago, and took her residency in obstetrics/gynecology at the West Suburban Hospital and McNeal Memorial Hospital, both in Illinois. She has been an attending physician at the Ravenswood Hospital Medical Center since 1972, and chaired its OB-Gyn department for five years.

She is a fellow of the American College of Obstetrics/Gynecology and a member of the Chicago Medical Society, Illinois Medical Society, and the American Medical Society. In 1979 she received the Golden Apple for Teaching Excellence from the University of Illinois, Abraham Lincoln School of Medicine where she was a clinical associate professor, and in 1986 the Public Service Award from the Chicago Medical Society. In 1993 she was named Physician of the Year by the Ravenswood Hospital Medical Center.

She is the author of the book *Look, I'm Flat Again.*

JOSIE OPEÑA DISTERHOFT has been involved, for almost half of her adult life, in helping working parents balance their dual human rights: the right to live and the right to work. She currently consults for the Interfaith Housing Development Council of Chicago to include center- and home-based day care and job training in a unique housing development for recipients of public welfare.

She has pioneered the design, development, and financing of day-care programs for children from infancy through schoolage, as well as the formation and professional development of their educarers. She has served as consultant to the American Medical Women's Association with whom she wrote and published a book, *Developing a Child Care Program: A Health System Decision-Making Guide.*

Serving on the boards of organizations such as those cited, and at the Center for Neighborhood Technology that works on issues at the intersection of environmental issues, community development, and economic development, is her way of reconnecting to her roots in the Philippines.

She is married to a brain researcher who wants to map out the cortical basis for behavior, especially among the ageing. He is, as well, a sculler, runner, golfer, and rehabber of old buildings, and is working to increase minority representation in the hard sciences.

The Disterhofts' elder child, Jason, is in Cambridge, Massachusetts, taking a course in global justice in his first semester of graduate studies in philosophy. Their younger child, Judith, graduated from high school six months early so she could experience some unprogrammed time in her life. She visited the Philippines to get better acquainted with her mother's family, after which she went to Guatemala to learn Spanish for eight weeks.

NARCISA "CHING" DE LEON ESCALER was in the Philippine diplomatic service for 10 years. She was the country's ambassador and permanent representative to the United Nations Office and other international organizations — in Geneva, Switzerland, from 1989 to 1992, and in New York from 1992 to 1994. While in Geneva, she chaired the Committee on Trade and Development for the General Agreement on Tariffs and Trade (GATT) in 1990, and in 1991 the Group of Three on Apartheid at the UN Commission on Human Rights, the GATT Working Party on German Unification, and the ASEAN Geneva Committee. She also served as second vice chairperson to the 61st and 62nd Councils of the International Organization for Migration (IOM) in Geneva in 1990 and 1991.

In 1994 she was elected to a five-year term as deputy director-general of the IOM. She is a board member as well of the Henri Dunant Centre for Humanitarian Dialogue in Geneva.

Born in Manila in 1944, she has a bachelor's degree in literary studies from Maryknoll College.

Before she joined the foreign service, she had worked in Manila as executive director of Ala-Ala Foundation, president and chief executive officer of the Business Resource Center, Inc., and public affairs manager of Benguet Corporation. From 1986 to 1988 she served President Corazon C. Aquino as appointments and social secretary, and then returned to the private sector as president and chief executive officer of the Jaime V. Ongpin Foundation Inc.

A widow, she has three children by the late Jose Ma. Escaler.

OFELIA GELVEZÓN-TÉQUI is a Philippine-born artist based in Paris. She has two bachelor's degrees — one in Fine Arts, the other in English — from the University of the Philippines, and a diploma in painting from the Accademia di belle Arti di Roma in Italy. She also took special studies in graphic arts at the Pratt Institute in New York City on a Rockefeller Foundation scholarship. She uses the following media in her art: colored etching on zinc or copper plates, engraving on copper, collage with handmade paper, aniline on silk, acrylic on paper or canvas, oil on canvas, and mixed media.

While in the Philippines, she taught humanities, art history, and printmaking at the UP, designed books for the UP Press, was a member of the UP President's

Council on the Arts, and was in charge of the UP Print Center. While living in Hong Kong, she worked at the Printmaking Workshop of the Hong Kong Visual Arts Center. She now works at the Atelier Francoise Bricaut in Paris.

She has won a number of awards for her art, among them first prize from the Printmakers Association of the Philippines, a gold medal for printmaking from the Art Association of the Philippines, the Mariang Maya Achievement Award for Graphic Arts from the Sigma Delta Phi Sorority Alumnae Association in Manila, and *quatrieme mention* in the XVIII Salon Ile-de-France, Bourg-la-Reine, France.

Besides participating in 66 major group exhibitions in various parts of the world, she has mounted 30 one-person shows since 1970 — in Manila and Iloilo City, Paris, New York City, and Monaco. Her work appears in several art books, among them *Art Philippines, The Printmakers, A Century of Realism in Philippine Art*, and *Conversations in Philippine Art*, all published in Manila; *Dictionnaire Critique et Documentaire des Peintres, Sculpteurs, Dessinateurs et Graveurs*, published in Paris; and *Who's Who in International Art*. International Bibliographic Art Dictionary, published in Lausanne, Switzerland.

SR. EMMA DE GUZMAN, ICM, is a missionary nun belonging to the ICM (Immaculate Heart of Mary) congregation. She was born in San Jose, Nueva Ecija, on Easter Sunday in 1945 and was educated by the SFIC Sisters of St. Joseph's College in San Jose and Quezon City. After her graduation, she taught English in Paco Catholic School in Manila and St. Louis Center in Baguio City for three years.

She joined the ICM Sisters in 1969 and took her first vows in 1972. Her first assignment was the Sisters' missions in Kiangan, Lubuagan, Bauang, and Tubao, La Union. In 1974, prior to taking up a new assignment in Cameroon, Africa, she was sent to the University of Lille, France, to learn French. She now speaks, teaches and writes French fluently. She was in Cameroon for more than 20 years. While there, she worked with the Diocesan Pastoral Team of the Archdiocese of Yaounde, was national coordinator of the Service Monde Meilleur (Better World Movement), and was elected team member of the Movement for French-speaking Africa. She has facilitated seminars for church renewal according to the spirit of Vatican II in Burkina Faso, Ivory Coast, South Africa, and Cameroon. She finished her pastoral studies in *Lumen Vitae* in Brussels, Belgium.

Sister Emma has written catechetical books for children in French and translated these into Ewondo, the language of Cameroon. She has also collected anecdotes, essays, and poems on her life as a Filipino woman missionary in Cameroon.

For the past two years she has been back in the Philippines, but "God willing," hopes to return to Cameroon in May or June 2000.

BETTY L. KING is an adjunct professor at the Lenoir Rhyne College in North Carolina, USA. She has a master's degree in Asian studies from the University of the Philippines and a diploma for advanced studies in economic development from the University of Manchester in England. She also did postgraduate studies at the University of Tokyo in Japan.

She is the author of *Girl on a Leash: The Healing Power of Dogs,* a psycho-social memoir about a Chinese immigrant family. Besides academic articles, she has written a regular column called "Eating Out" for the *Catawba Valley Neighbors* and the *Charlotte Observer*, "Lifestyles" for the *Lenoir News Topic*, and "Country Life" for *Caldwell News*.

In Paris where she and her husband, Dr. Ruben Santos Cuyugan, a commissioner at UNESCO, lived for many years, she earned a certificate in oenology from *L'Academie du Vin* and studied French cooking at La Varenne. She was president of the International Cooking Class at the UNESCO.

Now a vegetarian, she has become active in animal rights causes. She rescues abandoned and abused dogs and is often invited to speak at various animal welfare activities. In 1994 she introduced pet therapy for nursing and retirement homes.

She and her husband, now retired, live in North Carolina with their many four-pawed children.

MARIETTA ENRIQUEZ DE LA HAYE JOUSSELIN lives in Paris with her husband. She graduated from the University of the Philippines and Columbia University in New York with degrees in English and the humanities. In Manila she taught at the University of the East and St. Scholastica's College. She was connected with the Philippine Embassy in Paris as cultural attaché and as assistant to the Philippine member of the Executive Board at the UNESCO.

She has translated two historical books from **French**: *From Revolution to a Second Colonization: The Philippines Under Spain and the United States* in 1990, published by the National Historical Institute; and *The Diary of a French Officer on the War in the Philippines 1898* by Lieutenant X (Aime Ernest Mostch). The latter is dedicated to the memory of her father, Col. Manuel P. Enriquez, who died in the service of his country in 1944. The book was published in 1994 by the National Historical Institute.

LINDA R. LAYOSA is the editor of *Tinig Filipino International* (Voice of the Filipino), a magazine since 1990 for Filipino workers in Hong Kong, the Middle East, and Europe. A magna cum laude graduate of the University of Nueva Caceres in Naga City, she taught English after graduation and was cited as a model elementary school teacher. In 1986, forced by difficult economic circumstances to seek employment abroad, she went to Hong Kong to work as a domestic helper.

Before assuming the editorship of *Tinig Filipino*, she was associate editor of *Tinig ng Bayan* (Voice of the People), a newsletter funded by a missionary group in Manila.

She has received the *Bagong Bayani* (New Hero) Award from the Philippine government for being an inspiration and a model to other Filipinos abroad. In 1996 she was given a presidential award for exemplifying Filipino talent and industry.

She lives in Hong Kong but travels extensively for her magazine.

LOIDA NICOLAS LEWIS, a lawyer by profession, is chairperson and chief executive officer of TLC Beatrice International Holdings, Inc., a multinational food company that is a major manufacturer and marketer of ice cream in Spain and the Canary Islands and the leading manufacturer of potato chips in Ireland. The company also has convenience stores in China and a small bottling operation in Thailand.

She assumed the leadership of the company in February 1994, a year after the death of her husband, Reginald F. Lewis. She had previously been an informal adviser and confidante to him.

Mrs. Lewis earned her bachelor's degree, cum laude, from St. Theresa's College in Manila and finished law at the University of the Philippines College of Law. She was the first Asian woman to pass the New York State bar examinations without having studied law in the United States. In 1979 she won a discrimination complaint on the basis of race, sex, and national origin against the Immigration and Naturalization Service (INS) and thereafter served as general attorney with the INS until 1990.

She has written three books on US immigration law. The latest one, *How to Get a Green Card,* is a bestseller in that genre. In 1972 she established a monthly magazine for the Filipino-American community and served as its publisher until it merged with another publication in 1979.

She is one of the founders of the Asian-American Legal Defense and Education Fund, and a member of the Council on Foreign Relations and Jack and Jill. She is chairperson of the board of the Dance Theater of Harlem and is a member of the board of the National Foundation for Teaching Entrepreneurship. In 1998 she was a recipient of the "Outstanding Mother Award."

Besides Filipino and English, Mrs. Lewis speaks Spanish and French, and is learning Chinese.

She lives in New York City.

TINA LIAMZON is a freelance development consultant. She has had 22 years of experience working with civil society organizations in the Philippines, as well as at the regional and international levels, in both organizational management and executing programs and projects. She has also worked as a consultant to international organizations, including United Nations agencies, on evaluation of projects, project conceptualization, and process facilitation.

Among her clients are the UN Development Programme, the Food and Agriculture Organization (FAO), World Food Programme, and International Fund for Agricultural Development; nongovernmental organizations (NGOs) such as the Society for International Development, Inter Press Service, Development Networks and Innovations, Caritas Internationalis, International Council of Voluntary Agencies, Private Agencies Cooperating Together in Bangladesh, the Asian NGO Coalition on Agrarian Reform and Rural Development.

She has a bachelor of arts, major in economics, degree from the University of the Philippines and a master of science degree in human settlements planning, major in rural development, from the Asian Institute of Technology in Bangkok,

Thailand. She is currently working on her doctoral dissertation at the Pontificia Universita, Gregoriana, Rome, Italy.

She is the permanent representative of the Asian NGO Coalition for Agrarian Reform and Rural Development (ANGOC) to FAO in Rome, a fellow of the People-Centered Development Forum, a member of the Development Networks and Innovations (IRED) North, ANGOC representative to the Global Forum on Sustainable Food and Nutritional Security, a member of the NGO Working Group on Food Security for the FAO Committee on World Food Security, and a member of the working group to prepare the formation of an Economic Resource Center for Overseas Filipinos.

She has authored numerous papers for presentation at various international conferences.

She and her husband and their two children live in Rome.

ELIZABETH MEDINA works as a translator and interpreter in Santiago, Chile. Born in Quezon City in 1954, she studied at Assumption College in Manila, George Washington University in Washington, D.C., and the Universidad Catolica de Chile, but holds no degree. She has written the following books: *Rizal According to Retana: Portrait of a Hero and a Revolution*; *Becoming a Filipino: A Journey from Alienation to Identity*; *Thru the Lens of Latin America: A Wide-Angle View of Philippine Colonial History*; and *Messages from Chile: Essays and Poems on Country and Self*.

She lived in the United States for nine years, but moved to Santiago in 1986 after marrying a Chilean. Today she lives in Santiago with her two children.

LUCIA "CIAY" MISA has been teaching yoga since 1988. Her essay for this book is a product of 27 years of yoga practice and 20 years of training under world-famous masters. Her own brand of yoga was further fashioned in the solitude of mountains such as Mount Banahaw in the Philippines where she conducted her yoga workshops.

She runs an import company in Boston, Massachusetts, where she lives with her children, Cristina and Eric. She established the company in 1979, a year after she arrived in Boston.

EMELINA O. QUINTILLAN is a lawyer, political scientist, educator and international development advocate. She has been a litigation attorney for 17 years and a human rights activist for 25 years. She also taught law and political science for 13 years. An international consultant, she has directed human rights advocacy training programs in Asia, the Pacific, Central Asia, and Eastern Europe.

She is the co-founder and president of Donahue & Quintillan, Inc. International Consulting Company, in Washington, D.C. Previously, she was director of the Human Rights Advocacy Training program of Women, Law and Development International in Washington, D.C., and a partner in D.I.Y. Legal Services in Denver, consultant to the Organization for Economic Cooperation and Development in Paris, and regional coordinator of the Asia Pacific Forum on Women, Law and Development in Kuala Lumpur. She was also once a member of the teaching team at the Institute of Development Studies at the University of Sussex in Brighton, England.

While still based in the Philippines in the Eighties, she founded an all-female law firm in Davao City that contributed to criminal law jurisprudence by reversing a trial court decision on a murder case on appeal to the Supreme Court. Also while in Davao, she was executive director of the PILIPINA Legal Resources Center and a professor of law and political science at the Ateneo de Davao. She also worked as special assistant and chief legislative officer to Sen. Leticia Ramos Shahani.

She earned her bachelor's and masteral degrees, major in political science, at the University of the Philippines and her law degree at the Ateneo de Davao in Davao City. She was a fellow at the Institute of Development Studies, University of Sussex, in Brighton, England. She studied the US electoral process on the International Visitor Program of the United States Information Agency in 1986. She has also had special training in living trust and tax laws, labor laws for small business enterprises, and estate and financial planning.

Besides speeches, pamphlets, concept papers, and project proposals, she has authored the following: An Introduction to Women in International Law for PILIPINA Legal Resources Center, and "Advocating for Land Rights" in *Empowerment and the Law: Strategies of Third World Women* and "Gender, Community Development and Paralegal Training in the Philippines" in *Legal Literacy: A Tool for Women's Empowerment* for OEF International in Washington, D.C.

She is a member of the Philippine American Bar Association and the Association for Women in Development, both in Washington, D.C.

COCO QUISUMBING is a television broadcaster and writer who has been based in Singapore since 1994. She anchored the prime-time shows "Breakfast Briefing" and "The Asian Wall Street Journal on Air" for regional satellite broadcaster Asia Business News, which took the name CNBC Asia when ABN merged with its rival, CNBC. Her broadcasts have been seen throughout the Asia-Pacific region, Europe, the Middle East, and the United States.

Before moving to Singapore, she anchored the national news show "Newswatch" on RPN-9 in the Philippines and was a correspondent for Japan's NHK and Radio Australia. She now writes for the *Asian Wall Street Journal, Forbes Global*, the *Far Eastern Economic Review*, and other publications.

JUANITA SALVADOR-BURRIS, Ph.D. is a founder and the first executive director of Woodlawn Development Associates, a nonprofit community development corporation in the South Side of Chicago, Illinois. She has lived in that part of Chicago since 1966, except for two years of dissertation field work in her own neighborhood in Manila and a one-year sabbatical when she was chief of staff to then Philippine senator Rene Saguisag in 1987-88. Being a minority group member in America has shaped her work life fundamentally, for she has chosen to work in institutions which aim to advance the status of minorities in America.

She is married to Jim Burris, whose work has focused as well on community-based issues. They have one son, a college student.

IMELDA M. NICOLAS seems to have gone through several lifetimes and personas — from an idyllic, bucolic childhood in Sorsogon and life in a highly disciplined all-girls boarding school in Legaspi City run by the Benedictine sisters, to the intellectual and cosmopolitan environment of St. Theresa's College in Manila (where she majored in the humanities, graduating magna cum laude) and Columbia University in New York; from her activist years before, during, and after the Marcos regime as staff to then senator Benigno "Ninoy" Aquino, Jr., political prisoner, parliamentarian of the street, campaigner for presidential candidate Corazon C. Aquino and later presidential assistant to her (with an office next door to hers), columnist for the newspaper *Malaya*, to women's cause advocate as chair of the National Commission on the Role of Filipino Women during the Ramos administration.

Now she has taken on a corporate persona: first, as assistant to her sister, Loida Nicolas Lewis, chair and chief executive officer of the New York-based multinational TLC Beatrice International Holdings; and now, CEO and part-owner of TLC Beatrice (China), a rapidly growing and expanding chain of food retail stores in mainland China.

She remains active in women's groups. In January 2000 she helped organize the first Global Forum for Women Political Leaders in the Philippines. She has conceptualized and put in place a women's bank called MS Fund. Her publication of this book is itself part of her advocacy of the women's cause.

LORNA KALAW-TIROL is a freelance journalist and book editor. She has been connected with various magazines and newspapers in Manila since the Sixties (*The Manila Chronicle, The Manila Times, Philippines Free Press, Asia-Philippines Leader, Woman's Home Companion, Philippine Panorama,* and *Sunday Inquirer Magazine,* among others) and briefly with a regional newspaper, *The Asian,* in Hong Kong.

She spent half of her school life with Maryknoll sisters and the other half with Belgian and Filipino nuns at St. Theresa's College, where she majored in journalism and English.

In the last five years, three of the books she has edited — *Coming to Terms, Duet for EDSA,* and *The World of 1896* — have won National Book Awards from the Manila Critics Circle. She pursued the midlife theme of *Coming to Terms* with two more titles: *Women on Fire* and *Primed for Life,* which was written by men. Early this year, Anvil Publishing launched two collections of Mrs. Kalaw-Tirol's personality profiles: *Public Faces, Private Lives* and *Above the Crowd.*

She is a co-founder and member of the board of editors of the Philippine Center for Investigative Journalism. She also sits on the board of the Ateneo Library of Women's Writings, Policy Review and Editorial Services, Women's Feature Service, and Crossroads Publications.

Since turning freelancer four years ago, she has been working from her home in Antipolo City, east of Manila. She and her husband Vic, a newspaper publisher, have two sons.

LINA LLAGUNO CIANI is a visual artist based in Rome. She is a Fine Arts graduate of the University of the Philippines. When she was 23 and feeling that the world was too wide and promising to be left unexplored, she decided to fly to Europe on her meager savings and youthful dreams. Dreams do come true, she would find out, but one must work on them. Three days after landing in Rome, she met her future husband, an Italian named Umberto Ciani. For him it was awe at first sight; he thought he was looking at a straight-legged Japanese woman. Meeting him was the only thing that came to Lina without any effort. A few years later, a daughter, Maya, came with some labor pains, but she brought, according to her mother, "a whole new baggage of incomparable filial joy."

Mrs. Ciani worked first as an art director, then as creative director, and did freelance illustration on the side. She found a teaching stint at the European Institute of Design in Rome a most rewarding experience.

At a certain point, she says, doing as the Romans did became routine, and so she realized it was time to pick up her brush where she had left off. She has not stopped painting since.

The work on the cover, entitled "Just Go," was part of Mrs. Ciani's exhibition of paintings in Manila in March 2000.

The Pen-and-Ink Portraitist

LYNETT VILLARIBA is mainly a publication designer who has done magazine and newspaper makeovers for over 25 years. She is equally talented, however, as a pen-and-ink portrait artist. This talent was brought to the fore in 1992 with the publication of the book *Telling Lives*, for which she was commissioned to do pen-and-ink portraits of the women writers. She has since done other portraits for publication, which have been well-received because her old-fashioned black-and-white pointillist renderings bring out the human character of her subjects. Rather than duplicating the harshness of photographic detail, her portraits project a humanity that can come only from the controlled, deliberate hands of a sensitive artist (vis-à-vis authoritarian computer tools). The traditional pen-and-ink illustration she specializes in is a refreshing alternative to the impersonal, mechanical look of computer-generated art.

The Cover Designer

JOANNA RUIZ is a freelance graphic designer. She majored in philosophy at the Ateneo de Manila University and graduated in 1992.

She designed the covers for *Lina Flor: Collected Work; Alipato: Mga Bago at Piling Tula; Ochre Tones in English and Cebuano;* and *Balat ng Daga,* among other titles.

Editorial Assistant

MILA NACIONALES is the personal assistant of Imelda M. Nicolas in Manila, part of her work being coordination relating to TLC Beatrice (China).

She is a mass communication graduate of Far Eastern University in Manila. Outside of her corporate job, she is actively involved in her church's activities for children and youth.